Down the Tube

Down the Tube

(
An Inside Account
of the Failure
of American Television
)

WILLIAM F. BAKER

AND

GEORGE DESSART

BASIC
BOOKS
A Member of the Perseus Books Group

Designed by Elliott Beard

Library of Congress Cataloging-in-Publication Data
Baker, William F., 1942–
    Down the tube : an inside account of the failure of American
    television / William F. Baker and George Dessart.—1st ed.
        p.   cm.
    Includes bibliographical references and index.
    ISBN 0-465-00722-8 (cloth)
    ISBN 0-465-00723-6 (paper)
    1. Television broadcasting—Social aspects—United States.
2. Television broadcasting—Economic aspects—United States.
I. Dessart, George.   II. Title.
PN1992.6.B32   1998   97-31128
302.23'45—dc21   CIP

98 99 00 01 02 ❖/RRD 10 9 8 7 6 5 4 3 2 1

This instrument can teach, it can illuminate; yes, and it can even inspire. But it can do so only to the extent that humans are determined to use it to those ends. Otherwise it is merely wires and lights in a box.

Edward R. Murrow
OCTOBER 15, 1958

Contents

Contents

Foreword

I T COULD HAVE been different. As Bill Baker and George Dessart show in their thoughtful, pungent, and disturbing book, American broadcasting did not have to turn out this way. Decisions were consciously made, roads were purposefully not taken, regulations were energetically opposed or studiously ignored. It was not by accident that we, almost alone among the nations of the world, delivered virtually the entire command of the public airwaves—and the public mind and heart and soul—directly and freely into the hands of the hucksters, the hustlers, and the hawkers. It should come as no surprise that we have gotten so many messes of pottage in return.

Of course, commercialism in the media isn't anything new in the human experience, and it doesn't have to be nefarious. Sometimes the hope of making money is as effective a goad as genius or even perspiration in pushing the inventor and the innovator to take the next giant step.

Foreword

And people have always been able to figure out how to make a profit out of just about any process of communicating to others, no matter what its origin or motive. Six decades before the birth of Christ, when Julius Caesar, leader of the people's party, became consul of Rome, the very first thing he did was to order the government to communicate better. For centuries the senate, which met in private, had kept regular records of all its speeches, deliberations, and decrees, but they went straight to the archives, never to the public at large. Caesar ordered that the proceedings of the senate and a digest of other social and political happenings in the city be posted every day in public places where anyone (or at least anyone who was literate) could read them.

But if Julius Caesar invented C-SPAN, the entrepreneurs weren't far behind, busily creating the commercial news media and the tabloid press. In no time, resourceful scribes were making a business of copying the posters and selling them to people who were too busy, too distant, or too grand to stand around in the marketplace and read. Others began adding a compilation of news, information, and gossip to the official digests and sending the whole packet to subscribers in distant provinces.

The great orator and statesman Cicero, sent to take up a political post in distant Asia Minor, begged a friend at home in Rome to send him all the news—but what he got wasn't exactly what he had in mind. The professional scribe his friend had hired filled his packets with accounts of funerals, gladiatorial contests, legal trials, successes and failures on the stage, and other such "tittle-tattle" that "no one," Cicero huffed, "would have the impertinence to repeat to me when I am at Rome."

Two millennia later, our American empire can do something that even the most audacious Romans, with all their beautiful straight roads, swift runners, high-wheeled chariots, and sleek triremes, never dreamed of: we can communicate anything we choose almost anywhere in the world, and we can do it instantaneously, in a puff of electrons. But what the lords of the airwaves have usually chosen to

do with this amazing power is to send more tittle-tattle to more people in more places—tittle-tattle created not for the good it might do
but for the profit it might make. Every year in the American television business, it seems, the money is bigger, the stakes higher, the
competition fiercer, the penetration into every crevice of daily life
deeper, and, perhaps, the public tolerance for trivia greater—or at
least the public resistance to it wearier.

The pattern was set back in the early radio days: the message of
the medium was to justify the existence of the medium. Some of
America's very first radio stations were established by department
stores such as Gimbel's, Bamberger's, and Wanamaker's; after all,
what better way to sell radio receivers than to give away something
people could receive on them? Other early stations were established
by newspapers, which would then run special radio columns and sup-
plements. So newspaper readers would go out and buy one of those
radios they kept reading about, and radio listeners would go out and
buy the newspaper to tell them what it was they were listening to.

Given that long and—for the broadcasters anyway—successful
pattern, we should not be surprised at how the profit motive will col-
lide with the crucial duty of keeping the people informed now that
our four premiere broadcast news divisions—ABC, CBS, NBC, and
CNN—are all owned by parent companies with profit interests in
everything from aircraft engines and nuclear power to movies, major
league baseball teams, and gin. Surely we know enough by now to
scrutinize with special care what the newscasts say about these
issues—if we can remember who owns what. But as Sherlock Holmes
once said, let me draw your attention to the curious incident of the
dog in the nighttime. Will we be Holmesian enough to notice when
the dog does *not* bark in the nighttime?

The early radio executives did have something we don't: a sense
of delicacy. Not about *whether* to use the airwaves to sell, of course,
but at least about *how*. In an age when you can see eighty-one
corpses in a single movie, hear lyrics on your tape player about slit-
ting a woman's throat and then having sex with her body, and catch

anything from pro wrestling to pornography on a box right there in your living room—it's almost quaint to recall that a fierce debate once raged over whether a potential sponsor should be allowed to mention something as personal as toothbrushing on the air.

But the real danger nowadays to the American polity is not the coarsening effect of hearing about scrubbing one's molars—it's the alienating effect of being inundated, day in and day out, with this flood of tittle-tattle that panders to the lowest common denominator created by a communications industry that regards human beings as nothing more than mere appetites and America as nothing but an economic machine.

We should be better than that. Across the world and throughout the ages, communication has always been more than a way of exchanging information: it's been a ritual, a process, a way of building a shared culture, a way of working out what's important to a people and how they might accomplish that.

Communication can even be dangerous—especially to the powers that be. Cicero, it will be recalled, died because he communicated something he believed in. After he made a series of eloquent speeches against the rising power of Mark Antony, he was declared an outlaw and hunted down and killed by bounty hunters. His head and right hand were sent to Rome. In triumph, Mark Antony displayed them on the rostrum where the old orator had made some of his greatest speeches.

Bill Baker and George Dessart have communicated here something true, something powerful, something painful, something they believe in. They are lucky that the powers-that-be don't usually behead their critics anymore, for this is dangerous stuff, not easy to hear.

All the more reason, then, we ought to listen.

Bill Moyers

Preface

WHY IS TELEVISION SO BAD? For many years I was inclined to shrug off this persistent and annoying question, assuming my inquisitors were making small talk or demonstrating elitism. As the years have passed and I have worked my way through various assignments in the protean world of television, I have come to realize that this truly is a key question. Television does deserve to be characterized as "bad" in the sense that it has failed to achieve its potential to deliver a superior product or contribute to the public good.

I have been in the TV business for well over thirty years. Twenty-five of those years were spent in commercial television, where I started as a producer, mostly of talk shows. I was responsible for giving Oprah Winfrey her start as a talk-show personality. I moved on to television station management and to Hollywood, where for a brief period I was president of a television production company. We launched *PM Magazine* nationally, thus creating what was for many years the most successful program in syndication. My last commercial post was as president of Westinghouse Television (Group W) and chairman of its cable programming businesses. It was there we originated the Nashville Network, the Discovery Channel, the Disney Channel, the Travel Channel, Home Theater Network (a G and PG premium movie service), Satellite News Channel (a competitor with Turner's CNN), and others. Eight years ago I became the president of WNET, the PBS flagship station in New York.

People often try to please me by saying that our station looks better than ever. More in sorrow than in pride, I usually respond, "No, we just look better because everything else has gotten so much worse." Actually, I am enormously proud of the talent and dedication of the WNET staff.

Why is television so bad in the United States? Certainly one cannot blame the technology, which for forty years has only improved TV's communication capacity. And most certainly the medium does not suffer from neglect on the receiving end: Ninety-nine percent of American households have television, and the average set is turned on for more than seven hours a day. Television is undeniably the most powerful influence in our society today.

I've always been a staunch defender of both commercial and public television, but I am now forced to admit that this powerful communications medium has not lived up to its promise. I'm in a good position to see the industry's weaknesses, and I should be able to pinpoint what went wrong. We have no incentives or penalties that would make commercial television want to do anything other than go flat out to earn maximum profits. Yet I find it hard to blame only the commercial interests. At the opposite end of the television gamut, the public broadcasters are embroiled in internecine organizational politics. Fighting for their very existence—sometimes brilliantly—they inevitably find themselves trapped in an awkward system devised by the government with no mechanism for adequate funding.

Preface

From my perspective, the blame for all this lies squarely at the feet of our lawmakers, who never recognized the power of the medium or the need to make it responsible to the citizens of this country. Consequently, the industry has developed in accordance with laissez-faire commercial imperatives and without the benefit of constructive governmental focus or incentives to work for the public good.

This book reflects on the complex and often fascinating events that formed the multibillion-dollar colossus we call the American television industry. It will also look, somewhat critically, at the segment of the business I now toil in, public broadcasting. With the help of my able colleague, whose career in television is also extensive, we will try to answer the question, "Why is television so bad?"

William F. Baker

BILL BAKER AND I served together on the executive committee of the International Council, chartered by the National Academy of Television Arts and Sciences. The council's membership is made up of major television executives from nearly thirty countries on every inhabited continent. After one of our meetings, Bill took me aside and told me he was working on a book about the misregulation of television. I became excited as he described the central idea—that U.S. television is bad largely because of the history of laissez-faire regulation by the government, which has never recognized the power of this medium or made clear its responsibilities. Nor has the government acknowledged that the system belongs, in the final analysis, to the citizens of this country. When Bill asked me to join him in writing the book, I accepted eagerly.

We were in agreement from the beginning on the major thrust of the work. We believe our differences in emphasis, like the differences in our backgrounds, only enrich the discussion.

Like Bill and most American television executives, I had been confronted by the ambivalence of people, like those I met at dinner parties, who were impressed to learn that I was with CBS and wanted to learn something of the inner workings of the medium. Almost inevitably, The Question would arise.

Over the course of more than thirty years in commercial television, I had taken pride in working in an honorable, indeed, a distinguished company. For most of its history, CBS had a corporate culture that fostered identification with the company's finest achievements in both journalism and entertainment. Like many of my colleagues, I felt a personal sense of stewardship of a scarce public resource. Television has been called the national hearth. My colleagues and I felt we were responsible for maintaining both that perception and the reality behind it. In the 1960s we had seen television's enormous power to galvanize and inform the American public during the Cuban Missile Crisis; its power to heal following the Kennedy assassination; and, during the Vietnam War era, its power to expose and ventilate a generation's anguish. Having spent more than a decade successfully producing documentaries and other public affairs programs, I had personally known the empowerment of actualizing what the best of television could do. Later, as I moved through successive areas at the group vice-presidential level, I experienced the sense of impotence so many top managers cannot help but feel.

It was easy to believe that all was for the best in the television world. Our medium had its finger on the American pulse, and we were disseminating information in ways unimaginable in any previous age. And yet . . .

As the 1980s unfolded, I became increasingly uneasy. Something was fundamentally wrong. The three traditional networks and many stations had changed hands; broadcasting properties were no longer quasi-public institutions. They had become commodities, and the concept of private gain had, Gresham-like, pushed aside any vestige of concern for the public interest. The question "Why is television so bad?" could no longer be ignored.

Down the Tube shows how we got to where we are today. We

begin by looking at commercial television. The first chapter gives a broad overview of the industry and its major components and elaborates on our major theme. Chapter 2 provides a dramatic comparison between misregulation on the one hand and well-conceived public policy on the other. We look at the BBC and what made it possible for that institution and Britain's commercial television to become hallmarks of quality programming. The contrast with the development of our own broadcasting systems is inescapable and saddening.

In chapter 3, we look at the bottom line of the bottom line—at the essential business of stations and networks and how it came to be. In chapter 4, we explore why viewers have so few choices despite having so many channels available—and why that situation cannot change much over the foreseeable future.

We then devote a chapter to examining why television news has become such a pale residue of the splendid service it was not so long ago. Looking at the decisions that deprived viewers of more news and changed the definition of news is an important part of this analysis.

In chapter 6, we look at what is almost certainly television's most shameful shortcoming, its treatment of children. E. B. White once wrote that in the final analysis our civilization will be judged by its television. Clearly, to us and many others, this country's failure to demand that television be used in service of what should be our primary concern, the education of our children, represents a disgraceful squandering of resources.

Chapter 7 takes up the fascinating questions concerning the internationalization of television. This area may well prove to be the fastest-growing and most perplexing television phenomenon of our time. Does the sale of American television programs represent a source of significant profits? What are the implications of U.S. consumerism, the celebration of American lifestyles and brand names, when delivered to billions of people in dozens of countries simultaneously?

In chapter 8, we share our insights into how public television came to be what it is, why it has not become a stronger force, and whether it deserves the calumny of its critics or the adulation of its supporters. Most important, we look at some alternatives that may help it not only survive but serve as a major educational resource for the next century.

In chapter 9, we confront the next millennium. What options do we have? What prospects lie before us? How might television serve in actualizing the vision Americans have of a safe, healthy, happy future?

We believe that all of television's remarkable strengths and potential can be harnessed. We believe that commercial and public television can together build a better medium and assist in building a better world, for Americans and all people.

We hope that our optimism has stimulated your curiosity, kindled some hope, even roused your skepticism, and that this book prompts discussion. At the very least, we are convinced that the questions we raise merit prompt and serious public debate. I am convinced that at this late hour, without such discussion, the question "Why is television so bad?" will become moot. There will be nothing left on the screen to redeem.

George Dessart
DECEMBER 1997

W E HAVE TRULY BEEN BLESSED by the generosity, the candor, and the professional insights of so many friends, colleagues, and family members. Those who have given us support and encouragement are too many to begin to mention without making this book too heavy to hold and too costly to print. Surely, they know how much of their time and talents they have so graciously shared; we can only hope that they know how grateful we are. We do, however feel an especial debt to the following:

Eleanor Applewhaite; Jeanmarie Baker; Ward Chamberlain; Honey Cordon; Cory Dunham; John Fitzgerald; Arthur B. Greene; George Heinemann; Jane Henehan; Hal Himmelstein; Lynn Hollister; Loomis Irish; Art Kane; Colby Kelly; Paula Kerger; Georges Leclere;

Preface

George Miles; Marilyn Mohrman-Gillis; Kathy Napoli; Bob O'Reilly; Mary Kay Plowright; Michael Rose; Karen Rosen, Leslie Rosen, and her research staff in the WNET library; Karen Salerno; Ron Simon, Gayle Klinger, and their associates at the Museum of Television and Radio; Hudson Stoddard; William Tell; Ray Timothy; David Wilkofsky; and finally, the editors at Basic Books we have come to respect and rely on, Tim Duggan, Juliana Nocker, Chris Korintus, and Michael Wilde.

Down the Tube

(1)

What Hath Mammon Wrought?
The Illusions of Marketplace and Regulation

ARLY IN 1930 two executives of the Columbia Broadcasting System—as CBS was then called—met in London with the head of the British Broadcasting Corporation. The purpose of the meeting was to work out details on the use of BBC facilities and studios for a series of live transatlantic radio presentations by more than thirty British writers and statesmen, among them the poet laureate John Masefield, the future King Edward VIII, and George Bernard Shaw. Even the BBC was impressed with such an ambitious and unprecedented project.

Supported solely by license fees from radio sets, and established as a public corporation only three years before, the BBC had built a well-deserved reputation for excellence in technology and programming alike. Its highly educated programmers considered it their job to help shape public tastes and interests. What they had heard about American broadcasting, however, baffled them. Their associates brought back reports of "extreme commercialism" and competition between the several networks for programming, coverage of events, and, especially, advertisers. According to one of the CBS executives, when Sir John Reith, the BBC's director-general, heard about the CBS plan for the series, he commented: "What I'd like to know is how you Americans can successfully worship God and Mammon at the same time."[1]

One of the Americans, Cesar Saerchinger, was an experienced journalist who had covered London for several major newspapers before conceiving of the CBS project; the other, Henry Bellows, was a former commissioner of the Federal Radio Commission (FRC), the forerunner of the Federal Communications Commission (FCC). It is easy to imagine them taking offense at the biblical reference to money-grubbing. They were decent men, probably deeply committed to what they were doing—like most of the broadcasters we have known in our careers.

One of the most pernicious and deceptive myths about the American television industry is that its faults originate from the actions of a small group of greedy and villainous men and women living in Manhattan and Beverly Hills. Our argument with this myth is a keystone of this book. We frankly grant that the industry has its share of greedy villains, perhaps even more than its share. But the moral character of individual television executives is irrelevant to the quality of programming compared with the pressures that the system itself places on them.

The pressures are clear and implacable. Those executives who choose the great majority of the television programs available to Americans can do so only so long as they keep their jobs. And keeping their jobs depends almost entirely on the degree to which their choices satisfy the inexorable demand for ever-increasing short-term profits for their companies' shareholders. In short, these men and women are behaving as they should behave—as prudent, responsible managers in a free marketplace.

What Hath Mammon Wrought?

That is not to say that they may not wish to do otherwise. Les Brown, one of television's most distinguished critics, perceived a pattern more than twenty years ago: every year one or another network president, in a public forum, makes the clarion call for originality and promises to lead a new wave of creativity in the medium. It never materializes—because it cannot.

To our knowledge, the opinions of top industry managers on this matter have never been scientifically studied, or even polled. But anyone who has spent years in the industry knows an important secret: many of these seemingly omnipotent executives feel uncomfortable with much of the programming they present, and helpless to do anything significant to change it.

Some of these leaders make heroic efforts to create small, marginal pockets of quality programming—not golden works of genius, of course, those being rare in any medium, but programs of solid accomplishment. They do so knowing that the number of such pockets has been dwindling over the years and that they will someday be squeezed out altogether, usually sooner rather than later.

Many more of these leaders seem to have given up trying, having long ago armored themselves with a cynicism that cloaks any residual sense of failure or guilt. And constantly circling them, like sharks in a tank, are the true hustlers. Apparently oblivious to any motivation other than the need to maximize their own power and wealth, they have no need to develop cynicism.

Yet the question remains: given the immense amount of time and money spent on television, and given the real desire of so many within the industry to do fine work, why has there not been more solid quality programming? Why is there so little television to help our children discover the world, not just to distract them from it? Why has most news and public affairs programming, far from getting better, further declined into superficiality? Why has our national television not become a far more receptive showcase for our best writers, directors, musicians, and artists? If most of the men and women running this industry are responsible managers, why do so many of our country's television programs resemble junk food—most lacking nourishment and some actually poisoning us?

The answer, we believe, is that the system itself is flawed. And the primary responsibility for the flawed system belongs not to those who labor within it day by day but rather to those who set it in place. It was the U.S. Congress that made the rules—and failed to make other rules—that created the system we have labored under for seventy years. Sustained by certain widely held traditional beliefs, the government created the circumstances that gave rise to our national system of broadcasting. It then bequeathed that system entirely to private commercial enterprises. It is the government that, ever since, has monitored and regulated the system in ways that more often than not have been inconsistent, inadequate, and counterproductive.

Adam Smith, the father of economics who described and extolled laissez-faire capitalism, recognized that government has essential roles in provision for the poor, in building and maintaining public works, in education and public health, and in not encouraging merchants to join in "such assemblies . . . [as] end in a conspiracy against the public . . . much less to render them necessary."[2]

In that same spirit, we believe the U.S. government has always had a clear responsibility to help ensure the quality of our nation's television programming. Consistently undercutting that responsibility, however, has been a national bias toward letting the task be achieved through the "invisible hand" of market forces. This bias, sincere and bipartisan, is an understandable reaction to the dangers of governmental censorship and mind control. Indeed, the first—and most essential—amendment to our Constitution is a noble example of that impulse.

Our quarrel with applying this philosophy to television is that the government has never consistently and impartially explored the market forces at work in the broadcasting industry. We contend that from the first days of broadcasting, the government created an inadequate marketplace for television's operations by basing it solely on commercial competition. So long as the marketplace is limited to commercial enterprises, all of which are committed to the highest possible ratings in the service of ever-increasing short-term profits, the so-called competition will more likely create not diversity, and certainly not quality, but mere imitative mediocrity.

Let us make one point perfectly clear. We are not categorically opposed to regulation. We believe that our medium requires a modicum of regulation, as do many other industries. Both of us believe that in the historical, pendulumlike swing from regulation to deregulation in this country, television is best served somewhere in the middle of the cycle. What we deplore is the misregulation that has always plagued our medium and its predecessor, radio.

Examples of regulations with unintended consequences that impede or actually worsen what they seek to remedy are legion. So too are examples of effective policies and attendant regulations that represent the only way to accomplish what the public interest requires.

Philip K. Howard, in his recent best-seller *The Death of Common Sense: How Law Is Suffocating America,* cites myriad examples of unnecessary, cumbersome, ill-conceived, even dangerous regulations. He identifies exactly how and why the Cable Act of 1992 failed to achieve its objectives. For several years after cable rates were deregulated in 1984, members of Congress complained to each other about being besieged in their districts by constituents concerned not about the economy, foreign relations, or safety in the streets, but about the rising rates and declining services of their local cable systems. The 1992 act was designed to reinstate the right of the local franchising authority to regulate cable rates. The law, said to be "the most important consumer victory of the past 20 years," consisted of five hundred pages of detailed instructions on adjusting rates to reflect actual costs:

> The effect? Nothing except that prices edged up. Operators more than made up any decline in prices by increasing installation costs (which had previously been done below cost). They manipulated

the basic service charges by changing the number of channels a subscriber had to buy. It was hopeless: Trying to detail cable charges
just ended up giving operators a chance to blame increases on the
government.[3]

Howard points out that the rules were too detailed, and the attorneys for the operators too skilled in finding loopholes.

We see the failure of the Cable Act of 1992 as another example of
misconceived ad hoc regulation hastily put together to ameliorate a
temporary annoyance to the members of Congress. As had been the
case for nearly seventy years, the regulations failed because they were
not grounded in carefully deliberated, well-articulated public policy.

Because we believe that it is impossible to understand the present, let alone the future, without some notion of how the past got
us where we are today, we must now briefly review some ancient but
unavoidable history—the history, in fact, of radio. American television did not begin its meteoric rise to dominance until well after
World War II, but it inherited the ground rules laid down for radio
two decades before. The government's early regulation of radio
shows the same pattern of inconsistency and wishful thinking that
has characterized its treatment of television to the present day.

From the Wireless to the Radio

Radio was first regulated in the United States in 1912. Seventeen
years earlier, the long-standing dream of being able to speak to those
out of earshot had been realized by Guglielmo Marconi, a brilliant
Italian teenager. Later Marconi was summoned to demonstrate his
device to Queen Victoria. She wished to communicate with her son,
the Prince of Wales, who was cruising the southern coast of England
aboard the royal yacht while recuperating from a knee injury. The
demonstration was a success, thereby assuring Marconi of the English capital he needed to establish his business. It also secured him

another commission: relaying the results of the 1899 America's Cup race.

This would prove to be a far more important commission than it may first have appeared. The last few years of the nineteenth century represented a respite from the previous twenty-five years of economic swings between deep depressions and wild excesses. Entrepreneurs were opening up the West and building the railroads and telegraph lines that had fundamentally changed communication. Labor unrest was chronic, corporate concentration seemed to be the major organizing principle in the economy, and mergers had become a major concern. As the American studies scholar Susan Douglas put it, "Social conflict—between the city and the country, nativists and immigrants, workers and managers, the wealthy and the poor—had heightened many Americans' perception that with the rise of industrial capitalism they had lost control of their economy, traditions, and destiny."[4]

At the same time the United States had been flexing its international muscles. The Spanish-American War, which the press conflated into "a holy crusade," had demonstrated that the United States could exert its hegemony in the Atlantic and the Pacific simultaneously. Indeed, Admiral George Dewey sailed into Manila Bay and ended Spain's hegemony in the Philippines by sinking or crippling the entire Spanish navy without losing a single American life.

Three months before the millennium, Dewey arrived in New York for a spectacular celebratory parade on the last Saturday in September. The following Wednesday, Marconi's demonstration would take place. The race he was covering was the most publicized of any since the beginning of the series in 1851. Sir Thomas Lipton's *Shamrock I* was challenging *Columbia*, owned by J. P. Morgan, Edwin D. Morgan (not related), and C. Oliver Iselin. The race would take place off the shores of New York.

Getting the word of Dewey's victory back to the United States had taken a full week by ship and undersea cable. The *New York Herald* paid Marconi $5,000 to obtain the America's Cup results almost

9

instantaneously. Admittedly, the distance was in no way comparable. But the success of Marconi's Morse code dot-and-dash wireless telegraphy seemed a perfect metaphor for the end of the "Century of Progress."

That technology also caught the imagination of countless middle-class American men and boys in the opening decades of the twentieth century. Some would ascribe this fascination to the magic of penetrating wood and stone and "learning to launch our winged words,"[5] as the *New York Times* breathlessly editorialized; Susan Douglas has speculated that they were "seeking both technical mastery and contact with others in an increasingly depersonalized urban-industrial society."[6] Whatever their motives, the amateur operators had set up an informal grassroots network by 1910. They also were directly responsible for the first radio licensing law.

In 1907 Admiral Robley Evans was commander in chief of the U.S. fleet, which was returning from a successful round-the-world show-the-flag tour. As the ships neared their home base of Portsmouth, New Hampshire, the crew was not concerned about the incoming evening fog. They had wireless. But the wireless operator was unable to contact the base for assistance in coming in because of "amateur chatter." Identifying the ships, their mission, or the admiral was of no avail: some of the amateurs faked navy orders, and others made salty, inappropriate comments. We can only guess what the admiral had to say. We do know that he was soon in Washington pleading for legislation. The Radio Act of 1912 was the result.

During this period, from Marconi's first radio message to the 1912 act, radio was conceived of as point-to-point communication, a replacement for the telegraph or the telephone. Shortly after the passage of the licensing act a disaster captured the nation's imagination. The HMS *Titanic*, a huge, supposedly unsinkable ocean liner, struck an iceberg on its maiden voyage and disappeared into the North Atlantic. Guglielmo Marconi had been booked for passage among the host of socialites and other celebrities on board, but canceled.

What Hath Mammon Wrought?

This was not, however, his only brush with the fate of the *Titanic:* the radio technology he pioneered was credited with saving the more than eight hundred survivors among the twenty-two hundred persons aboard. Indeed, after the young radioman David Sarnoff picked up the signal in New York and relayed the news to the press and the authorities, he became a national hero.

David Sarnoff's skills became increasingly important and his fortunes would improve considerably over the next few years. When World War I broke out less than two years after the *Titanic* disaster, point-to-point radio equipment was in great demand. At the beginning of the war President Woodrow Wilson was determined to loosen the British armlock on radio technology. Accordingly, he forged a consortium of the U.S. Navy, Westinghouse, General Electric, and other leading corporations. From their combined technological and organizational skills, the Radio Corporation of America (RCA) was created soon after the war ended. By 1930 David Sarnoff would be its president.

Among all the booming enterprises of the Roaring Twenties, radio was the champion. In that decade alone sales of radio sets went from zero to nearly $850 million per year. The price of RCA stock rose, in one year, from $85.25 per share to $549. It was an economic go-go era whose extremes were strikingly similar to our own excesses in the 1980s. Once again, mergers of industrial corporations and banks were at an all-time high. Rumors abounded, and each seemed to drive the market even higher.

The age blended a shameless financial boosterism with ingenuous religious uplift. As the historian James Truslow Adams put it, "The younger generation . . . want a religion but for them a mere sentence in the Bible can no longer be appealed to . . . for an ethical idea or a code of conduct *that has no other apparent reason for being.*"[7] For both 1925 and 1926, America's best-selling nonfiction book was Bruce Barton's *The Man Nobody Knows,* which depicts Jesus as history's greatest executive, an "outdoor man" and "the most Popular dinner guest in Jerusalem," who "picked up twelve men from the bottom ranks of business and forged them into an organization that conquered the world." Clearly, "He would be a national advertiser today."[8]

The same promise that doing well was synonymous with doing good appeared in every pronouncement on the future of broadcasting. When RCA formed the National Broadcasting Corporation in September 1926, it announced:

> Any use of radio transmission which causes the public to feel that the quality of the program is not the highest, that the use of radio is not the broadest and best use in the public interest, that it is used for political advantage or selfish power, will be detrimental to the public interest in radio, and therefore to the Radio Corporation of America.[9]

Sarnoff spoke of radio as the "greatest educational tool in history," and Harry P. Davis, vice president of Westinghouse, told a Harvard School of Business Administration audience in 1928 that the rector of Pittsburgh's Calvary Episcopal Church had done more than any other person on earth to help mankind simply because his sermons were carried on KDKA—America's first full-service broadcast station (founded by Westinghouse). Radio, he concluded, had come "as a voice from another world . . . [bringing] humanity a new and heavenly vision, if not a new world."[10]

But this heavenly vision would be achieved by means that were quite earthly. As Davis explained to the Harvard students, Westinghouse was convinced that it had the best and most efficient communications medium ever devised. Nor were there any doubts concerning who would pay for this blessing:

> [Radio's] advertising value has always been recognized, and it was evident from the beginning that sooner or later this would be . . . the answer to the question. [The] firm that can bring the subject of its activities in an adroit and satisfying way to the listening millions is

employing a means for great commercial possibilities . . . and can
justify the expenditure of large sums of money in its development.[11]

This argument was welcome in the White House of Calvin
Coolidge, whose abiding maxim was that "the chief business of the
American people is business." It was no less welcome to his secretary
of commerce, Herbert Hoover, a distinguished engineer and world-
famous humanitarian with the face of a middle-aged cherub. No one
better exemplified the distinctly American faith that, in great men of
industry, the works of heaven and Mammon were serenely compatible. For example, Hoover openly opposed the use of radio broadcasting for direct sales effort, saying, "It is inconceivable that we
should allow so great a possibility for service and for news, for entertainment and education and for vital commercial purposes to be
drowned in advertising chatter."[12] Yet he also insisted that any problems with advertising on radio should be left to the industry to solve.
Neither direct government oversight nor legislation would be necessary, Hoover claimed.

Nevertheless, some form of regulation was already unavoidable.
By the mid-1920s the number of transmitters—commercial, amateur, civic, and military—had skyrocketed, creating a crowded bedlam of overlapping signals. Government would have to intercede if
"the heavenly voice" were not to become a pandemonium of whistles and static.

So it was that the Radio Act of 1927 was passed. It created the
Federal Radio Commission, which would parcel out licenses to trans-
mit on frequencies within the limited radio bandwidth. Nowhere in
the legislation did the words *advertising* or *education* appear. But it
did affirm the necessity of serving the "public interest," whatever
that might mean.

Early on, a few public interest advocates demanded that the commission expand noncommercial broadcasting. As Joy Elmer Moran
of the National Educational Association wrote in *Harper's* in 1931:
"There has never been in the entire history of the United States an

example of mismanagement and lack of vision so colossal and far reaching in its consequences as our turning over the radio channels almost exclusively into commercial hands."[13] His organization, the National Committee on Education by Radio, demanded that the broadcasting frequencies be reallocated, with 15 percent granted to schools and colleges.

In response, John D. Rockefeller Jr. created his own organization, the National Advisory Council on Radio in Education, which urged that the entire matter be left to the commercial broadcasters. One member of the Federal Radio Commission was even more direct. Harold A. Lafount, a Utah businessman, wrote: "Commercialism is the heart of broadcasting in the United States. What has education contributed to radio? Not one thing. What has commercialism contributed? Everything—the life blood of the industry."[14]

This faith in self-regulation by the great men of radio was probably shared by most Americans throughout the Coolidge-Hoover era of prosperity. It was, after all, an age of heroes: Knute Rockne and Red Grange, Jack Dempsey and Gene Tunney, Will Rogers and Rudolph Valentino. Babe Ruth hit sixty home runs, and when Charles Lindbergh returned from his thirty-six-hundred-mile solo flight to Paris, New Yorkers threw more than three and a half million pounds of confetti in the air. Into the same air the stock market seemed to be forever climbing, and popular songs underlined the faith—"Blue Skies," "My Blue Heaven," "Let a Smile Be Your Umbrella."

Then, just two months before the new decade, it all burst like a beautiful soap bubble. By mid-November 1929, the leading industrial stocks had fallen by more than half. U.S. Steel was selling at 262. By July 1932 it had fallen to 22. General Motors went from 73 to 8.[15] Billions of dollars of personal wealth suddenly vanished. Factories closed, homes were foreclosed, and breadlines and soup kitchens appeared everywhere. During those three years, as the bottom fell even further, President Hoover continued to preach the same gospel he still devoutly believed: conditions are "fundamentally sound." "Prosperity is just around the corner."[16]

What Hath Mammon Wrought?

But it wasn't. In 1932 America elected a new president and a new Congress. Amid the hurricane of legislative activity, one proposal, attached to a new communications bill, would have radically altered the world of broadcasting. The Wagner-Hatfield Amendment called for the annulment of all broadcast licenses and their redistribution to those enterprises that had consistently shown a regard for the "public interest"—with a full 25 percent to be allocated to nonprofit associations.

Yet it came to nothing—the amendment lost in the Senate 42–23. And the Roosevelt administration's rewrite of the radio act, the Federal Communications Act of 1934, did little to reduce the commercial domination of radio. Perhaps the president was too busy with other aspects of the economy. Perhaps, knowing that his own genius with a microphone was his greatest political asset, he calculated that a battle with the networks would not be a high priority for his administration. Whatever the reason, the New Deal for radio was largely the same as the old one. As the January 1935 *Harvard Business Review* stated: "While talking in terms of the public interest, convenience and necessity, the [Federal Communications Commission] actually chose to further the ends of the commercial broadcasters."[17]

Nevertheless, certain boundaries were drawn. With the end of Prohibition, the FCC announced that the advertising of hard liquor would be "taken into consideration during license renewal" for a radio station. As a result, radio's self-regulatory arm, the National Association of Broadcasters (NAB), added the abolition of liquor advertising to its code of good behavior. Often the most effective results came, then as now, not from actual FCC rulings, but from what has often been referred to as "regulation by raised eyebrow": vague threats lurking on the horizon. When in 1935 the commission spoke of a possible investigation of CBS's monopolistic tendencies, the founder and then president of CBS, William S. Paley, quickly instituted a new Monday evening series during the summer: *The Columbia Workshop,* which presented, among other programs, Archibald MacLeish's *The Fall of the City,* narrated by Orson Welles.

NBC joined in the cultural race, programming in the same Monday evening time slot Toscanini's NBC Symphony Orchestra or Shakespearean plays performed in condensed form by John Barrymore.

A number of well-meaning regulations backfired with unintended consequences. All during the 1930s NBC comprised two separate networks: the Red Network (emanating from WEAF in New York) and the Blue (from WJZ in the same city). For years the FCC had studied the question of whether NBC should be forced to sell one of these networks to another company. In 1941 FCC Chairman James Lawrence Fly announced an antitrust policy against networks, or, as they were then called, "chain broadcasters." Fly emphasized that the FCC had no desire to censor or control programming, only to use its licensing powers to prevent monopoly, thereby fostering competition and creating diversity. Paley replied that such a policy would make broadcasters "impotent vassals."[18] The industry's trade journal, *Broadcasting*, warned that an antitrust policy would wreak "destruction" on "the existing system of broadcasting."[19] *Collier's* magazine called Chairman Fly "public enemy number one."[20] Martin Dies, the chairman of the House Un-American Activities Committee, attacked the FCC as "subversive."[21] Finally, in 1943, the Supreme Court upheld the commission's right to regulate the networks. Immediately thereafter, RCA sold its Blue Network to Edward Noble, chairman of the board of the candy company Life Savers Corp. and owner of New York City's WMCA.

Ironically, a decline in programming quality resulted from this increase in "competition." From the beginning, Sarnoff had used his Red Network for profits and devoted the Blue to cultural programming such as classical music and drama. Under Noble, the Blue Network became the American Broadcasting Corporation. Hopelessly behind NBC and CBS in the number of affiliated stations and in profits, ABC was forced to scratch its way upward with an almost total reliance on mindless mass-market programming. In hearings before the FCC, Mark Woods, a former NBC vice president who was the president-to-be of ABC, made this dynamic clear. When Fly asked what the new network would do if a news program regularly reflected the ideologies of the sponsor, Woods replied: "We are in the advertising business, gentlemen, and that business is the business of selling goods to the American people."[22]

The New Deal made its final reform effort a year after FDR's death, when the FCC issued its report *Public Service Responsibility of Broadcast Licensees*, popularly known as the "Blue Book." Among its suggestions were certain minimal standards for public-affairs and other noncommercial programming, along with a reduction of commercial clutter. Broadcasters hated the report, not least because it had been written by an Englishman, Charles Siepmann of the British Broadcasting Corporation. A typical reaction was that of CBS's Paley, who called it: "Snobs preaching to fellow snobs . . . who apparently want public discussion programs, political talks, symposiums, social controversy and so on to take the place of popular entertainment."[23] Paley needn't have bothered to comment. The only result of the FCC's recommendations was that the NAB tightened its code of so-called self-regulation a bit, to little discernible effect.

Talking Movies in the Home

The truly dramatic changes that followed had almost nothing to do with the FCC. First, the end of World War II meant that at last the long-deferred dream of television could now be made a reality. As early as 1928 a Westinghouse executive had claimed that "radiovision, whereby we shall see as well as hear by radio, is an accomplished fact; talking movies in the home [are] nearly here."[24]

During the thirties the "accomplished fact" was much more a reality in England than in the United States. American commercial broadcasters were so fabulously wealthy from radio alone that they may have felt little incentive to make the necessary investments. Both NBC and CBS had set up experimental demonstrations as early as

1928. But the first demonstration to the American public did not occur until the 1939 New York World's Fair, just before the outbreak of the war.

Once the manufacture of television sets began in 1946, however, the growth of the new industry was as explosive as radio had been in the 1920s. In 1950, 10 percent of American households owned a TV; in 1955, 67 percent; in 1960, 87 percent; and in 1965, fully 94 percent were television households. Since the early 1980s, that percentage has gradually inched up to its present 99 percent. (What's more, nearly two-thirds of those households now have two or more sets.)

During the early years of the cold war, the national obsession with threats to the United States from internal subversion caused the attitude toward broadcast regulation to change. Calls for reform were viewed as unnecessary, even suspicious. In 1949 Congress made the FCC rescind a ruling that would have required competitive bidding whenever a station license was transferred to a new owner. Two years later Congress went a step further: it blocked the FCC from considering any license applicants other than the proposed transferee. The commission did call, in 1952, for seventy VHF television channels, with some reserved for educational channels, but its decision was rendered moot when Congress failed to create a funding apparatus to make such channels possible.

The only pressure for reform came quite a while later, and only as the result of inside scandals. In 1958 Richard Mack, an FCC commissioner, was found to have accepted bribes to change his vote on granting a license. He was dismissed and died in disgrace. At the same time, FCC Chairman John C. Doerfer was charged with receiving improper honoraria from broadcast companies. He eventually resigned and accepted an executive position with one of the companies that had been so generous to him.

Far more damaging in the public's estimation were the 1959 quiz show scandals. National heroes such as Charles Van Doren admitted that they had been given correct answers beforehand by the programs' producers. In penance, all three networks canceled the discredited programs. CBS, which had killed Edward R. Murrow's *See It Now* to make space for a quiz program, started a new documentary series, *CBS Reports.* The network also promised, in the interest of total truth, to identify on-screen the use of canned laughter and applause—a promise it never kept. NBC promised to start new public affairs programming. And all broadcasters promised to tighten their standards of self-regulation.

Congress went further, however, by amending the Communications Act of 1934. This amendment was seen as a codification of the so-called fairness doctrine. At first blush, there may be no apparent connection between the quiz show scandals and the codification of the fairness doctrine. To opposing forces, however, in what Ginsburg, Botein, and Director describe as "A Great Experiment" that had gone on since 1929, the two events must have epitomized what each side feared most.[25]

The scandals demonstrated to many Americans how irresponsible it had been to entrust something as important as broadcasting to those who applied only one standard, profitability, to the venture. At the same time, many felt that a formal fairness doctrine signaled the first massive government intrusion into electronic media programming.

Fought by broadcasters for the next quarter-century as an infringement of their First Amendment rights, the fairness doctrine had two parts. First, as one of the responsibilities of holding a license granted by the FCC, each station was required to broadcast programs that dealt with controversial matters of public importance. Second, if a station presented any material on one side of a controversial issue, material on any other significant viewpoints had to be aired—not necessarily in a single program, but over a reasonable period of time. Theoretically, this doctrine could be used to revoke the license of an unresponsive station. The FCC chose, however, to use it only as a standard at the time of license renewal—and even then with the greatest reluctance.

Over the next decade the fairness doctrine would survive two major tests, both of which affirmed the rights of the public over the preferences of stations. In 1964 the United Church of Christ, led by its communications director, the Reverend Everett C. Parker, taped months of broadcasts by WLBT-TV (an affiliate of NBC and ABC) in Jackson, Mississippi. The tapes proved that although the station was licensed to serve an area whose population was 45 percent African American, all network programs on desegregation were replaced by "noncontroversial programming." The FCC, with only two dissenting votes, ruled for the stations and against the church, saying that because the commission alone could represent the public interest, the United Church of Christ had no legal standing in such a case.

The Reverend Mr. Parker went to the U.S. Court of Appeals for the District of Columbia Circuit, which unanimously ruled that WLBT had lost the right to renew its license. The Mississippi station went back to the FCC claiming that it had improved its behavior. The FCC, with the same two dissents, agreed; it voted to award WLBT a full three-year renewal. Finally, the U.S. Supreme Court overturned the FCC's renewal and awarded WLBT's license to a biracial, nonprofit organization.

The other case, even more definitive, concerned WGCB-TV in Red Lion, Pennsylvania. That station carried programs featuring the televangelist Billy James Hargis. When one of the Reverend Hargis's broadcasts charged a journalist, Fred Cook, with a lack of patriotism, Cook asked for airtime to defend himself under the personal attack rule, a subsection of the fairness doctrine. The station refused. Cook sued, and the case eventually was carried all the way to the Supreme Court. In May 1969, the Court shocked the television industry by delivering a unanimous decision read by the newly appointed chief justice, Warren Burger, supporting Cook's right to respond on the air to the attack against him. The decision included this crucial passage:

> A broadcaster seeks and is granted the free and exclusive use of a
> limited and valuable part of the public domain; when he accepts that

franchise it is burdened by enforceable public obligations. . . . [A] broadcast license is a public trust subject to termination for breach of duty.

The critical point concerning the fairness doctrine is that it was never a restraint on the First Amendment, but a stimulus to it. It was not censorship, but rather the public's best protection against censorship. The Mississippi station did not lose its license because it advocated racial segregation. Neither did the Red Lion station lose its license because it attacked a journalist's reputation. Thanks to the fairness doctrine, as enforced by the courts, these stations lost their licenses because they were clearly and beyond any doubt censoring viewpoints other than those they espoused. They were denying vital information to their viewers—in effect, disenfranchising a significant portion of their communities.

These stations were claiming First Amendment rights for themselves but denying those rights to their communities. They were shirking their public trusteeship—a responsibility that derives from the very nature of the television medium. Not everyone—not even every billionaire—can own a television station. Laws of physics tell us that only a limited number of frequencies can carry television signals. That limitation brought about the Radio Act of 1927: the government, to ensure that the airwaves were efficiently used in the public interest, had somehow to choose among those who wished to own stations, selecting some and rejecting others. Because broadcasting stations generate incredibly high profits on the revenues they bring in, many entrepreneurs wanted to own one. (This would be affirmed in the winter of 1990 when the FCC proposed adding as many as one thousand low-power television stations. The commission received more than five thousand applications. And in many of the top one hundred markets it received up to ten applications for every opening.)

With the election of John F. Kennedy, the National Association of Broadcasters naturally expected that the new FCC chairman would be compatible with the regulatory phase of the cycle. What it did not expect was the tumult created when it invited Newton Minow to address its annual meeting. He challenged the industry leaders to sit down before their television sets and watch for one day, sign-on to sign-off. They would find, he promised, "a vast wasteland." This phrase won Minow the fury of the industry, although his brief tenure on the commission produced little in the way of lasting, productive policies. Nevertheless, he remains one of the more enlightened chairmen in the FCC's history. Many would say that even the perceived threat he represented to the stations and networks invigorated television programming for some years to come.

In 1963 an FCC study showed that fully 40 percent of American television stations exceeded the NAB's own code of behavior in the number of commercials they broadcast per hour. In response, the NAB argued that whatever problem there might be could be solved only by its own self-regulation, which punished code violators by revoking their right to display over the air the NAB's "Seal of Good Practice"—a display that was never noticed by the overwhelming majority of viewers. In addition, the FCC learned that not once in the NAB's history had any station, whatever its code violations, suffered the removal of its seal-display rights. In response, the new FCC chairman, E. William Henry, proposed in 1964 that the NAB code of behavior be codified into law, allowing the commission to use the broadcasters' own professed standards to judge a station's performance at license renewal time. Clearly, this would not do. The NAB sent out a furious memorandum to all U.S. stations, stating that such a law "would open the door to unlimited governmental control of broadcasting."

That same year the association fired its new president, former Florida Governor Leroy Collins, soon after he publicly agreed that restrictions on cigarette advertising were needed. That issue returned to the forefront in 1967. In what may be the most important fairness doctrine case ever, a young lawyer, John Banzhaf III, acting as a private citizen, challenged WCBS-TV, New York, the CBS flagship station, under the doctrine to air public-service announcements (PSAs) against cigarettes, arguing that its cigarette commercials should be counter-balanced by a presentation of the evidence of tobacco-related disease contained in the 1964 Report of the U.S. Surgeon General. After the station refused to do so, Banzhaf appealed to the FCC.

The commission concurred with his argument but denied the principle of equal time, requiring only "a significant amount of time." Generally, this meant that one anti-cigarette commercial was broadcast for every three or four commercials that promoted smoking. Once again, major reform came neither from a crusading FCC nor from a self-regulating television industry (which understandably feared losing tobacco advertising income of nearly $220 million per year). Instead, true reform came, ironically and most reluctantly, from the tobacco manufacturers themselves. Despising the mandated antismoking commercials, and apparently believing that no news is better than bad news, they successfully lobbied Congress to pass legislation that banned all televised cigarette advertisements after 1970. When the commercials disappeared, so too did virtually all the PSAs, precisely what the tobacco industry had hoped for since the announcements had proven astonishingly effective. However, the number of smokers, already down to some extent from its high in 1965 of 42 percent of all American adults, decreased exponentially during and immediately after the mandated public service announcement campaign (and has continued to decline ever since). It is reasonable to suggest that Banzhaf's use of the fairness doctrine was instrumental in saving more than twenty million Americans from premature death. (Let it be noted, as a rare and shining example, that one group of stations, Westinghouse's Group W—Bill Baker's former venue—led by its maverick chairman, Donald H. McGannon, canceled all its cigarette commercials eight months before the legislation was passed.)

As these examples clearly show, the FCC has often supported business interests against any others. One particularly egregious instance occurred in 1966 when the FCC narrowly approved, by a vote of four to three, a petition by ITT and ABC stockholders to merge the two corporations. The petition argued that the merger was necessary because ABC badly needed the cash that ITT could provide. The FCC's approval was overturned by the Justice Department, which had discovered an internal ITT document that noted: "ABC's cash throw-off through 1970 will approach $100 million, almost all of which will be available for reinvestment outside the television business."[26]

Despite this revelation that the merger was clearly not designed, as had been represented, to benefit the public by ensuring that Americans would have three viable network sources of television programming, but rather to take advantage of ABC's profits to help ITT, the FCC, once again by a four-to-three vote, reapproved the merger. When the Justice Department continued to disagree, however, ITT backed off.

Yet another example of misregulation leading to unintended consequences took place in the mid-1970s when the FCC ruled that stations in the top fifty markets could present only three hours of network programs each night during the four most popular hours. As we examine in detail in later chapters, the prime-time access rule (PTAR), as it came to be known, would change network programming, local news, and viewer habits in ways not foreseen by the regulators.

The results further demonstrated the FCC's failure to understand, and therefore to improve, the television marketplace. Implementation of PTAR began with an initial period of chaos because CBS chose the 7:30–10:30 period (6:30–9:30 in the Central time zone), while ABC and NBC opted for 8:00–11:00. ABC and NBC, however, soon had second thoughts: they realized that CBS could schedule popular one-hour programs at 7:30 each night, thus changing the viewing patterns of a large segment of the prime-time audience and setting a pattern of successful program flow that would dominate the ratings throughout the week. The FCC calmed the waters by "suggesting" that all three networks select the 8:00–11:00 period for prime-time programming.

What Hath Mammon Wrought?

Quite apart from the scheduling details, the access rule soon led to a series of fiascoes. First, the FCC had vastly overestimated both the capability and the eagerness of the local stations to produce their own programs. As Les Brown observed in *Television: The Bu$iness Behind the Box*, the local stations have always been "as much to blame as the networks for the calibre of prime-time programming."[27] Some tried putting public affairs and other locally produced programs in the time period, but few stations were willing to put up the money to ensure their success. Most stations simply opted for reruns until the new made-for-access products began to arrive. Not too surprisingly, these consisted almost exclusively of game shows, which could be produced in Canada at a rate of five per day on a weekend at far lower cost than any other prime-time format.

There were notable exceptions, such as *PM Magazine*, produced by Westinghouse, and *The Muppet Show*, produced in the United Kingdom at the instigation of CBS-owned and -operated stations. *PM*'s format was licensed to other stations; *The Muppet Show* was syndicated by the Jim Henson organization throughout the United States and the world. Overall, however, giving stations the task of programming hours of prime time each week produced almost no local creativity.

The access rule also increased commercial clutter. Prior to PTAR, the networks were generally holding themselves to a limit of three minutes of advertisements per prime-time half-hour, while local stations were carrying twice as much advertising per half-hour in time they programmed locally. Once the rule went into effect, networks needed to achieve their profit goals with less inventory to sell: instead of having twenty-four minutes of announcement time exclusive of the news broadcast, each network now had only eighteen minutes to offer the advertisers every evening. Since overall advertising demand for access to a nationwide market is relatively constant, prices went up. This increase, in turn, prompted advertisers to replace many one-minute announcements with thirty-second, even fifteen-second, commercials. Although actual commercial time did not increase, the number of announcements certainly did.

Deregulation: The Pendulum Swings

Today, of course, many of these regulations are only memories. The fairness doctrine, for example, despite the expressed belief in Congress that it should be taken up again, fell victim to the deregulation fever that prevailed in Washington in the late seventies and throughout most of the next decade. According to the advocates of "pure" marketplace economics, a government has few roles to play other than the military one. They argue that in virtually every other area, commercial competition provides greater consumer choice at lower cost if government "gets out of the way." Our fortieth president, Ronald Reagan, stated in his first inaugural address: "Government is the problem, not the solution." Ten years later, well into the wide-open eighties, the George Bush White House was still persuaded that industries can police themselves, with no additional ethics regulations. They seemed to think that all we really need is the Ten Commandments, the only problem being that some people haven't read them yet.

Indeed, that problem did exist. In its heyday, the motto of the deregulatory movement seemed to be "greed is good." Suddenly there were more deca- and centa-millionaires, as well as more billionaires, than in any time in our history. Deregulation played a significant role in this transfer of wealth.

For the general public, the going was a bit more mixed. Among the first industries to be freed of the government's chains were America's airlines. President Carter's economics adviser, Alfred Kahn, dismantled the Civil Aeronautics Board. In the short term, entrepreneurial energy exploded: 176 new airlines entered the marketplace with cut-rate prices. Laissez-faire policies seemed to have unleashed a traveler's paradise. But trouble lay ahead. The airline industry is too investment-heavy (and, many would argue, too essential to the nation's infrastructure) to survive simple cost competition. By 1986 the top six airlines controlled a higher market share than in the early seventies, and prices adjusted for fuel costs were rising far faster than in the days of regulation. By 1991 all but one of the 176 new airlines had disappeared. The sole exception, America West, rested in bankruptcy. By 1992 four U.S. airlines controlled two-thirds of the domestic market—up from 42 percent in 1985. And it cost less to take a taxi ride (ninety cents per mile) than to fly (one dollar per mile) from St. Louis to Kansas City.

Other essential industries were deregulated just as successfully. The savings and loan associations were freed from bureaucratic restrictions against speculative investments. Thus unencumbered, they managed to lose half a trillion dollars in ten years.

Soon it was television's turn. Leading the deregulatory charge on television (or, as he preferred to call it, "unregulation") was Mark Fowler, the FCC chairman from 1981 to 1987. Fowler, a lawyer and former disc jockey known as "Mad Mark," was blessed with a talent for the pungent phrase. He referred to the FCC he inherited as "the last of the New Deal dinosaurs." In meetings with broadcasters, he contended that the commission had no business thinking about programming, let alone any such concept as the public interest. "TV," he said, "is a toaster with pictures."[28]

Armed with this philosophy of the public interest, his FCC in 1984 abolished the anti-trafficking rule, which had required that anyone buying a television station had to keep it for at least three years before selling it. Networks and stations were subsequently swept up into the maelstrom of stock speculation, mergers, and leveraged buyouts. Very quickly, those broadcasters who wished to remain independent of buyers with deep pockets were forced to go into unprecedented debt in order to buy back their own stock. Ultimately, all three major networks were purchased by new owners— CBS and NBC by companies with little or no experience in television programming. The networks thus fell victims to a common business school myth: that management skills are interchangeable and generic.

Thus, most of American television has now passed through the three-step cycle that has troubled a multitude of our industries: the passage from the hands of the *creators* (such as Ernst Alexanderson and Edwin Armstrong, who invented, respectively, AM and FM radio); to those of the *leaders* (the Sarnoffs, Paleys, and Stantons), who know and love their businesses, take personal pride in their programs, and feel responsible for their operations; and finally into those of the *managers*, the business school graduates—often financial wizards—who regard their new acquisitions as cash cows to be milked for a creamier bottom line.

W. Edwards Deming is the American guru of quality; his Zen-like teachings are revered by the Japanese, whose industries he helped revive after World War II. According to Deming, profits pursued as primary goals are fickle phantoms. They become long-term rewards only to the company that knows its products, respects its customers, and wins their abiding loyalty by providing them with a product of the highest quality. Unfortunately, this goal is beyond the vision of most MBA matrix-managers.

The other media have now been struck by the same fate. Listen to the cry of betrayed leadership by Arthur Temple, a board member of Time Inc., arguing against the merger of Time with Warner: "If all you want to do is make money by whatever means, let's just open a string of whorehouses across the country!"[29]

At least one of Mark Fowler's ambitions was frustrated while he ruled the FCC. While overturning the anti-trafficking rule, he announced his determination to crush the fairness doctrine as well. "The marketplace of ideas," he wrote with Jeffersonian passion, "is too important to be subject to the grease pencil of a censor." For this cause, he gained judicial support from two members of the U.S. Court of Appeals for the District of Columbia Circuit—the not-quite future Supreme Court justice Robert Bork and his more successful colleague, Antonin Scalia. They ruled that the concept of the fairness doctrine embedded in the 1959 amendment to section 315 of the Communications Act of 1934 was subject to nullification by the commission. Congress sought to overturn this decision by legislation in 1987, but President Reagan vetoed the bill. By then, the FCC was under the chairmanship of Dennis Patrick, who thereby won the race against Fowler to abolish the fairness doctrine. In a 1989 decision, *Syracuse Peace Council v. FCC,* the D.C. circuit court again upheld the FCC's right to terminate the doctrine. Since then, Congress has been unable to muster enough votes to override a presidential veto.

Even if the fairness doctrine were to be reinstated, the good that it might do would depend heavily upon the regulators' will to enforce it. The FCC's record on almost any form of regulation is not encouraging. By the end of 1995 there were 1,544 full-strength and 1,772 low-power American television stations, each with a three-year license subject to renewal. And yet, after forty years, the FCC has denied, or dismissed without regranting, the licenses of only ten stations. As we have seen, even the more activist commissioners have continually fallen back on the "invisible hand" power of competition to accomplish what is necessary. Time and again, the assumption has been that competition leads to diversity, which ensures quality. This formula has always been an illusion.

More than thirty years ago a former FCC commissioner, Charles H. King, defended the networks against the would-be reformers. In a conference on "Freedom and Responsibility in Broadcasting" at the Northwestern University School of Law, King (who was then a Detroit College of Law professor) sarcastically declared: "All I can say is, I'm sure that [the chairmen of ABC, NBC, and CBS] would be extremely surprised to learn that they are no longer in competition with each other, that between them they're just a big fat monopoly! They're just about as much a monopoly as Ford, Chrysler, and General Motors!"[30]

In retrospect, King's choice of analogy is particularly appropriate. Of course the networks were "competitive"—with each other. Just so, the Big Three of Detroit were competitive—with each other. But neither the television nor automobile marketplace produced for Americans a broad-based set of consumer choices. Television viewers who wanted noncommercial programs of high quality were in precisely the same fix as consumers who wished to buy an excellent, economical, energy-efficient, safe, long-lasting, nonrusting, domestically manufactured automobile. The ferocious competitiveness of these two marketplaces tended to produce neither diversity nor excellence, but rather a shoddy sameness—caused, again, not by the moral or intellectual failings of individual American executives, but rather by the pressures of the system. A survey of Fortune 1000 CEOs by the MIT economist, James Poterba, and Laurence N. Summers, undersecretary of the Treasury for International Affairs, showed that American "firms had systematically shorter time horizons than their major competitors in Europe and (especially) Asia." They suggest that this is "not 'managerial paranoia'" but comes from the fact that U.S. investors—even during recent years, when real debt cost has averaged only about 2 percent—demand 12+ percent inflation-adjusted profits—much more than Germany or Japan (whose respective research and development investments are about 60 and 50 percent long term—in contrast to the United States's 20 percent).[31]

Not only are media executives, and especially television executives, subject to the same pressures, but their companies are expected to generate more profit per dollar of revenue than virtually any other industry. Newspapers, for example, generated 24–34 percent profit during the 1980s. During the 1990s their profitability dropped for a number of reasons, including what Veronis Suhler & Associates, the media brokerage and consultant company, refer to as the "ballooning growth in newsprint prices" and increased distribution expenses.[32] In 1996 it cost about three dollars to print and deliver a copy of the *New York Times*, and five dollars for the Sunday edition. Higher production costs have forced newspapers to rely more and more on advertisers for their revenue. A record fifty-nine million papers were sold in this country each weekday in 1994, but the last fifteen years have seen an 8 percent decrease in the number of American adults who read newspapers. Nonetheless, newspaper profitability now averages 14 percent—roughly three times the profitability of the Fortune 500 companies.

Television station profitability, on the other hand, is rising. In

1996 the average commercial station was expected to make a profit of 35–55 percent of revenues. Expectations of that magnitude put enormous pressure on the general management of a commercial television station. Indeed, they put pressure on the industry as a whole, so that public television is affected as well. It is our contention that this unremitting pressure proceeds directly from the shortcomings of regulation, especially as it has failed to insulate a vital national information and cultural resource from speculators.

When Mark Fowler attacked the fairness doctrine as an affront to the marketplace of ideas, he was pressing a powerful button. The marketplace of ideas is a metaphor that resonates deeply in our national ethos; one of America's proudest traditions, the concept in fact predates the Bill of Rights, the Declaration of Independence, and the Federalist Papers, going back to John Milton's *Areopagitica* of 1644. Unfortunately, the marketplace of ideas remains only a metaphor in the television industry. As the sociologist and media scholar Todd Gitlin has argued: "They are not *trying* to stimulate us to thought, or inspire us to belief, or remind us of what it is to be human and live on the earth late in the twentieth century; what they are trying to do is 'hook' us. Meanwhile, the government regulatory agencies have been persuaded that 'the marketplace' is its own regulator, which means that no interest that cannot be expressed as Nielson numbers counts."[33]

(2)

The Road Not Taken
The British
Broadcasting Corporation

BROADCASTING BEGAN at about the same time in a number of industrialized countries. And yet the two largest English-speaking countries made very different choices with respect to the infant medium. For several reasons—the American tradition and how we interpreted it, the zeitgeist of the twenties, the sense of urgency that so often drives commerce—we made our choice. Or more precisely, we made decisions that amounted to a choice.

Although it had seemed to Herbert Hoover that radio, unique among American industries, sought governmental regulation, the zeitgeist favored laissez-faire. Once the basic problem of frequency allocation was solved, industry and government went their separate ways. A widely held belief of the period was that government should play as small a role as possible in the affairs of business and industry.

The Road Not Taken

What if that belief had proved to be flawed? What if the idea that government is a natural enemy of radio and television and that all regulation is harmful had turned out to be a myth? What might have happened had we taken the other road?

The British Pioneers

These are not just speculative questions, for we have only to look at the United Kingdom, which took the other road, to learn much about where we went wrong and what our television might have become. From the very outset, the United Kingdom—unlike the United States—recognized the new medium as a major cultural and informational resource whose development should be nurtured through periodic review by concerned, impartial, and informed citizens.

At precisely 3:00 P.M. Greenwich Mean Time, on Monday, November 2, 1936, the world's first regularly scheduled television service began broadcasting under the same network management as it does today. Only four hundred receivers within thirty miles were capable of receiving the 240-line-per-inch service, referred to at that time as "high definition," in contrast to some other early systems with their barely discernible 30-line resolution. During the two hours a day of broadcasts in the first week, viewers were able to see a preview of the marvels that early television would present—a famous aviator, a pair of equally renowned tennis players, two popular American comedians, as well as tap dancing, boxing, a ballet, pictures of a London art show, a musical, champion German shepherd dogs, and a bus driver who displayed the model he had made of Sir Francis Drake's ship, the *Golden Hind*.

But they saw no commercials. BBC television—for that was the network in question—has never yet carried advertising.

Unlike the United States, most countries of the world do not have predominantly commercial television systems. Programming is content-driven rather than profit-driven. To most Americans, if they think about this at all, the obvious example of such programming is the output of the United Kingdom's British Broadcasting Corporation, or "the Beeb," as it is frequently called.

How did the BBC come into being, and how did it manage to avoid the traps of Mammon? Paradoxically, fourteen years before its first regularly scheduled television broadcasts, the BBC's senior service, radio, began operating as a *commercial* network. Like the Americans, the British had considered radio a point-to-point communications medium—one they had long been awaiting. When the Italian youth Guglielmo Marconi beat out the world's electrophysicists and found a way to piggyback Morse code dots and dashes on Herzian waves, the British were first in line to finance his development and marketing of the equipment that would make communication beyond the horizon a reality. No one was surprised at the eagerness of the British: at the beginning of the twentieth century, schoolchildren around the world were accustomed to maps dominated by the color red, assigned to the far-flung empire on which, it was proudly said, the sun never set. The world's most successful and largest imperial power, the Queen of the Seas, had a great need for the latest communications technology because of its obvious interest in keeping in touch with its more than one hundred colonies, territories, protectorates, and dominions.

In 1897 Marconi received his patent and British investors joined him in establishing what would become Marconi's Wireless Telegraph and Signal Company, Limited. Marconi had already shown a nose for news-making as well as news-gathering. The combination of his services to the queen and his coverage of the Kingstown Regatta for the *Dublin Daily Express* and the America's Cup yacht races for the *New York Herald* made him an international figure and helped solidify his company's position in the growing race for domination in the communication field. By the time World War I began in 1914, the United Kingdom was a leader in radio equipment manufacture, and Marconi's company led the pack.

The royal navy demanded radio equipment for all its ships, the

RAF for its planes, and the army for communications from trench to trench and back to headquarters. The Marconi firm and others were pressed into service to meet these demands, as were American companies making radio receivers, transmitters, and parts.

When the war ended, there was an excess production capacity, a vast cadre of trained radio operators, and pent-up interest on the part of radio amateurs and other potential listeners. Marconi and the other companies began experimental broadcasting of music, news, and lectures to satisfy that demand and to expand the market for their products. Along with its historic role in overseeing and operating telegraph and telephone services, the British Post Office had long held licensing authority for radio frequencies. At first, the post office was concerned that the broadcasts were "frivolous" and rescinded the Marconi license. Soon the postmaster general was confronted with a petition from some sixty wireless societies. They expressed their outrage over being denied weather reports, news, and music provided to the wireless societies by competent companies that were willing to do so without interfering with the national defense. The postmaster general saw fit to renew the Marconi license and to encourage the station's management to develop a popular service of several hours a week of both speech and music. Asa Briggs, in his definitive work *The Birth of Broadcasting: The History of Broadcasting in the United Kingdom*, suggests that these young and creative managers were so motivated and so successful, they virtually "guaranteed the future of broadcasting in Britain."[1]

That future took the immediate form of a commercial company, the British Broadcasting Company, established in December 1922 with Marconi's Wireless and seven other companies as shareholders. It was licensed to build and operate eight stations that would be financed by fees of ten shillings per receiver and to operate to "the reasonable satisfaction of the Postmaster General." The company would send half of the revenue from the license fees to the government, retaining the rest.

The newly formed company hired a twenty-three-year-old Scot,

John Charles Walsham Reith, as its first chief executive. Reith, ultimately Lord Reith, proved a nearly perfect choice. The son of a Presbyterian cleric and a mechanical engineer by training, Reith had been severely wounded in the war, withdrawn from combat, and sent to the United States to facilitate the purchasing and delivery of war materiel. His familiarity with the United States and its emerging broadcasting system would prove invaluable. Reith almost immediately enunciated his "classic trinity of broadcasting principles," as John Scupham, the future BBC controller of educational broadcasting, would call Reith's succinct description of the role of broadcasting in British society: "Broadcasting represents a job of entertaining, informing and educating the nation, and should therefore be distinctly regarded as a public service."[2] Reith continually reminded his colleagues that the three principles overlapped, a judgment reaffirmed by a succession of committees of inquiry and governments.

Whether or not the British Broadcasting Company met the "reasonable satisfaction" of the postmaster general during the two years of its first license may be beside the point, since that minister was undoubtedly preoccupied and beleaguered by the many other questions raised by those with conflicting interests. True to his political calling, he decided to resolve them by convening a committee that would conduct a formal public inquiry. The committee was chaired by Major General Sir Frederick Sykes, and its members included representatives of the postmaster general, Parliament, the press, the Radio Association of Great Britain, and the British Broadcasting Company. Thirty-four meetings and countless interviews later, the committee's report concluded that because "broadcasting holds social and political possibilities as great as any technical attainment of our generation . . . the control of such a potent power over public opinion and the life of the nation ought to remain with the State."[3]

The report was adamant that such an important national service not be allowed to become an unrestricted commercial monopoly. Nevertheless, the Sykes Committee recommended, and the government approved, an extension of the commercial British Broadcasting

Company's license through 1926. Terence O'Brien, looking at this period a decade later in *British Experiments in Public Ownership and Control*, reasoned that the option of monopoly control "was undoubtedly influenced by the experience of the broadcasting boom in the United States which had led to a condition bordering on chaos in that country as a result of competition for and in the air between a large number of independently-owned stations."[4]

During this second license period, the number of radio receivers increased by 50 percent and the nine stations reached 80 percent of the country. Citing both practical and theoretical objections to leaving broadcasting in the hands of a private company composed of radio equipment manufacturers, O'Brien noted the widespread belief that the time had come to introduce a more impartial operation and a more definite form of public control.

The postmaster general appointed another committee.

The committee, under the Earl of Crawford, opted to continue monopolistic control, but in the hands of a public corporation "acting as trustee for the national interest in broadcasting." This spelled the end of the commercial British Broadcasting Company and of the profits shared by the seven manufacturers and their shareholders. Henceforth, the license fees would go entirely toward funding the work of the new corporation. To this day, the concept of funding public broadcasting primarily from a fee paid by the consumer for each receiver prevails in the United Kingdom. The license fee (currently approximately $150 for a color set, virtually all of which goes to fund the service) has been a source of stability for the BBC, as it has been for the many other fee-supported systems, including those of twenty members of the European Broadcasting Union from Scandinavia to Turkey.

The postmaster general informed the House of Commons that the government agreed with the Crawford Committee, a royal charter was sought and issued, and the British Broadcasting *Corporation* began a ten-year license term of operation on January 1, 1927. Reith, by then Sir John Reith, was to be at the helm.

Enter the BBC

The year 1927 was significant for broadcasting on both sides of the Atlantic. The British had gone so far as to permit a for-profit company to operate the system; the United States had seen seven hundred for-profit stations become increasingly commercial. Moreover, both countries had new regulatory schemes in place. Yet even taking into account the inevitable differences due to the relative sizes of the two countries, their approaches to broadcasting still presented a marked contrast. In the United States, a succession of industry-initiated and -dominated conferences had been followed by brief congressional hearings. In the United Kingdom, two government-appointed committees made up of leaders from many disciplines and perspectives had been extensively covered and discussed in the national press. There the issues, including broadcasting's potential for educating and informing, had become the subject of national debate; in the United States, the 1927 act had passed through Congress in record time. The major difference, however, was that the U.S. law was strongly anti-monopoly while continuing to keep radio in private hands, and the British opted for a monopoly, but in the hands of a public trust.

The nature of the monopoly established in the United Kingdom is little understood by Americans. "'The government-controlled BBC'—how often I used to read those words when I was working in the United States, and how often I gainsaid them, to no discernible effect," recalled Leonard Miall, the longtime chief BBC news correspondent and director of its New York office. "Many people assume that if an organization is not private enterprise it must be government, though the American Red Cross is an exception to that rule. Certainly the BBC is not private enterprise."[5]

Underscoring that point, the British are proud to explain that the BBC has sued the government and succeeded in collecting several million pounds. Surely, the British argue, you can hardly sue the government if you are part of it. They also point out that BBC employees are not civil servants, and that the government does not tell the BBC what it may or may not broadcast, although like all governments in all Western democracies, Miall reminds us, it sometimes tries to lean on the media.

All governments have several inescapable interests in television. Since the electromagnetic spectrum is limited, only so many television and radio signals can be sent through the air at any one time. Because the electronic media play such important roles in military and public safety issues—the emergency broadcasting system and the weather channels, for example—setting aside portions of the spectrum for those and other nonbroadcast purposes requires government attention. Similarly, assigning frequencies to broadcasting and land-mobile communications and determining who will have their exclusive use requires a licensing authority. Further, governments are parties to international treaties on the allocations of spectrum.

All those considerations stem from physics; politics dictates others. The mass media can serve as informed observers and surrogates for the public in keeping government both attentive and honest, and they have often used that capacity. When it serves their ends, governments make use of the media's capacity to reach the entire body politic. But even the most open and democratic of governments often tries to keep some information from reaching the media. How a government interacts with the media depends on how it has traditionally interacted with the public. The traditional relationship of the three forces—the government, the public, and the media industries—is the most accurate predictor of how a nation's television system will be established. Ultimately, a nation reinvents broadcasting in its own image.

Under Reith's stewardship, there was little doubt about what the British image required: "As we conceive it, our responsibility is to carry into the greatest possible number of homes everything that is best in every department of human knowledge, endeavor, or achievement."[6] In making the choices they did, the British were reflecting their own history and setting the ground rules for the future relationship among the government, the public, and the media.

There are only three options open to any government:

1. It can operate the television system and thus control the content.

2. It can license the frequency to private interest.

3. As the British did, it can establish a public institution to operate the system.

Parliament's unusual choice of a royal charter to establish the corporation granted the BBC a certain independence of government and the status of association with the crown. The original charter was granted for 1927–1936; subsequently, with very few changes, it has been renewed seven times, most recently in 1996. The charter establishes and sets forth the "Objects of the Corporation," specifies the number of governors (currently twelve, including one governor each for Northern Ireland, Scotland, and Wales), includes its constitution, and provides for general advisory committees as well as national broadcasting councils. The charter also requires the corporation to obtain a license from the secretary of state for the Home Department, the successor minister to the postmaster general.

In addition to details on financing and technical matters, the charter also sets out the so-called reserve powers—the prerogatives the government reserves unto itself. It specifies that the home secretary may order the corporation not to broadcast "any matter or matters of any class specified in such notice." This chilling passage was behind the bizarre practice of having actors voice-over the words that television viewers could see were being spoken by Gerry Adams and other IRA leaders.

In the first fifty years of broadcasting in the United Kingdom, the government chose to exercise these powers only five times. Two of the five directives remain in place—a 1927 ruling against editorializing, and another prohibiting subliminal messages. It has also been noted that the government has never withheld funds in order to influence or control the BBC's policies or broadcasts.

From the outset, the emphasis in the BBC was on programming. Its managers were the *creators,* and their leader, Sir John Reith, clearly qualified as one of the world's broadcasting *leaders.* Invoking his "trinity" of broadcasting principles, Sir John warned the nation that the entertainment provided by the service needed to be balanced with information and education. The BBC followed that advice in 1927 when radio was established, and again, still under Sir John's leadership, when television service began in 1936.

Lord Reith, as he was to become, would leave the BBC in 1938 to establish British Airways, but his philosophy remained in place. Fifty years after television service began, Alasdair Milne, the incumbent director general, summarized the system put into place by his first predecessor.

> BBC television has always rested on four assumptions; you have to have security of income; you have to have the freedom to choose the most creative people to do your programs; once chosen, you have to trust these people and let them get on with it; and finally, you must not divide the public into permanent majorities and minorities, when every one of us belongs temporarily to one or the other group depending on the subject in view.[7]

The fundamental imperative of the BBC for most of its history has been public service rather than profit, and a service driven by content rather than by schedule. A commercial network, in the interest of maintaining its *audience-in-being,* must reject some programs because of their probable effect on the programs that follow in the schedule. Not so the BBC. Being free to choose programs on their merits, the BBC built a tradition and a record second to none.

When World War II forced BBC television to go dark, less than three years after it began (the television transmitter tower would have provided the Luftwaffe with a perfect homing device), it was reaching twenty thousand licensed television receivers and an audience estimated at more than one hundred thousand regular viewers, a more than tenfold increase. As it went off the air in 1939, a Mickey Mouse cartoon was in progress. In June 1946, in typically British fashion, BBC television resumed at the exact point in the interrupted cartoon, "to emphasize continuity," the BBC's research historian points out, and "just in time for London's Great Victory parade."[8]

The BBC also, of course, picked up where it had left off. Reith had charted a clear course: "That broadcasting should be merely a vehicle of light entertainment, was a limitation of its function which we declined to accept. It has been our endeavor to give a conscious, social purpose to the exploitation of this medium."[9]

The Monopoly Ends

At first, postwar television had the same wide-eyed eclecticism that had characterized its first two weeks on the air. Peter Black, the long-time television critic of the *London Daily Mail,* recalled:

> It exploited the fact that any picture of an activity was interesting. As it probably had not been seen before this was usually correct. The program-builders hated the regularity of schedules. They sought the unexpected. Thus, the visit to the glass-blowers would be followed by the comedian Terry Thomas, or a piano recital by Pouishnott, or a demonstration of omelette cooking.

Viewers who had never attended a concert in their lives responded enthusiastically to the piano recital. In Black's opinion, "Anything outstandingly good could be recognized as such by audiences to whom it was a new experience."[10]

By 1954 the BBC was on the air for forty hours a week with nightly audiences of more than five million people. There were three dramatic productions a week. Trollope's *The Warden* had appeared in 1951, and the BBC was soon embarked on a regular production schedule of dramatizations of classic novels that would become a signature of British television. Documentaries covered such subjects as homelessness, child abuse, marital difficulties, and alcoholism. Situation comedies were particularly popular, as was *Animal, Vegetable, Mineral*. In this adaptation of a CBS program, archaeologists, anthropologists, and art historians tried to identify mysterious objects from museum storehouses. The BBC version, however, played in prime time, while CBS ran the program in what was then known as the "cultural ghetto" of American television, Sunday afternoon.

Although television households did not proliferate as rapidly in the United Kingdom as in the United States—Britons had very little discretionary income after the war—by any other measure the first postwar decade was a glorious time for the BBC and its audiences. Lord Reith, appearing before the Beveridge Committee in 1949, ascribed the corporation's success largely to one significant factor: "It was the brute force of the monopoly that enabled the BBC to become what it did; and to do what it did; that made it possible for a policy of moral responsibility to be followed."[11]

Not everyone in the United Kingdom was as pleased with that monopoly as was his lordship. Indeed, the call to ask that very question, and to explore the alternatives to monopoly, had prompted the formal investigation undertaken by the Beveridge Committee in 1949. The Labor government, after a period of deliberation that lasted from the end of the war, when the party came into power, until 1951, finally came out in support of Beveridge and the continuation of the status quo. However, a very persuasive group of Conservative members of Parliament succeeded in changing the new Labor government's thinking about private enterprise—and particularly about commercial broadcasting.

In May 1952, the Labor government announced its decision: BBC radio would remain a monopoly, but the government would favor "some element of competition" in television. Reith, "still an unrepentant monopolist" eight years after the fact, described the decision with characteristic tact: "The Conservatives quickly pushed the wretched maggot of commercialism into the body politic of broadcasting; and that was that."[12]

Commercial television had come to the United Kingdom and with it an elaborate but logical system for isolating the creative from the regulatory and technical processes. The Independent Broadcasting Authority, IBA (originally the Independent Television Authority but given a new name when it was given a mandate to set up commercial radio in 1972) was set up as a public corporation with no stockholders and with a government-appointed board, but unlike the BBC, it does not have the cachet or the latitude of a royal charter. The IBA's "formal powers are to regulate programming in the public interest," as the Pilkington Committee stated.[13] In addition to its regulatory role, especially with respect to advertising, it was charged with building, maintaining, and operating transmitters throughout the United Kingdom, making possible an interconnected national network. IBA oversees and coordinates scheduling of that network, and all other commercial broadcasting. The commercial network began broadcasting in August 1954, under a ten-year license from the postmaster general, once again the licensing authority.

Programming and advertising are the province of ITV, the term for the fifteen regional companies it franchises.

There are only fourteen regions, but London's service is divided between two companies. For many years Thames Television provided service from Monday to Friday; London Weekend, aptly named, programmed the remaining two days. The Big Five companies—those with the largest populations—include the two London franchisees and those serving northwest England (Granada), the east coast (Yorkshire Television), and the Midlands (Associated Television, or ATV, later Central Television). Other regional companies operate in Scotland, Wales, Northern Ireland, the Channel Islands, and other regions in England.

The ITV companies set up a joint news service, Independent Television News (ITN). In a typical recent year, centrally produced news programs (essentially national and international news) filled 7 percent of the total broadcast day, and regional programs another 8 percent. The bulk of the network schedule comprised programs from the Big Five (49 percent) and programs acquired from outside sources (28 percent). Programming for the remaining 8 percent of the schedule was provided by the other regional broadcasting companies.

The IBA charges each company for the use of the transmitting facilities on a sliding scale based on the size of its audience and therefore its ability to pay. The authority receives none of the advertising revenues, which go to the regional companies and pay for their programming, but it does regulate all advertising. Advertising time is restricted to six minutes per hour at most and is not permitted to interrupt programming, as it does in the United States.

Within the first two years of commercial competition, 1954 to 1956, the BBC lost two-thirds of its audience. Some of this loss was undoubtedly due to the novelty of choice, but at least part of the shift was due to the BBC's program-driven, paternalistic policies. ITV behaved more like a fast-food chain than like the BBC's four-star gourmet restaurant. It offered the dishes most of the customers wanted at times convenient to them.

Part of the erosion of audience was undoubtedly related to certain criticisms of the BBC dating to the earliest Reithian days. There is little doubt that Reith, who likened the BBC to a ship with himself as the chief pilot, "securely articulated the values, standards and beliefs of the British upper middle-class, especially that part educated at Oxford and Cambridge," as Ien Ang points out in *Desperately Seeking the Audience*.[14] BBC policy was deliberately to raise the level of musical taste and to encourage serious, attentive, and purposeful listening, eschewing any notion of using the radio as background noise. The paternalistic, moralistic tone of the pronouncements of Reith and others also underscored how seriously the executives of the radio period took the threat of the Americanization of culture so feared by many critics. Popular music, much of which came from across the Atlantic, was perceived as inferior to the music the educated knew and appreciated. One 1930s Labor MP alluded to the class bias of the BBC when he told Parliament that the network "was run very largely by people who do not know the working class point of view, do not understand the working class point of view, but are seeking evidently to mould the working class" (p. 108).

Reith had been undeterred by such criticism. Indeed, according to Ang, Reith believed that

> public service broadcasting was meant to be a form of enlightened cultural dictatorship, in which a single set of standards and tastes was imposed on the entire national audience. . . . What Reith strived for was the creation of a common national culture: the BBC's self-conception was that of a "national church" to whose authority all citizens must be subjected.

Reith's flinty single-mindedness has already been seen in his characterization of commercialism; Churchill used to refer to him as "that withering height" (p. 109). It is understandable that his critics sometimes painted him in villainous hues, but Ien Ang cautions:

> Such rightminded [sic] authoritarianism should not be too easily dismissed as manipulative or elitist. Rather, these ideas were linked to a well-intentioned stance on broadcasting as a means for the democratization of culture and society, in the sincere belief that democracy was directly related to principled and conscientious cultural leadership and guidance, to giving people access to established cultural forms from which they were previously excluded. (P. 109)

One countertrend, however, was already evident. During World War II, the BBC's value as a link to home for the troops was clearly realized and exploited. But it soon became apparent that modifying the BBC schedule in favor of light music and popular entertainment would greatly improve morale. The resulting service, Forces Program, proved to be so popular not only with the troops but also with those at home that after the war it forced a modification from single to tripartite service: BBC Light, BBC Home, and the BBC Third Service, as determinedly meaty as the Light was frothy. Later the transnational Radio Luxembourg and pirate radio stations operating in the North Sea would prompt another revamping of the radio playlists.

By the 1950s it was popular, even among young intellectuals, to refer to the BBC, both radio and television, as "Auntie." The moniker was often used affectionately but nevertheless denoted a caretaker with a certain fustian aura. Now Auntie had to contend with what ITV was promoting as "people's television." Faced with the drastic loss of audience and the reality of competition, the BBC was forced to reexamine some of its practices.

For one thing, it realized that although it did not have to compete for advertising revenues, as American broadcasters did, it did have to compete for audience attention. Traditionally the BBC had engaged in rigorous research designed to determine the level of "satisfaction" the audience derived from its various programs. Using a standard sample size of 2,250 with a different panel each day, standardized questions were asked on what they had heard on BBC radio or seen on the television service in the previous twenty-four hours. From these answers an index of audience appreciation was derived. The BBC had no desire to abandon this measure, which had been helpful over the years, but it did begin to examine the size of its audience as well. As the *BBC Handbook, 1957* admitted, it was "of obvious importance to the BBC to know how those of the television public who have a choice of programmes divide their evening time" (p. 114).

There was no doubt that the ITV had hit a nerve with its populist appeal. Ien Ang's analysis is that "commercial television's most significant impact was the breaking of the BBC's cultural monopoly in defining what broadcasting should be about" (p. 115).

The BBC had both some time to respond to the challenge ITV

represented—it would take nearly a decade before the new network was entirely in place—and many resources, not the least of which was a highly professional staff. There is some dispute as to what turned the tide. Some contend it was competition, arguing that a monopoly engaged in repeated activities, day after day, is bound to become stale and any competition will reinvigorate it. Sir Frederick Ogilvy, who followed Reith as director general of the BBC from 1938 to 1942, asserted in a letter to the *London Times* in 1946 that "monopoly of broadcasting is inevitably the negation of freedom, no matter how efficiently it is run, or how wise or kindly the boards or committees in charge of it. It denies freedom of choice to listeners."[15]

From the vantage point of the 1970s, Anthony Smith assessed that earlier period:

> For many in the BBC competition brought enormous creative opportunities. Under the leadership of Sir Hugh Greene, the BBC responded to the competitive situation by not adopting the programmes or criteria of the commercial system but by acquiring a new impetus of its own. Producers within the BBC were more often conscious of an internal competition between the different sections of the BBC, producing an enormous flowering of talent and inventiveness which became characteristic of the broadcasting in the first half of the 1960's; the coming of commercial television had undoubtedly produced a mood of competitiveness, but the changes which occurred within the BBC were not to any great extent imitative of independent television.[16]

Lord Reith had been gone from the BBC for more than twenty years, but the paradigm he had established remained in force during the beginning of the competitive era. If anything, the coming of commercial broadcasting in the late 1950s prompted the BBC to become even more "serious" in its programming. Reith saw the BBC variously as a ship or a church. The audience was either the passengers or the congregation, and the broadcaster the captain or the priest. A new paradigm was to appear with the selection of Hugh Greene as director general. Greene held the post from 1960 to 1969, a period in British history "when the hierarchical idea of society as a cultural pyramid gave way to a more liberal vision of cultural pluralism," as Ang saw it.[17] Greene's metaphor for the BBC was a mirror: "I don't care whether what is reflected in the mirror is bigotry, injustice and intolerance or accomplishment and inspiring achievement. I only want the mirror to be honest, without any curves, and held with as steady a hand as may be" (p. 115).

The implications of the change were enormous. For the previous four decades the BBC had been avowedly paternalistic, transmitting its own values, tastes, and habits in the assumption that they should be adopted by all. A mirror cannot concern itself with public betterment. Holding a mirror with a steady hand would not require moral certainty but carefully developed professional skills. Contemporary accounts bear this out. The historian Asa Briggs reports that within the BBC in the 1960s "there was as much talk about professional standards of the producer and of the team of people who worked with him as there was of the 'social purposes' of broadcasting."[18] T. Burns, in *The BBC: Public Institution and Private World*, observed that the shift to an "ethos of professionalism, in which the central concern is with the quality of performance," was tantamount to "a shift from treating broadcasting as a means to treating broadcasting as an end."[19]

The public broadcaster would soon have the opportunity to put its newfound professionalism to the test. The BBC had long sought a second television channel, which, it contended, was essential to its operation. As proof, it offered its radio experience. The ability to shift programming from one radio network to another had multiplied the BBC's effectiveness. BBC television's case, however, was weakened by its 27 percent audience share—ITA could have made a stronger claim for a second commercial channel—and by the unseemliness of competing for audience.

An opportunity to compete arose as criticism of the new commercial channel mounted. Members of Parliament railed against what they saw to be excessive profiteering; newspapers saw their advertising monopoly eroding; others complained about the quality of the commercials. Once again, history was on the side of the BBC.

The Power of Periodic Review

The history of British broadcasting is paginated by the distinguished committees that have looked at the state of the art whenever problems arose, and particularly when the time has approached for charter renewal. Both the BBC and the IBA charters came up for renewal in 1964. The Pilkington Committee was convened, and the BBC was given, in Peter Black's term, "a respectable motive to compete." Among the competitive strategies it selected were moving the "classic drama series to teatime on Sundays where they found their audience. Thirteen week schedules were adopted for primetime, even as they had been by ITV. The BBC share of audience rose."[20]

Sir Henry Pilkington's committee considered more than eight hundred written statements and held seventy-eight days of public hearings. Of the succession of committees and reports, Sir Henry's *Report of the Committee on Broadcasting 1960*, issued in June 1962, may have had the most far-reaching consequences. Its work demonstrates the British penchant for rigorously examining the role of broadcasting and translating the results into public policy. Arguably, that periodic review and the respect accorded it by British society have been key to ensuring Milne's four conditions and making the BBC the exemplar it has remained to this day. It is worth looking at the Pilkington Committee's work in some detail.

The Pilkington Committee examined British television as it had emerged with its private-public duality and focused on several issues, including "triviality," news on the two competing services, commercialism, and, most tellingly, "the disquiet and dissatisfaction" about television. The "dissatisfaction" generally referred to a kind of sameness, a "lack of variety in treatment"; some viewers felt that "the range of subjects was too narrow" and that there was little "effective choice," especially since the range of subjects in prime time "was markedly narrower even than the overall range."[21]

The cause of "the disquiet about television," the committee reported, was that,

> for the sake of easy appeal, television portrayed too often a world in which the moral standards normally accepted in society were either ignored or flouted, and that for a similar reason it showed excessive violence. There is no doubt that concern is widespread and acute. It cannot be dismissed as the unrepresentative opinion of a few well-meaning but over-anxious critics, still less as that of cranks.

Further, it concluded, "the way television has portrayed human behavior and treated moral issues has already done something and will in time do much more to worsen the moral climate of the country."[22]

This question is particularly poignant to us now when the American networks, the production studios, and Congress are putting on another routine performance of their pas de trois about violence on television. Far from settling for "parental advisories," the British, ever since the Pilkington report, have long taken the subject very seriously. "People in the U.S. think the Brits have no standards because we aren't bothered by nudity or language," Eileen Opatut, executive vice president of Lionheart Television International, the BBC's syndication arm, told a seminar of graduate students in New York,

> but there are any number of programs appearing in prime time in the United States that we can't possibly present in the U.K. Even the most tasteful love-making can't be shown here on broadcast television but you think nothing of seeing someone's throat being cut. That is absolutely unacceptable in the United Kingdom. Absolutely.[23]

The British review process characteristically goes beyond the details of broadcasting behavior and reaches toward a societal position on its purpose. Consider, for example, how the Pilkington report dealt with one theme that emerged from its initial surveys of audience concerns. "The criticism of triviality," as the committee described the audience's concerns, was thought to be a sin of omission. Trivial programming was seen as failing to realize television's potentialities. But the committee pointed out that it was also a sin of commission. Too many broadcasts that sought to explore controversial issues avoided doing so and thus reinforced complacency and prejudices. Emotional and intellectual values were cheapened by programs that embraced "emotional tawdriness and mental timidity." The committee also criticized serials that portrayed a "candy-floss world" by failing to deal with human problems.[24]

The committee cited the testimony of experts in several disciplines that such programs teach that it is slickness that really counts in life, thus having a more subversive influence than the portrayal of violence.

The committee also looked at the relative amount of prime time devoted by BBC and ITV to "serious programming," which they defined as news and current affairs, talks and discussions, documentaries, live coverage "of national importance and other major events of a non-sporting character," religious broadcasts, ballet, and opera and music other than "light music." It found that over a two-year period the commercial broadcasters had devoted 11 percent of prime time to serious programs, and the BBC 33 percent.[25]

The report was highly critical of ITV on nearly all counts. The committee called for "major changes . . . in the constitution and organization of independent television" with respect to program planning, the sale of advertising time, and the relationship between the Authority and the program companies. It further called for a period of "family viewing time" prior to 9:00 P.M., a specific policy on violence set forth by the Authority and not by the programmers, and a tightening of all policies on the acceptance and scheduling of commercials.[26]

Significantly, the Pilkington report recommended that the BBC remain "the main instrument of broadcasting in the United Kingdom." It also recommended that on occasions when only one camera team could be present, "the BBC should have the right and the duty of undertaking the broadcast."[27]

The work of the Pilkington Committee has had far-reaching effects. As a result of its concerns about advertising, the Authority voluntary code became a matter of law, and indeed, British controls are recognized as "among the most comprehensive in the world." Not only must the frequency, amount, and nature of the advertisements comply with the Broadcasting Act of 1954 and the many rules and principles laid down by the Authority, but the frequency and length of commercial breaks are strictly regulated by the IBA "to ensure that they do not detract from the value of programmes as a medium of information, education, and entertainment."[28]

Finally, the report recommended that the next program channel be given to the BBC, as soon as possible, and that the BBC's charter be renewed for a twelve-year term.

BBC2 came on the air on April 20, 1964. Finally, the BBC could have its biscuits and eat them too. Martin Jackson, for twenty years the television critic for the *London Daily Express*, would later observe: "The BBC has always been most adept at entertaining, and a good deal more adept than the opposition. Whether it is at International Festivals, or by the more accurate and competitive gauge of audience ratings, BBC entertainment consistently outpaces its commercial and supposedly popular rivals."[29] With the second channel, the BBC could continue to entertain without forgoing the chance to uplift. *The Guide to the BBC 1992* notes that "40% of the total BBC income goes to BBC1 and 20% to BBC2." The task of BBC1, it points out, is to create "a distinctive mix" of entertainment and information for a broad national audience. BBC2 embraces music and the arts, new talent and ideas, documentaries and drama, and "is a forum for debate."[30]

With two channels, not only could BBC1 become directly competitive with ITV, but the BBC could, as one observer put it, "try adventures on BBC2" that could be shifted to BBC1 if they proved successful.[31] Many of these adventures came to the United States. *The Six Wives of Henry VIII* won the British equivalent of the Emmy in five categories and played in prime time on CBS. Alistair Cooke's *America,* Kenneth Clark's *Civilization,* and *Life on Earth* with David Attenborough were carried by PBS.

Alasdair Milne's historic warning that the BBC's "mental profile must not divide the public into stereotypes" was now moot. As he pointed out:

> A great many BBC series started out as a well-kept secret of a few enthusiasts and ended as a national talking-point. A current arts program often boasts a bigger audience than a football match. Maximize the cultural choice of your audience and you'll be surprised what interests you can nourish and sustain.[32]

In 1977 yet another report on the future of television was released. The Annan Committee recommended a fourth broadcast network for the United Kingdom, to be operated by a new entity, the Open Broadcasting Authority. "Not only could it be a nursery for new forms and new methods of presenting ideas," the report explained, "it could also open the doors to a new kind of broadcast publishing."[33]

This latter recommendation appears to have been too open and too new for many. Debate on the idea in the Houses of Parliament and in the press was still vigorous in 1981 when the Labor Party lost the elections and the Conservatives came in. The new government rejected the notion of an "open authority" but concurred with the committee's recommendation that another network with a mandate for innovation be established. The United Kingdom would now have two BBC channels and two commercial networks. The Broadcasting Act of 1981 assigned oversight of the new network, Channel Four, to the Independent Broadcasting Authority, the public corporation that had been overseeing the initial commercial service, ITV.

The Road Not Taken

The 1981 Broadcasting Act, consistent with the British regulatory tradition, carefully spells out what that oversight means. The IBA must ensure:

- proper balance of information, education and entertainment;

- a high standard in all respects;

- accuracy in news;

- impartiality in matters of political and industrial controversy;

- avoidance of offence to good taste and decency.[34]

Chastised in its earliest days for bowing to commercial interests, the IBA had at one point refused to renew the licenses of eleven of the fifteen stations for failure to present quality programming. In 1982, in the spirit of the law's mandate that the IBA and the stations put public service above commercial interests, the IBA hiked up ITV transmission fees and funded the launch of Channel Four.

Channel Four is unique in that it is advertiser-financed but not solely dependent on advertising income. It is designed to complement the ITV and to provide a choice of programs to appeal to different minority interests. Its founding coincided with a resurgence of Welsh nationalism, and it therefore has been given the mandate to produce programs in that language. The Welsh service, S4C, in addition to providing twenty-two hours a week of programming in Welsh, also carries most of Channel Four's programming in English on a delayed basis.

At first the press was highly critical. The service, after being debated for nearly twenty years, had failed to attract the audience its proponents predicted, despite the fact that its first-year programming included such publicity-garnering programs as *Nicholas Nickleby,* which would later play throughout the English-speaking world, and *Superbowl XVII,* which gave the United Kingdom its first exposure to American football. In its second year Channel Four programs were nominated for three International EMMY Awards and won two of them. But it took two years for the channel to find its audience. By that time the service was reaching an average of one of every three Britons each day, and four out of five each week. By 1985 the average viewer was spending three hours a week with the service. While Channel Four's share of audience had risen dramatically, it had not diminished the audience for BBC2, also designed to cater to minority tastes. The other two British services, BBC1, the more popular public channel, and the ITV, both experienced a loss of audience.

Unlike the BBC and the ITV, Channel Four creates no programs but commissions or buys sixty hours of programming a week. Thus, it has followed its mandate to seek out and develop new ideas and new talent. Channel Four Films, which commissions or purchases filmed programs, has become a significant source of films not likely to be financed or distributed by other motion picture companies throughout the world. Both *A Room with a View* and *My Beautiful Launderette*, after their appearance on Channel Four, attracted great attention when distributed internationally on television and in movie houses.

The Entrepreneurial Future?

By any measure, the BBC places at or near the top of any list of broadcasters. Not only its entertainment programs but its documentaries, dramas, and arts programs have shone in every international competition. Equally important is its role in motivating its competitors to become the most discerning programmers in commercial television. The BBC's preeminence is particularly apparent in the International EMMY competition, the most prestigious international award, for which any broadcast not originally seen in the United States may compete: the BBC has won more awards (thirty-eight) than any other broadcaster in the world. The BBC is the standard to which all public service systems' broadcasters aspire and against which all broadcasters should be compared.

The Road Not Taken

This year marks the seventy-fifth anniversary of the BBC, but the organization can hardly pause to celebrate. Unfortunately, trying times lie ahead for the BBC and for all broadcasters in the United Kingdom. Margaret Thatcher chose to ignore both the recommendations of the Peacock Committee—which she had initiated—and of her ministers and opted to require the BBC to pay much of its own way and the commercial broadcasters to pay a considerable premium in exchange for the right to maintain their licenses. On June 1, 1991, an auction of commercial licenses was held. The ground rules were far from clear, and the results were far from satisfying to many observers. Each incumbent and each competitive applicant filed a sealed bid with detailed information on how it would meet its responsibilities in programming as well as in financial and business matters. Supposedly the amount of the bid was not to be the only criterion.

When the day for delivering bids arrived, Central Television, the incumbent serving one of the less populated regions, sent its representatives, with two different bids, to watch for competitive bidders. When none had arrived by the end of the day, the Central team destroyed the bid they had prepared based on what they thought would be competitive and filed the other. They got their license for the minimum possible figure, two thousand pounds. Granada, the incumbent serving the northwest region, bid what it thought would be required to ensure its license renewal. It is now reported to be suffering greatly under the burden of debt involved.

Besides the amount of the bid, such "quality" factors as the nature of the schedule, the record of an incumbent, and the experience of the respective bidders were also to have been considered. Yet when the dust settled, Thames Television—which had been providing the Monday to Friday service in the London area for twenty-three years and was considered by many critics to have been the best commercial broadcaster in the world—had lost the franchise. Thames bid £31 million; a newcomer with no broadcasting experience won with a bid less than £2 million higher. Sometime after the fact, and after Thames had laid off more than fourteen hundred first-rate professionals, Thatcher wrote one of the major broadcasters to the effect that she had made a mistake. She became enraged, however, when he released to the press what she described as a "personal letter."

The BBC was not left unaffected by the Thatcher government's eagerness to change the face of television. The corporation was put under an injunction, as of April 1, 1993, to purchase 25 percent of its programming from the private sector. Further, as studios and support facilities have been cut back to respond to the outside production requirement, BBC program makers are now encouraged to purchase services from outside vendors rather than from the corporation if doing so is more cost-effective. Beyond those measures, the BBC is now required to aggressively seek markets for existing programs and for new products that might be developed. The next charter review committee will even contain a subcommittee on entrepreneurship.

The BBC describes one such entrepreneurial initiative, the launch of twenty-four-hour World Service Television into Asia on November 15, 1991, as "opening the most significant chapter in the history of BBC overseas broadcasting since its inception in 1932."[35] Carried on the AsiaSat satellite, the news and information channel is available in fifty countries from the Red Sea in the West to the Yellow Sea in the East, although it lost its entrée into mainland China after some news reports angered the Beijing authorities.

Since its founding in 1932, BBC External Services Radio has been a significant source of information throughout much of the world. Originally established as the Empire Service, operating with funds generated by domestic license fees, it soon moved from rebroadcasting domestic programs for British subjects in colonial outposts to establishing its own news service and doing foreign-language broadcasting in sensitive areas like the Middle East. When World War II broke out, the Empire Service took on the duties of entertaining the troops and maintaining a line of communication with millions in occupied Europe.

BBC overseas broadcasts continue to constitute a significant source of news around the world. When Mikhail Gorbachev was held prisoner in his Crimea dacha in August 1991, he found a radio in the basement, rigged an antenna, and followed the course of the coup against him on the BBC World Service. Terry Waite, the bishop of Canterbury's emissary held hostage in Beirut in the early 1990s by the Islamic Jihad, somehow managed to get hold of a radio. He later credited the BBC with helping to keep him "mentally and spiritually alive" during his last long year of captivity.

Despite its heritage, the World Television Service represents a new venture. Set up as a self-funding subsidiary corporation in April 1991, it immediately began broadcasting to Europe an eighteen-hour-a-day subscription service including, as well as news, light entertainment, drama, documentaries, sports, and children's programs culled from both BBC domestic television services. At the same time it began an eleven-hour-a-day service for Africa in collaboration with a South African entertainment service, M-Net.

In 1996, the sixtieth anniversary of BBC television, the royal charter was renewed after yet another vigorous public discussion of British television. Much of the discussion would have been astounding to Lord Reith—the age of monopoly in British communications is long over. But many inside the BBC and within the ranks of its audiences would unblushingly agree, even today, with John Scupham's dictum: "Every broadcast is a moral act."[36]

Nonetheless, many Britons must be startled by some of the ways in which the BBC has been responding to "the pace of competition." In the 1995 *BBC Annual Report,* the current director general, Sir Michael Checkham, announced the launch of a satellite service, BBC Select, to be beamed to the United Kingdom and "funded by a mixture of subscription and advertising." BBC Select is a joint venture with Thames Television—now solely a production company—drawing on classic programs from the archives of both institutions as "the backbone of the channel." Sir Michael added:

Down the Tube

> The BBC has to think of itself as a multi-funded organization. We have a commercial turnover from BBC Enterprises of over 200 million pounds [from the sale of programs to other countries, including the United States], we attract events sponsorship. . . . We are ceaselessly looking at ways of expanding supplementary income to the license fee.[37]

Consistent with those statements, the 120 members of the BBC's staff detailed to prepare for the formal charter review formed themselves into fifteen task forces. Many of these were charged with examining the activities of the BBC that have provided the familiar framework for the review process—the BBC as "The information provider, The entertainer, The cultural patron, The educator, The children's programmer, The standard setter." For the first time in the BBC's history, however, one task force was charged with looking at the BBC as "The entrepreneur."[38]

The word *entrepreneur* has many connotations. Some are noble, alluding to the vision, energy, and courage to take risks in pursuit of clear objectives, the steadfastness that marks enterprise at its finest. But the word has other connotations as well; some American observers may fear that the entrepreneurial mission now being pressed upon the BBC could take the British far down the road we have traveled.

We see little danger of that. The British have a remarkable capacity for adaptation without capitulation, as we have been privileged to see in a succession of *Masterpiece Theater* series from the BBC and from the ITV companies as well. That capacity served them well in World War II, in the divestiture of the empire, and in the move from a homogeneous, class-bound society toward the culturally diverse, far more egalitarian society that some observers see developing. In part, that capacity seems to rest on a practice of clearly determining and articulating societal goals, as we have seen in the periodic reevaluation of the nature of broadcasting and of the accomplishments of the nation's broadcasting systems. The safeguard of principled regulation and the ever-evolving concretizing of the concept of the public interest will continue to serve the BBC and its audiences. For them, the public interest has never been "the vague penumbra" that U.S. Supreme Court Associate Justice Felix Frankfurter described, but rather a vivid reality.

Although the BBC may have been coerced into adopting some of Mammon's ways and means—many British television shows are trivial, if not meretricious—there is little chance that it will adopt his values and less that it will serve him. The disturbing question remains: What if we had taken the same road? What might American television look like today? Might we have a system that all Americans—regardless of educational level or any other demographic marker—would consider a source of national pride?

The United States is currently in a deregulatory mode. But if history remains a reliable guide, the pendulum will soon be swinging in the opposite direction. A new regulatory climate combined with the technological change already under way may give us a chance to reengineer some elements of American television. If so, could we benefit from the British experience? The debate over the V-chip has already demonstrated that many Americans want more information about programming. Could we benefit from the British experience with quality ratings and with third-party evaluations at license renewal time? Could we dare to hope that the debate about the new media, now confined within the Washington Beltway and the boardrooms of New York and Hollywood, might be opened to involve television's ultimate stakeholders, the American public?

(3)

Eyeballs for Sale
The Best-Kept Secret in Television

THE STORY IS probably apocryphal, but like many apocryphal stories, it serves a metaphorical purpose.

Every Monday evening during the fall of 1954, the Eastern NBC Network—initially, New York, Philadelphia, and Schenectady—carried *The Voice of Firestone*. (It was not broadcast coast to coast, since the coaxial cable linking the two coasts had not yet been laid.) The program was a concert, and arguably the first television classic. Carried over radio every Monday night since 1928, *The Voice of Firestone* had been simulcast on television since 1949. It had changed little over the years. The grand opera singers who appeared on the show (with a sprinkling of Broadway musical stars) wore formal evening clothes, just as they had since 1928, and they stood in one place before a fixed microphone, as they had when the broadcast was on radio alone. The opening and closing theme songs had been composed by none other than Mrs. Harvey Firestone herself.

Eyeballs for Sale

Over the years *The Voice of Firestone* had built a very small but devoted Monday-night audience. In an effort to increase its overall Monday-night audience, NBC wanted to move *Firestone* to another time and day. Because the broadcast was fully sponsored and had been on NBC for so long, courtesy demanded that the news of the change be given not to the advertising agency but to the sponsor himself. Accordingly, a personable and senior network executive was dispatched, so the story goes, to see Harvey Firestone.

When the network executive told the tire company president that NBC wished to move the program to another time period, Firestone informed him that "I like it just where it is." The TV executive pointed out that the program could attract even more people were it to move to another time, which NBC's research had identified specifically as "a time when families like to be together."

Firestone seemed interested. "And what time would that be?" he asked. The salesman took a deep breath and blurted out, "Three o'clock Sunday afternoon." Firestone was incredulous: "Three o'clock Sunday afternoon? Absolutely unacceptable: at three o'clock Sunday everybody's playing polo."

Despite his objections, NBC insisted on reprogramming Monday night. *The Firestone Hour* moved to the newly emerging ABC, where it played at its usual time, 8:30 Monday night, for the next three seasons.

Before discussing the implications of this story, let's look at a more recent event. During the 1994–95 season, the *New York Times* reported that NBC was dropping the sitcom *Madman of the People*, the eleventh most popular program with a weekly audience of nearly seventeen million households. Despite its ranking above more than fifty other shows in prime time and a steady roster of advertisers happily buying time for their commercials within the program, it left the air.

These two incidents have three things in common. First, they show that satisfying a steady audience may not guarantee a program's survival. Second, having advertisers willing to buy up all the time in a broadcast also will not ensure a show's survival. As the earlier case demonstrates, a fully sponsored broadcast whose sponsor was completely satisfied with how well it attracted an audience could be summarily taken off the air.

The third and determining factor these two shows have in common is standing on the wrong side of a major paradigm shift. In each instance the business of television itself was undergoing major change. And in each case that change was a direct result of the regulatory philosophy embodied in the Communications Act of 1934.

It used to be said—and the data backed up the statement—that more people were watching the test pattern when the channel went on in the morning than could fit into Yankee Stadium. The myth that people will stare at whatever is on the tube, however, has long since been put to rest. It was true, of course, when that myth arose in the 1950s, that all those television sets were turned on. But the statistic masked actual viewing behavior, as uncovered by the so-called people meters of the 1980s: many people turned on the television set when they first got up in the morning and left it on until something interesting came on that might bring them back into the room to watch.

The simple fact—and it bears repeating—is that people watch programs. If the program is something they want to see, they will watch, but to update Samuel Goldwyn, nothing can make people watch a television program they don't want to see.

The least understood—or most *mis*understood—question is, What business is commercial television in the United States really in?

Commercial television is not in the business of presenting programs; commercial television is not in the business of selling advertising. Nor is it in the business of selling time to advertisers. Commercial television is, quite simply, in the business of aggregating and then selling audiences.

Saint Augustine warned against what such an activity might lead to: the reification of persons, one of the two greatest sins. Treating people like things, the fourth-century philosopher cautioned, goes hand in hand with the second sin, treating things as though they were people. Today social scientists call it the commodification of persons. Ien Ang, the British media scholar, refers to the principal activity of the broadcaster in the United States as "desperately seeking the audience."

In its simplest terms, the business of television in this country is the buying and selling of eyeballs.

The Beginnings of Commercialism

That single fact mandates a very different economic outlook, a very different social outlook, and a very different programming agenda for commercial broadcasting networks and stations and for advertising-based cable networks and other commercialized means of reaching the public.

Even now some advertisers choose to devote a small portion of their public relations budget to building goodwill among customers and potential customers by identifying with worthy causes or supporting quality programming. But even they are like all other companies when it comes to the advertising budget. The overwhelming majority of sponsors reduce the viewer to a single statistic: each of us represents a minuscule, predetermined percentage of the total number of viewers the sponsor knows from previous experience must be reached in order to meet its market share target for the quarter. Marketers know that if their commercial is seen by x number of people, y number of boxes of cereal will be sold. Therefore, they can compute how many commericals positions they must buy to hold or improve their share. For the sponsors and their agents, it is as simple as that.

To the broadcaster, the viewer is reduced to a different but equally precise number—the exact price the station or network will charge the sponsor, that is, how much the sponsor is willing to pay to reach any single viewer. Thus, in the marketplace model, programming has only one function: each program must attract as many viewers as possible. The sole criterion becomes how effective the program is in attracting the number of viewers needed to enable the broadcaster to meet its profit goals.

Although they may not have consciously analyzed the role of advertising in their lives, Americans have become accustomed to its pervasiveness, its seeming power, and its ingenious opportunism. For example, no one appeared shocked with the latest mutation in magazines. For decades we had seen the number of advertising pages increasingly dwarf the editorial matter in successful magazines. We barely noticed when, about ten years ago, numerous magazines began to choke our mailboxes. They were different in that they were free to the consumer and stripped of all editorial content. Similarly, most of us paid even less attention when the logical extension of the silent, two-dimensional catalog followed. Such is the media environment in which we live that the Home Shopping Network (HSN), the Quality and Value Cable (QVC), and the other overlords of the zirconium and kitsch industries now seem to have *always* been there. This environment has been facilitated by seventy years of increasing commercialization of the electronic mass media.

Let's take a close look at that environment. How did it arise? Again, we have to examine the early radio period, when so many fundamental decisions affecting television were made—most of them, in fact, long before television became available. Long before pictures enhanced the pitch, commercialization had come to stay.

Nobody quite intended that outcome. Far from it, as Secretary of Commerce Herbert Hoover testified before Congress in 1924:

> Radio communication is not to be considered as merely a business carried on for private gain, for private advertisement, or for entertainment of the curious. It is a public concern impressed with the public trust and to be considered primarily from the standpoint of public interest to the same extent and upon the basis of the same general principles as our other public utilities.[1]

Eyeballs for Sale

As early as 1912 it had been decided that radio had something to do with interstate commerce. Since the Department of Commerce had jurisdiction over interstate commerce, Hoover presided over the mad scramble in the early 1920s to establish broadcasting. Yet despite his testimony, which he doubtless believed in, Hoover was arguably the single public figure most responsible for the commercialization of broadcasting.

What may be surprising is that Hoover came to broadcasting—and with him the government and, indeed, regulation itself—at the specific request of the broadcasters themselves. This time it was not amateurs interfering with the navy, as we saw in chapter 1, but professional broadcasters interfering with each other. There were simply too many of them operating in a limited spectrum.

Radio had been dismissed as the province of fifteen-year-old boys and admirals. It was the tinkering adolescents' delight and the realization of the admirals' centuries-old dream of point-to-point, over-the-horizon wireless communication. Nothing more. But World War I brought radio into the consciousness of millions of other people. The marvels of military technology—the E-boats, R-boats, and U-boats—paled to insignificance in the imaginations of Americans compared to the wireless. Not too surprisingly, by far the greatest interest in this technological wonder was shown by the manufacturers of radio equipment. They had been asked to share their patents to serve the war effort, and many companies emerged from the conflict with full radio-receiver manufacturing capability. Westinghouse, Crosley, General Electric, and Atwater-Kent were eager to supply what they perceived as a pent-up market demand.

There was just one hitch in their plans for radio consumers: aside from static and occasional techie talk, there was nothing to listen to.

It was Westinghouse that solved the manufacturers' problem. Like most other equipment manufacturers, Westinghouse had long been operating experimental stations to test and perfect its products. Frank Conrad, an engineer at its Pittsburgh station, inserted a microphone into the huge horn-shaped speaker of a windup phonograph and broadcast the sound of a record. By prearrangement, a downtown department store was tuned to Conrad's frequency, and its customers were able to enjoy the experiment. The department store advertised the "Air Concert"—and the radio sets that had picked it up.

The story might have ended there were it not that Conrad's supervisor happened to read the department store ad and experienced a marketing epiphany. He had found the answer to the manufacturers' dilemma. Regularly scheduled programming would sell plenty of Westinghouse sets.

Six weeks later the experimental station had become the nation's first broadcasting station, KDKA. Newspapers in Canada as well as in the midwestern and northeastern United States published the station's one-hour-a-night music and talk schedule. Not coincidentally, the station's November 2 debut was timed to occur on the very night of the 1920 presidential election. As periodic returns came across the telegraph wires, they were phoned in from the local newspaper and read on the air. In between announcements, phonograph records alternated with live banjo music from the studio.

With KDKA established as the world's first radio station, Westinghouse lost no time in looking for other opportunities. Within the year its Newark, New Jersey, station, WJZ, would carry the World Series, and its KYW station in Chicago would build its premiere around the popular soprano Mary Garden of the Chicago Civic Opera. There were only thirteen hundred radio sets in all of Chicago that night, but by the end of the opera season twenty thousand sets were tuned in, the largest regular audience yet.

Meanwhile, back in New York City, Marconi's American operations had been folded into the Radio Corporation of America. RCA changed its focus from point-to-point and made David Sarnoff general manager in April 1921. By the end of that year RCA had sold $11 million worth of radios. The radio boom was under way.

Radio manufacturers, department stores, and even newspapers

began bringing in potted plants and pianos, ample mezzo-sopranos, and lean poetry readers and converting their experimental facilities into stations that deliberately sent out signals far and wide to reach anyone with a receiver. Someone, in the Midwest no doubt, likened the process to a farmer sowing crops by reaching into a bag of seeds and casting them about widely. Farmers called this method of seed dissemination, so very different from placing one seed at a time into a prepared hole in the ground, "broadcasting."

The term caught on, and so did the practice. On January 1, 1922, there were 30 authorized stations, but only one on the air. By the end of the year 576 stations were on the air. More than 100 universities and colleges had opened avowedly educational stations, but the vast majority were commercial in purpose and depended on indirect revenue—the sale of receivers, for example.

There was one startling exception. The American Telephone and Telegraph Company thought it had found a way to bring in direct revenue without worrying about programming. As the press release announcing the opening of WEAF, the AT&T-owned "toll broadcasting" station in New York City, said: "Just as the company leases its long distance wire facilities for the use of newspapers, banks, and other concerns, so it will lease its radio telephone facilities and will not provide the matter which is sent out from this station."[2]

During the station's first month in operation, only three customers showed up. WEAF took in only $550, but it made history.

Commercialization was taking its course. On the afternoon of August 28, 1922, between 5:00 and 5:30 P.M., WEAF carried a ten-minute broadcast supplied by a real estate developer with a number of unsold co-op apartments on its hands. Even though a new elevated rapid transit line was reaching eastward across the meadows of northwestern Long Island, no one was buying the train ride or the neighborhood or the houses. The announcer came on the air to introduce a Mr. Blackwell, who would "say a few words concerning Nathaniel Hawthorne and the desirability of fostering the helpful community spirit and the healthful, unconfined home life that were the Hawthorne ideals."

Mr. Blackwell began: "It is fifty-eight years since Nathaniel Hawthorne, the greatest of America's fictionists, passed away. To honor his memory the Queensborough Corporation, creator and operator of the tenant-owned system of apartment homes in Jackson Heights, New York City, has named its latest group of high-grade dwellings, 'Hawthorne Court.'" After a few minutes extolling "God's great outdoors . . . within a few minutes by subway from the business section of Manhattan," Mr. Blackwell came to the point: "The fact is . . . that apartment homes can be secured."[3]

That particular Hawthorne sermon set back the Queensborough Corporation $50. Queensborough paid for four more broadcasts on subsequent afternoons and one, at $100, for one evening that week. Clearly that deal was a bargain, because by the end of the six broadcasts, $27,000 worth of units had been sold. So had the efficacy of commercial broadcasting.

By 1926, although WEAF was making $150,000 a year in net profit, AT&T had come to realize that it could make more money out of broadcasting by charging other broadcasters for the use of its long-distance lines. The company gave up its retail common carrier approach, sold WEAF to RCA, and retired from the increasingly crowded field of broadcasting. That overcrowding was not lost on anyone, especially Herbert Hoover, who had foreseen trouble almost from the time of his appointment three years earlier. Despite an economy that year in which twenty thousand businesses would fail and three and a half million Americans would be unemployed, radio caught the public fancy: more than one hundred thousand sets were bought in 1924. Many of them cost only $9.75, but that was more than a week's wages for most people.

From its Pittsburgh location, KDKA had made radio a national phenomenon, which the press termed "Radiomania." In the 1919–23 edition, *The Reader's Guide to Periodical Literature* had no listings at all under "Radio"; in the next edition (1924), there were ten pages of radio-related entries. In 1921 prospective set owners were lining up four and five deep at department store counters, and prospective broadcasters were besieging the Commerce Department for information.

The Government Steps In

Secretary Hoover convened the first Washington Radio Conference in February 1922, "to inquire into the critical situation that has now arisen through the astonishing development of the radio telephone."[4] Hoover gathered up the usual suspects: the American Radio Relay League, RCA, AT&T, General Electric, and Westinghouse Electric and Manufacturing. He told them he needed new legislation; they agreed that the airwaves were "a mess." The conference passed a resolution recommending that Hoover be given "adequate legal authority," and Congressman Wallace H. White, Jr., of Maine began drafting legislation. A delighted Hoover averred that "this is one of the few instances where the country is unanimous in its desire for more regulation."[5]

An increasingly agitated industry would call for three more annual conferences. Only twenty-two persons attended the 1922 conference; by 1925, four hundred were on hand. By that time the entire system appeared to have broken down. Commerce had assigned commercial radio to two very narrow bands on the spectrum. The first was for usual station use. Stations had to change to the second band when they broadcast weather and government messages. When distress signals were believed to be coming in, the stations had to cease broadcasting and keep the frequencies open to relay them. Since stations in the same vicinity could not operate at the same time, they were expected to work out a shared schedule. To accommodate listeners who wanted to tune in to the legendary KDKA and other major stations, broadcasters were expected to observe so-called silent nights, periods when they went off the air so as not to block the majors. That arrangement did not work out as planned. Some competitive stations would jam the frequency, others would exceed their allotted power, and still others would jump from their assigned frequency to another, drowning out one or more stations in the process. Worse yet, when Hoover brought suit against a Zenith station in Chicago for using a different frequency and power than it had been assigned, a federal court ruled that the secretary was exceeding his authority under the antiquated 1912 law. More than two hundred new stations came on the air operating wherever and whenever they chose—thirty-eight stations in New York City alone, and forty in Chicago.

Sales of radio sets began to plummet. Listeners complained of "aural bedlam"—their radios sounded like peanut roasters with assorted whistles. The problem was "almost hopelessly involved" and "without parallel," as the Federal Radio Commission (FRC) later described the situation.[6]

Hoover sought support for accelerating the passage of new legislation. "The whole service of this most important public function has drifted into such chaos as seems likely, if not remedied, to destroy its real value," President Coolidge would say to Congress in late 1926. "I most urgently recommend that this legislation should be speedily enacted."[7] The result was passage of the Dill-White Federal Radio Act of 1927, which set up the FRC on a temporary basis to bring order out of the chaos.

The 1927 legislation recognized "this most important function" by establishing the trusteeship model under which broadcasting, both radio and later television and cable, would operate for nearly the next fifty years. The trusteeship model rested on three principles. As to the first, there was no choice: the simple physical fact is that only a limited number of frequencies can carry radio waves. The second principle stemmed directly from that physical limitation: since not everyone could make use of this public resource so essential to national safety and of such promise to the national culture, it followed that whoever operated a radio station would do so in the best interests of the public. The third principle rested on the belief that radio and television are so powerful that great damage could be done were they to fall into the wrong hands. Therefore, the operators had to be carefully chosen to ensure that their broadcasts did no harm to the public.

Unlike British lawmakers, Congress did not specify what the public interest was, but left it ambiguous. The closest that body came to elaborating its notion of the public interest was in a quaint phrase that occurs several times in the 1927 law and again in its successor. Senator Clarence C. Dill's staff had crafted the Interstate Commerce Commission bill for the same congressional committee that would pass on the radio act. When they needed a phrase to describe the station licensee's duty, they simply reused the phrase they had written to describe the duty of a railroad: to operate "in the public convenience, interest and necessity." Later the sequence was changed, in most uses, to place the public's interest before its convenience.

Over the last seventy-eight years, Congress, the executive branch, and the courts have often been criticized for the decisions they made that allowed American broadcasting to follow the route it has. To be sure, although we now recognize that the decisions made during the very earliest days of radio made total commercialization of the audience inevitable, that outcome could not have been foreseen even if the discussion had taken place in a less pressured atmosphere. Hundreds of stations, commercial ventures all, were already in operation, as were other interests, such as the set manufacturers. In retrospect, the system seems to have been improvised against a framework of such increasing consumer dissatisfaction as to doom the entire enterprise unless decisions were made almost instantly. The complications of dealing with a new technology in a relatively nontechnological age were monumental. William Howard Taft, the chief justice of the Supreme Court at that time—and also a former president—said: "I have always dodged this radio question . . . and have told the other justices that I hope to avoid . . . the subject as long as possible."

When asked why, he explained: "Interpreting the law on this subject is something like trying to interpret the law of the occult. It seems like dealing with something supernatural."[8]

Hoover had boasted of "helping business help itself," a laudable goal for the head of a cabinet-level department whose mission was to foster commercial activity. Also, the 1920s were dominated by a laissez-faire ideology. The nation had been built on unfettered capitalism, the argument went, so get government out of the way of the new industry and let it grow.

Ironically, many latter-day critics of broadcasting policy find that capitalism did not go far enough. R. H. Coase, for instance, argues: "A private enterprise system cannot function properly unless property rights are created in resources, and . . . someone wishing to use a resource has to pay the owner to obtain it."[9] In this view, frequency allocation would therefore not have required regulation, and we would all be better off for it. But that option did not appear to be much discussed in 1927.

The broadcast license itself became and remains the only instrument of regulation. It is logical to presume that any station must serve the public in order to survive. But does it necessarily follow that the station thus serves the public interest? Indeed, a federal appeals court stated in 1946 that "it would be difficult, if not impossible, to formulate a precise and comprehensive definition of the term 'public interest, convenience and necessity,' and it has been said often and properly that the facts of each case must be examined and must govern in determination."[10] In a case nearly thirty years later, another federal appeals court wrote:

> The only way that broadcasters can operate in the "public interest" is by broadcasting programs that meet somebody's view of what is in the "public interest." That can scarcely be determined by the broadcaster himself, for he is in an obvious conflict of interest. . . . The Congress has made the FCC the guardian of that public interest.[11]

Under the circumstances, the public interest standard was doomed to fail; commercial imperatives would win out. For a variety of reasons, some of which we have already commented on, the marketplace model was destined to displace completely the trusteeship model in this country.

Sponsorship Takes Hold

Even as we might have preferred a regulatory schema that was thoroughly discussed and painstakingly developed, it would be comforting to believe that American mercantile ingenuity envisioned the process by which the budding electronic mass media business became today's vast merchandising engine. To be sure, there would be visionary businessmen who saw it in part. And engineers were already able to foresee terrestrial if not satellite-delivered television. But most practitioners were proceeding step by unforeseen step. We have seen how the first two or three steps were taken. KDKA had shown that an audience could be assembled if interesting programming were available and promoted. WEAF had made it clear that the increased sale of radio receivers might not be the only revenue stream available. And the 1927 radio act had done away with the maddening technical interference. The other problems—distribution, the professionalization of advertising, fulfillment assurance, and pricing—would all be solved. Not immediately of course. The business of broadcasting would only incrementally—but inevitably—become the aggregation of eyeballs.

In the beginning, radio program sponsorship was acknowledged as discreetly as it would be on public television prior to 1989. In the days before broadcasting, many department stores, such as John Wanamaker in Philadelphia and New York, had open spaces where musicales could be given. Wanamaker's even had a pipe organ. Following the success in selling the Queensborough Corporation's Hawthorne co-ops, the Wanamaker organ concerts were broadcast over WEAF and identified as such. Other department stores that provided recitals to refresh (and perhaps even to attract) lady shoppers followed suit. But it fell to the supersalesman Harry C. Smith, who had put together the Queensborough deal, to break the mold. He persuaded another store, New York's Browning King, a haberdasher, to sponsor a weekly concert on WEAF. Browning King did not put on musicales in its store. It had no pipe organ, no vast open space, no roster of musicians who had been playing in the store. No problem: Smith arranged for the Anna Byrne Orchestra to appear under the store's name. *The Browning King Orchestra* became a weekly feature with no gratuitous lecture and only the liberal use of the orchestra (read store) name by way of a commercial.

Soon the Great Atlantic and Pacific Tea Company, a chain of groceries, was sponsoring *The A&P Gypsies; The Lucky Strike Orchestra* was formed; a soft drink company provided *The Cliquot Club Eskimos;* and a soap company came up with *The Gold Dust Twins,* who sang on the program of the same name. A male duet under contract to WEAF sang variously as *The Interwoven Pair* for a sock company, *The Happiness Boys* for a similarly named candy company, and *The Taystee Loafers* for Taystee Bread.

Brand-name awareness, goodwill, and sales went up for each of the sponsors. Usually only the brand name was identified. Browning King, for instance, did not mention that it sold clothing. One company went even further. In December 1923, listeners to WEAF heard the following dignified announcement:

Tuesday evening means *The Eveready Hour,* for it is on this day each week that the National Carbide Company, makers of Eveready flashlights and radio batteries, engages the facilities of these fourteen radio stations. Tonight, the sponsors have included in the program actress Elsie Janis, who will present hits-and-bits of former years, and guest Arthur H. Young will tell some of his experiences while hunting wild animals in Alaska and Africa with bow and arrow.

The program was a great success. *The Eveready Hour* would air for a number of years and feature a variety of upscale offerings, including a monthly original drama, concert, or, occasionally, dance music and even the wedding of a singer. It was the first time a sponsor's name had been attached to a program rather than to a performer or a band, and probably the first program series identified by any sort of name.

The Eveready Hour made one even more significant contribution to broadcasting history. The program traveled from city to city. National Carbide, through N. W. Ayer, the advertising agency that produced the program, was interested in reaching other markets. At first the musicians would pack up their instruments, take a train to another city, unpack instruments, music, and script, and repeat the entire program at another radio station. This made no sense, especially since the technology to broadcast from more than one location simultaneously was already in place and had been tested. After all, WEAF was owned by AT&T. By early 1924 a two-station linkup had been arranged. As the WEAF announcement cited earlier confirms, the ad hoc network would soon comprise no fewer than fourteen stations.

Networking was an idea whose time had come. In 1925 AT&T was publishing a rate card with the prices for linking up any or all of its stations, which ranged from Boston to Washington, D.C., and as far west as Minneapolis. Long-line hookup for New York cost $500 an hour; Washington, Cleveland, and Davenport, Iowa, cost only $150. At least two sponsors contracted for $100,000 or more.

AT&T's net profit in broadcasting reached $150,000 that year. That was nothing, however, compared to what lay in store for the telephone company. In January 1926, the RCA board of directors approved the organization of a new company. RCA would own half, GE 30 percent, and Westinghouse the remainder. The new company would purchase WEAF from AT&T and draw up a contract with the phone company for the use of its long lines. It took six months of complex and secret negotiation to put the deal together. RCA announced the incorporation of the new company on September 9, 1926, in full-page announcements whose headlines proclaimed: "*Announcing the National Broadcasting Company, Inc.*" The text promised that "*National radio broadcasting* with better programs [was] permanently assured by this important action of the *Radio Corporation of America* in the interest of the listening public," and then went on, for more than twenty-six column inches, to make a number of exciting, if self-serving, points. Among them:

> To day the best available statistics indicate that more than 5,000,000 [households] are equipped [with radios], and more than 21,000,000 remain to be supplied.
>
> *Radio receiving sets of the best reproductive quality should be made available for all, and we hope to make them cheap enough so that all may buy.*
>
> The day has gone by when the radio receiving set is a plaything. It must now be an instrument of service.

The announcement then described the new company:

> *The purpose of that company will be to provide the best program available for broadcasting in the United States. . . .*
>
> *It is hoped that arrangements may be made so that every event of national importance may be broadcast widely throughout the United States.*

Before announcing the formation of a "Public Advisory Committee" and identifying the new company's president, RCA addressed the likely concerns of a Congress still reeling from the effects of the Teapot Dome and other Harding-era scandals; for the record, it vowed that communications should not ape the oil cartels:

> The Radio Corporation of America is not in any sense seeking a monopoly of the air. That would be a liability rather than an asset. It is seeking, however, to provide machinery which will insure a national distribution of national programs, and a wider distribution of programs of the highest quality.

Eyeballs for Sale

> *If others will engage in this business the Radio Corporation of America will welcome their action, whether it be cooperative or competitive.*

The announcement concluded:

> *We have no hesitation in recommending the National Broadcasting Company to the people of the United States.*
>
> *It will need the help of all listeners. It will make mistakes. If the public will make known its wants to the officials of this company from time to time, we are confident that the new broadcasting company will be an instrument of great public service.*[12]

NBC's spectacular premiere in November included the expected New York Symphony and the New York Oratorio Society as well as unexpected remote broadcasts. Will Rogers was picked up in Kansas City, Mary Garden in Chicago, and no fewer than four of the big bands that would become a staple on the medium. NBC's president, Merlin H. Aylesworth, noting that the stars were donating their talent, is reported to have prophesied that thenceforth sponsors would pick up all the costs.

Not quite yet, however. AT&T would make $800,000 on long-line service during the next year; NBC would bring on a second network based at another New York station, WJZ; and a potentially competitive network, United Independent Broadcasters (UIB), would struggle to get under way. Getting into the network business—developing an extensive program schedule and lining up advertisers—was costly and difficult. NBC had a set-manufacturing corporate parent that not only had deep pockets but knew it was likely to make money from NBC even if the network ran in the red. The upstart UIB begged and borrowed, took on a partner to provide programming, and changed its name to the Columbia Phonograph Broadcasting Company, but fourteen months after going on the air it was still operating in the red at the rate of $4,000 a week. Something had to be done.

A Young Man Changes the Rules:
An Industry Is Born

Enter William S. Paley.

Paley, twenty-eight years old, with a degree from the prestigious Wharton School of the University of Pennsylvania, was approached by family friends who had invested in the hapless UIB. Knowing that Paley had demonstrated an interest in radio when he developed a successful radio advertising campaign for his father's cigar company, they urged him to buy the company and straighten it out.

Paley bought the company for $400,000 and proceeded to reinvent modern commercial broadcasting.

NBC had essentially been offering a program service to its affiliates. It charged them $90 an hour for prime-time unsponsored programs. Since tradition held, at that time, that advertising should be confined to the daytime, this fee constituted a substantial tariff.

Paley proposed a four-part modification of the standard broadcasting contract of the day. First, he would provide all nonsponsored programs—termed "sustaining" since the network sustained them in the absence of a sponsor—*for free*. He would pay the same amount as NBC, $50 an hour for commercial programs. Second, the stations would not be paid for the first five hours of commercial programs each week but he would "compensate" the stations with a guarantee of 20 hours per week. Third, CBS would have an option on all other time, thus enabling Paley to guarantee a prospective buyer that he would be able to deliver all the affiliates. Fourth, the contract was exclusive. The station could not sign up any part of the day with another network. Additionally, the station was required to identify itself as an affiliate of CBS.

With these changes in place, Paley's network grew from sixteen to forty-nine stations by the end of 1928. Even more impressive, while NBC's profit had been $1.2 million in 1928, CBS made $1.6 million that year. Almost overnight NBC adopted the same rules. In fact, with the exception of the option rule, which the courts pronounced to be in restraint of trade, all networks since that time have adopted CBS's contract provisions. Paley had established himself as the father of modern commercial broadcasting. His "compensation" idea is still the model for network television.

The effects of networking were profound and immediate. Radio set sales had fallen off in 1927 but rebounded by more than 50 percent to an astounding $650 million in 1928. Over a five-year period, Americans spent more than $2 billion to be able to listen to the radio—far more, by any estimate, than the manufacturers or programmers had invested in broadcasting. With respect to expenditures on television as well as radio equipment, the same imbalance exists today.

An even more significant result of the establishment of networks was the exponential increase in advertising. After the success of *The Eveready Hour,* other sponsors followed suit. *The Maxwell House Hour, The Palmolive Hour, General Motors Family Party, Stetson Parade, The Wrigley Review,* and a host of other sponsored programs went on the air. So many sponsors signed up that NBC would show a net profit in 1931 of $2,325,229; CBS, with fewer stations, would nevertheless show even more: $2,346,766. The next year a number of newspapers throughout the country joined forces—they were understandably concerned about the shift in advertising dollars from their medium—to conduct a study of radio advertising on 206 stations. The results showed an average of 5.3 "interruptions" in every hour of programming.

The interruptions were certainly proving effective for the advertisers. Sales of Haley's M-O, an over-the-counter pharmaceutical product, jumped "several hundred percent" during the first month of that company's sponsorship of *The Voice of Experience.* More than four hundred thousand fans mailed in the leaflet from their Ovaltine jars to get a picture of Little Orphan Annie, and Kellogg's had to put on thirty-eight people to handle the one hundred thousand box tops sent in each week for *The Singing Lady*'s songbook. Kellogg's was so delighted that it placed an ad in the grocers' trade journal, *Chain*

Store Management, that foretold the changes radio advertising was bringing about: "This entire program is pointed to *increase consumption*—by suggesting Kellogg's cereals, not just for breakfast but for lunch, after school and the evening meal."[13]

Also changing were the who, what, where, and when of advertising. The first advertisements had been very dignified, institutional announcements. Stations had from the beginning developed their own standards and maintained them scrupulously; advertising was to be tasteful and "indirect." Direct references—citing the color of the package, offering samples, giving store locations or, especially, prices—were strictly taboo. Indeed, in 1925 the future radio commentator H. V. Kaltenborn, writing in the *Brooklyn Eagle*, would confidently report: "Direct advertising has already been abandoned by most advertisers who have tried radio as a medium."[14] Even three years later the National Association of Broadcasters' ethics committee institutionalized the widely observed time ban: "Commercial announcements, as the term is generally understood, should not be broadcast between 7 and 11 P.M." Their rationale, as the historian of broadcasting Eric Barnouw put it, was that "daytime hours belonged to the business day . . . but the evening did not."[15]

That restriction, along with many others, was soon to fall. Competition between NBC and CBS for advertisers intensified, while jingles and dramatized commercials proliferated. "The art of radio advertising" was advancing, Paley would say, adding: "Our contribution toward this end is the permitting of price mention."[16]

Nor was the relationship of advertising to audiences overlooked. The first rating service was established in 1930. Commissioned by the Association of National Advertisers, the Crossley ratings—named after the deviser, Archibald Crossley—were based on telephone interviews. By 1932 all the elements of today's commercial broadcasting were in place.

One of these elements was the advertising agency. Union Carbide, when it first thought of putting together a sponsored radio series, sought out the expertise of its advertising agency N. W. Ayer to create a vehicle. The resulting *Eveready Hour* had been, in 1929, the first major program series produced by an agency. Ayer shaped the program; selected, contacted, and hired the talent; wrote the copy; provided a director; and collected a 15 percent commission for the sixty minutes of broadcast time it purchased from the station. The client liked the professional product, and the agency made a handsome profit. Indeed, it made an unexpectedly high profit— which was the basis of the advertiser-supplied shows that predomi- nated throughout the 1930s on radio and in the early decades of television. The agencies had discovered a business that was far more lucrative than merely buying time on a radio station could ever be.

This lesson came home with great clarity to one of the authors of this book, George Dessart. Early in his career, he worked on a net- work presentation of a circus broadcast from Philadelphia every Sat- urday at noon. Among his duties was setting up the displays that formed the visual component of the live commercials. On one occa- sion he discovered that the shipment of milk for the Sealtest com- mercial was two containers short. Normal protocol was to inform N. W. Ayer, the New York advertising agency, and then wait for the two bottles to be hand-carried by courier on the Pennsylvania Railroad hours later. During the two days before the weekly broadcast, at least three and sometimes five or six such couriers would arrive in the course of any given day.

Since he had theater tickets and did not want to risk being late while waiting for the courier to make the two-hour run, he went to the nearest grocery store, bought two containers of Sealtest milk, and set up the commercial. He sacrificed several hours of overtime, but the job was done. The next day he could barely wait for the agency representative to arrive. When he proudly told the agency man of the money he had saved, he was astonished by the response. "Don't ever do such a thing again," he was told. "You're jeopardiz- ing our business." Patiently and firmly, the man from N. W. Ayer explained how the advertising agency made its living. It charged 15 percent on every dollar it spent for the client. Two bottles of milk may have cost about $1 in those days; the agency would have made only 15¢ on that part of the transaction. But a courier cost $25 plus train fare, which was about $8 round trip. Instead of charging 15¢, the agency could have billed the client $34 plus $5.10 in commission.

Faced with economics of that kind, the agencies could hardly be expected to turn down the production business in the 1930s. Not only could they bill the client for 15 percent on the airtime, perhaps $6,000 an hour, they could also bill commissions on the producer, the director, the talent, and all other production expenses: Fifteen percent on production costs that ran as high as $15,000 could bring in up to $2,250 over and above the $900 commission on the airtime. It would take nothing short of a congressional investigation of the quiz show scandal, some thirty years later, to get the agencies out of the production business.

A few advertisers that could not afford, or did not need, the exposure from sponsoring a regularly scheduled program made use of individual announcements, but the bulk of prime-time radio advertising took the form of program sponsorship. Full sponsorship made for strong brand identity. Weekly sponsorship built brand loyalty as people began to set their evening agendas by the day and time their favorite programs were on. Moreover, sponsorship through their advertising agency assured sponsors that they were buying into programs that would bring them into direct contact with the audiences. It also permitted some sponsors to indulge their own tastes. *The Lux Radio Theater* associated the soap with the glamorous stars of Hollywood and the theater by starting with an informal chat between stars who traded observations on the product. *The Bell Telephone Hour,* like *The Voice of Firestone,* presented pop classic music for the benefit of those who could afford their own telephones. For those who could afford automobiles, Texaco presented *The Metropolitan Opera,* a Saturday-afternoon classic still going strong in its fifty-seventh year.

Networks could also program what they were particularly inter-

ested in, or what they thought middle- and upper-middle-class listeners wanted. Although many have pointed out that the networks
liked to cite the unsponsored programs when called on to defend
their stewardship under the "public interest, convenience, and necessity" standard, it would be both unfair and oversimplifying to suggest that this was the only reason sustaining programs were produced. During 1931, the FCC would later announce, only 66
percent of NBC's programs, and 78 percent of CBS's, were sustaining. The best time periods went to commercial programs, but the
networks did not even attempt to find sponsors for every hour. A
70–30 ratio was held to be just about right. Nor did the networks
keep sustaining programs to budgets so low that nothing more than
one-on-one interviews could be done. The 70 percent of the schedule the networks sustained included a broad range of program types
that were often innovative and sometimes even grand in scope: for
instance, the NBC Symphony Orchestra played just for radio under
the baton of Arturo Toscanini, arguably the best and certainly the
world's most celebrated conductor, and on CBS *The Columbia Workshop* pioneered original radio drama and provided a training ground
for writers and directors such as Orson Welles, Norman Corwin, and
John Houseman.

Television Commercials:
Perilously Live and Safe in the Can

Radio remained a major mass medium, dominated by the networks,
throughout World War II. When television emerged in the early
postwar years from its nearly twenty years of experimental broadcasts, it began with a limited program schedule designed to attract
those buying the new sets coming on the market as well as those who
already owned the less than one thousand receivers in the metropolitan New York area. The FCC had awarded the earliest television fre-

quencies to radio broadcasters on the inescapable assumption that they possessed both the skills and the incentive to establish the new medium. Unlike other investors, broadcasters would perceive the considerable investment in equipment and in audience building as an opportunity to expand and protect their core businesses.

Understandably, the broadcasters brought over their commercial practices intact. Network and station programmers and sales forces, as well as advertising agencies, geared up to do new business as nearly as usual as possible. They established the same program formats and the same fifteen-minute, half-hour, and one-hour time slots, and they even broadcast a number of the same programs. Some sponsors, such as Firestone, simply added cameras to the budget and produced simulcasts of what had previously been successful radio programs. Full sponsorship was the rule, and as in the early days of radio advertising, many program titles bore their sponsors' names. *The Gillette Cavalcade of Sports* and *ESSO Newsreel* appeared on NBC's 1946 prime-time schedule; *Kraft Television Theater* and *In the Kelvinator Kitchen* appeared the next year. Bigelow, Chevrolet, Cities Service, Colgate, Ford, Philco, and Texaco joined the program roster in 1948.

For nearly a decade there would be no way to produce a broadcast-quality recording. Commercials had to be made live. Unable to summon up the grandeur of the Rockies, the allure of Paris, or the kinesthetic of water sports, advertisers were forced to rely on the product and its spokesperson. Mistakes were inevitable, and spokespersons became celebrities. The actress Betty Furness had been the commercial announcer for several years on the prestigious drama series Westinghouse sponsored on CBS, *Studio One.* "You can be sure when it's Westinghouse," her tag line, had already passed into the language when, on one occasion, she took a night off. Her replacement simply could not succeed in opening the refrigerator door during a live commercial. So strong was Furness's image that the audience credited her with the error. Years later, when Lyndon Johnson appointed her the nation's first consumer affairs director, a reporter brought up the old incident at the press conference. "I can't wait until I've been in this job for three weeks," she replied. "Then I will have made another mistake and I won't be asked about that refrigerator door ever again."[17]

One of our favorite examples of the hazards of live commercials came to us from the late Mike Ziegler, the first director on the landmark NBC series *Home*. Ziegler had not met the producer before the series went on the air but did get a phone call from him about a week before the premiere. The producer had read all the memos and was impressed with what Ziegler had been doing to ready the production. He then confessed that he had gotten the producer's job because his family owned several NBC radio affiliates. He himself had never seen a television show all the way through, but he promised to learn quickly. Could he please come into the control room and watch the opening broadcast?

On the appointed day the producer showed up, impeccable and eager, and reported that he was absolutely delighted with the first hour. He then asked to spend the second hour on the studio floor. He stationed himself on the perimeter, well out of the way, near the setup for a dog food commercial. He donned headphones, listened to the instructions from the control room as a pair of cameras moved into position for the commercial, heard the stage manager give a two-minute cue, and admired the splendid-looking dog waiting to be fed the sponsor's product in one of the preset areas. The producer also watched as the dog relieved himself in the middle of the "glory shot," the beautifully lighted display of the product that was to have been the opening and closing shot. The producer heard the stage manager's urgent and repeated message to the control room, "Stay off camera 2!" He watched as the frantic stage manager waved his arms to catch someone's attention through the control room windows. All to no avail.

Thirty seconds before the commercial was to begin, the producer took off his headset, whipped out his silk pocket square en route to the glory shot, and, hardly breaking stride, used it to scoop up the offending offal. Brandishing the trophy before the transfixed stage manager, he remarked, "This is the difference between a producer and a stage manager."

Whether or not the incident occurred the way Ziegler swore it had, the three non-prime-time series NBC introduced, *Today* in 1952 and *Home* and *Tonight* in 1954, would have a lasting effect on television.

All three were the vision of Sylvester L. "Pat" Weaver, whom Sarnoff had lured from Young & Rubicam to become vice president in charge of NBC television. It had taken nearly three years of development, but Pat Weaver had finally succeeded in bringing to the airwaves the first format original to television. Each of the three programs were daily magazines of the air, not only in their program content but in their commercials. The bulk of their advertising was in the form of spot announcements. No single advertiser could afford to sponsor any of the three broadcasts all week long, and no agency had a broad enough roster of clients to do so.

Pat Weaver's innovation would not have succeeded even a year or two earlier. The new format depended entirely on the availability of filmed commercials; accommodating live commercials from a dozen or more sponsors on a single show would have been logistically impossible. The first use of film to establish a locale on a popular prime-time series, *T-Men in Action,* would be a major event in the fall of 1951. (Videotape would not even be demonstrated until 1956, five years later.)

Quite apart from the obvious advantages of no longer being tied to a studio, advertisers and their agencies had eagerly seized on the reliability, improved quality, and reuse possibilities of film. But it took a season or two to build up a critical mass of advertising campaigns sufficient to supply the three magazine series. By that time, filmed commercials were all over the schedule.

Market researchers had long known that sponsors liberated from a single weekly sponsorship could extend both the frequency and the reach of their commercials, both essential criteria for any successful and efficient advertising campaign. The rule of thumb is that seven or eight impressions are required before an advertising message even registers, let alone changes consumer behavior. Commercials encountered throughout the broadcast day achieve that aim faster than messages seen only once a week. Scheduling announcements in several programs is desirable because a campaign must reach as large a proportion of the target audience as possible, and not everyone is watching any one program, no matter how popular it is. For the marketer, the greatest advantage is in being able to reach entirely different segments of the population with a campaign based on selected placement of individual spots.

Pat Weaver's trio of program series ushered in the era of demographics in advertising. Sophisticated market research techniques enable an advertiser to determine exactly where a prospective customer—defined by age, gender, educational level, or family size—is most likely to be found on the dial at any given time. Since some programs have more appeal to men than to women, or to persons living in different geographical areas, advertisers can target their advertising schedules to reach their most desired potential customers.

There is a dark side to Pat Weaver's legacy, which changed industry practice from program sponsorship to spot insertion. Before 1952, schedules were set up around the fixed time slots of sponsored programs, which were regarded, if not as sacred cows, at least as cows that generated more than their share of cash. The audience for a particular program might have aged along with the series and its cast, and younger audiences might have rejected the program for the competition, but as long as the sponsor was happy, the network was generally happy as well.

Not that the sacred cows could expect immortality as well as veneration. Production costs were rising (see chapter 4), and few sponsors could afford the luxury of full sponsorship much longer. From a purely business perspective, Weaver undoubtedly sensitized advertisers to the paradigm shift that recorded commercials represented.

Inventories of spots would build up to fill the magazine shows and an emerging market that could flourish only with the certainty of filmed or taped commercials. National advertisers increasingly realized that they needed to supplement their national campaigns in certain markets. Also, there were some products that needed to be advertised in a limited number of markets. Advertising snow tires to markets in the South hardly made sense. Network advertising could meet the objective of brand-name recognition, but reaching the snow tire customer could best be done in local station breaks and locally produced or scheduled broadcasts. Recorded commercials would prove to be an enormous stimulus to what local stations refer to as their national sales.

Where Has It All Led Us?

But the most profound business change was in the nature of prime-time competition. Then as now, the real business of television was the sale of eyeballs, the aggregation of audiences. Finally divorced from the security and the hobbles of full sponsorship, each program had to stand on its own. Weaver's contribution to natural selection would be the idea that every single minute of airtime had to be exploited, had to be captured, had to return maximum revenue.

Advertisers had come to recognize that women between the ages of eighteen and thirty-four controlled 70 percent of all consumer buying decisions. That demographic, that specific cohort of viewers, could now be reached with great precision. Access to the audience could be sold on the industry's standard basis, the CPM, cost-per-thousand (M is the abbreviation for *mille*, the Latin word for thousand). The advertiser could express a demographic preference and place advertising on the one station in the market, or the one network that represented the best buy. Every minute of airtime took on the same significance. If it beat out the competition, either for total audience or for the preferred demographic, it would maximize its revenue potential. This remains the primary criterion for program, station, and network success. Every minute, every second, is golden.

None of this potential could be realized without a system for measuring the audience—or rather, a system that everyone could agree on. When radio began, there was plenty of anecdotal evidence—the mail response to the Kellogg and Ovaltine offers, for example—but little hard empirical data on which to base advertising decisions. The advertisers themselves provided the impetus and set up the first objective, finding a systematic audience measurement process. Archibald Crossley, who headed the market research firm that bore his name, described how the Crossley ratings came into prominence:

> The thing that gave us the most publicity was the origination of radio ratings in 1929, which, having never been done before, created quite a stir. Dan Starch, about the same time, had done a survey, asking people what kind of programs they liked. But he didn't ask, "What program did you just listen to or listen to in the past few hours?" We did that.[18]

Advertisers needed to know where their dollars were going, but eventually it was the broadcasters who would pay the freight for the ratings and set up monitoring committees to straighten out discrepancies between competing services. Many companies, each with a different emphasis, entered the business over the ensuing decades, and methods for gathering data proliferated. Today several companies offer "co-incidentals," phone calls seeking information on what is actually being watched at that moment and by whom, and "overnights," prime-time ratings that appear on executives' desks the following day. "We get a daily report card. This is one of the few businesses in the world I know where a guy comes to work in the morning and looks to see how he did the day before," a harried CBS executive once commented.[19] Meters supplied by Nielsen are attached to the sets of a representative sample population, record which channels the sets have been tuned to, then provide the data for the overnights as well as other reports.

Until 1993, a random sample of television households filled out ARB diaries that were submitted to the Arbitron Ratings Company at the end of the month for which they had been selected. Arbitron also conducted the dreaded "sweeps": monthlong surveys of forty thousand viewers in two hundred markets, conducted in November, February, May, and July, that determined the pricing for local stations' commercial time for the coming year. Now, Nielsen Media Research, with its *Viewers in Profile*, continues to conduct and disseminate sweeps period research.

By the mid-1980s, dissatisfaction with the crudeness of the measuring systems was widespread. Their inadequacy was not so important when only three networks and a few independent stations vied for advertising dollars, but as cable reached the magic 50 percent penetration of television households—the critical mass advertisers claimed would trigger their significant entry into basic advertising— the industries could no longer ignore the deficiencies of the Nielsen and ARB figures. Diaries had long been suspect: viewers were unable to record their viewing faithfully. Children's viewing went especially unreported, and some audience members misstated their actual viewing record and used diaries to assure the continuation of their favorite programs.

The setmeter could record only that the set was on, not who was watching it—or, for that matter, whether anyone was in the room at all. Cable companies argued that their programs were being undermeasured. Also, zapping, or channel-surfing, was not being recorded. Enter the British research firm AGB with its PeopleMeter. Nielsen brought out its own version, the Homeunit. These devices promised to clear up the problems by installing what amounted to a modem connected to a central computer and having individual buttons for each member of the family and several more for guests. The networks protested that the system was too disruptive to install and to operate, and that both its sample and its daily use would be biased in favor of the computer-friendly cable user. The networks refused to accept the PeopleMeter, and AGB withdrew, as did Arbitron, which experimented with a people meter that tied viewing to product usage and consumer behavior. Complaints against people meters persisted. William Rubens, vice president for research at NBC, summed them up: "People meters go against human nature. You can't expect people to work on data entry during their leisure activity of watching TV. Either they take a leisurely approach to data entry, or TV viewing becomes work—and they may ease the burden by watching less."[20]

Several alternative technologies have been discussed: computer chips in the navels of family members, a heat-sensitive device on the chairs and sofas where people sit to watch television, and ultrasonic devices to recognize and distinguish among household members. Nielsen itself has tested a sophisticated image detector, developed with the David Sarnoff Research Center in Princeton, New Jersey, that can recognize faces and determine whether they belong to family members or other people and whether they are watching television.

Since the economics of television is totally dependent on the number of eyeballs watching, the stakes in accurate ratings on which all can agree are enormous. A single rating point difference in a prime-time half-hour series can mean as much as $4 million in revenue over the course of the season. One rating point represents 1 percent of all households with television sets, now held to be 98 million. The rating quoted for any given program is the percentage of those 98 million households watching that particular program.

Ratings, which are absolute numbers of households viewing, are the most important figures at the network level, but stations generally think in terms of shares, the other figure routinely quoted in audience reports. Share figures are analogous to market shares in any business. A department store measures its share of all the retail dollars spent in department stores over a certain period; a television station needs to know what proportion—share—of all the households watching television at a given time are tuned to each of its competitors.

Down the Tube

Veronis Suhler & Associates, the media brokerage and consulting company, estimates that television broadcasting revenues in 1997 reached $34 billion, more than 40 percent of which went to the networks. Cable took in only $7 billion dollars from advertising. But that was nearly three times what cable advertising revenues were in 1991. And by 2001, Veronis Suhler forecasts, cable advertising revenues will be at $15 billion, only $2 billion less than those of the broadcast networks. Little wonder that the networks are concerned about the quality of the research that determines their pricing.

Much of the advantage that advertisers obviously believe the broadcast networks hold over cable networks is the greater efficiency with which they can reach the desired target audiences. Historically, a pool of approximately 545 companies have had products that appeal to a nationwide mass audience, as well as the manufacturing capacity and delivery mechanisms to benefit from national television. They buy time in what is essentially an auction market, with certain assurances that they will be compensated with make-goods—free commercial positions at other times—should a new show or a newly rescheduled show fail to live up to the networks' audience estimates.

The estimates are, of course, only that, though the methods are scientific, with predeterminable margins of error. Billions of dollars rest on them. And that may be part of the problem. Commercial television must appeal to the majority in order to survive.

This is particularly noticeable at the local level. With station owners no longer prohibited from selling the station at any time, sales of stations have increased. Nearly every sale is heavily if not exclusively financed, thus burdening the station with enormous debt. A premium is placed on always—in every time period, on every day—putting on the program that will bring in the largest possible audience and thus maximize its profitability. Much of the success of the tabloid news programs rests on that simple imperative. Similarly, neither stations nor networks are much inclined to schedule broadcasts that will almost certainly garner smaller than usual audiences or incur unusually heavy production costs. Once upon a time a station or network may have felt able to do so, but no longer. The first rule of general management is to protect the bottom line. In today's climate, that means making certain that every possible eyeball is in the audience.

Broadcasting has come a long way from *The A&P Gypsies* and *The Eveready Hour*. But it does seem to be following a predictable track. We certainly have more variety now than we did when there were only two or three stations in any one community. Talk of the information superhighway conjures up visions of five-hundred-channel systems. With so many options, will television finally fulfill its promise? Will we be commodified no longer, but satisfied? Will we have an unimaginable variety of mind-expanding, genuinely fulfilling entertainment, information, and education in music, art, and the sciences?

Or will the industry continue to provide a degraded product, only—with the profits on five hundred channels—on a grander scale? Stay tuned.

(4)

The Scarcity of Abundance
More Networks, More Stations, More Cable, but Not More Programs

A T LEAST SINCE THE Academy of Music moved to West Forty-second Street, bringing with it the vaudeville houses and theaters that would become known as Broadway, New York's Times Square has been the home of hoopla.

On December 31, 1995, prior to the descent of the golden ball to mark the very first second of the new year, a new element appeared. All evening long, as the crowds assembled in Times Square, an exuberant announcement dominated the five-story Sony billboard on what has become the Allied Building. The sign promised all manner of delights to anyone fortunate enough to be watching television the next week. Three letters, UPN—repeated over and over—announced the arrival of a brand-new television network.

The Scarcity of Abundance

For more than twenty years, friend and foe alike had seemed to agree that the networks were dinosaurs, an endangered species, incredibly decrepit relics that would soon embarrass us all before their inevitable demise. Hadn't ABC, CBS, and NBC slipped from attracting 98 percent of the prime-time television audience to a mere 63 percent in less than two decades?

And yet, here was a new network willing to spend huge sums to get into the business. Not only that, but it was the third new network—or wannabe network—to emerge in the previous decade. Fox, not quite a network according to the FCC, had started just nine years before, and already it had developed an audience that for the 1995–96 season would average 6.2 million television households, nearly two-thirds of the average traditional network's audience. The other new network, Warner Brothers' WB, had come on air with the beginning of the 1995–96 season.

If the networks were doing so poorly, why would three seasoned companies wish to enter the field? Didn't they know that for the previous ten to fifteen years at least one of the three networks was running in the red? And that media investment authorities predicted that network revenues would grow only 4.8 percent annually for the rest of the century, while cable advertising's compound annual growth would be more than double that?

What was going on? Hadn't they heard of the information superhighway? Didn't they know that soon we'll all have five hundred television channels to watch?

The fact is that cable television in *any* form is not a reality for thirty-eight million American families. Forty percent of all households must still rely on over-the-air broadcasting to watch television. And that figure probably won't change. These households are simply too spread out, too disinterested, or too poor for cable companies to pursue profitably.

However disappointing cable's prospects for expansion may be, the fact is that we have expanded television service greatly in this country since television's beginnings. The 1948 plan drawn up by the FCC promised two channels for most of the country. The FCC froze the process from 1948 to 1953 and then released a new allocation plan calling for more than three stations in the top five markets, three in the next, and an average of fewer than three throughout the rest of the country. Many of the stations were in the UHF band—channels 14–83—and required the set owner to provide a special tuner. By 1994 the average television household had seven channels available in the broadcast bands alone, even though fewer than 10 percent of the markets in the United States have five or more stations. (Most of the population is in big cities, which have more stations than smaller markets.)

Cable increases the number of channels available considerably. The nation's 11,660 cable systems offer anywhere from 12 to 150 channels, depending on the age and location of the system. Even the oldest cable systems, with 12 or fewer channels, increased the availability of broadcast stations in most markets. No longer did set owners have to go to a different tuner to watch stations broadcasting in the UHF band. The cable tuner did not discriminate but brought in channels 14–83 with as much clarity as stations in the VHF band broadcasting on channels 2–13. Indeed, in just the last ten years, many cable subscribers have seen their capacity raised to 17, 30, 70, even 150 channels of programming.

Where do programs come from? How do they get on cable or on the air? Who controls the process? How did it come about?

The last question is the easiest to answer and the most unsatisfactory to hear. Once again the answer is, not by design, as in the United Kingdom, but by happenstance and inadvertence. Misregulation and the failure to regulate at all are largely to blame. The advertising agencies controlled program development from the late 1920s until the quiz show scandals. Then Congress demanded that the networks take control and responsibility. They did so until 1975, when the Justice Department determined that they were acting in restraint of trade and ordered them out of production and ownership of prime-time entertainment for the next twenty years. Ownership and production of prime-time programs passed to the six or seven major studios. In 1995 the twenty years were up, and the networks were once again able to own and produce programs. The studios are still the major players, but network-produced programs are now coming on line.

The economics of television programming can be quickly expressed in terms of a circular relationship. Sales revenues are a function of both what the advertiser will pay for an audience member and distribution. Distribution—being able to get the programming to the audience—is a function of programming (a program must be attractive to viewers). Because there must be money to produce broadcasts, programming becomes a function of sales. And sales . . . you get the idea. As Deep Throat counseled Bob Woodward and Carl Bernstein of the *Washington Post* during their Watergate investigation, to understand the business, you have to follow the money.

The average American subscriber paid $360 in 1997 for the privilege of having cable programs brought into the house. What did they get for their money? What were the inducements to spend $30 a month?

Whatever the total number of cable channels available in a community, the channels themselves fall into a relatively narrow range of types in terms of how they serve their audiences. Subscribers can use cable networks in much the same way they use broadcast television, radio, libraries, boutiques, and movie houses.

The most successful channels, by far, are those that permit audiences to watch their favorite network programs at different times— whether hours, seasons, years, or even decades later, as typified by the entertainment programming of USA, the Family Channel, and TNN. ESPN permits time-shifting of major sports events previously broadcast in real time and of events similar to those on network television but of less widespread interest. The ESPN Olympics coverage from Barcelona in 1992 was a case in point. Aficionados of archery or soccer or equestrian events could see their favorite sports while the rest of the country tuned in to NBC for gymnastics, track and field, and other events that draw large audiences.

The next most popular type of cable programming imitates radio in content and audience use. Viewers tune in CNN or CNN Headline News to get a quick fix on the news of the last hour, complete with pictures. CNN usually garners an audience of fewer than 1 percent of the potential television audience at any given time. Over the course of a week, however, many viewers will have tuned in for one or more short bursts of information. Other cable networks also seem to imitate radio: MTV, the Country Music Channel, and MSNBC (the NBC/Microsoft information service) are obvious examples.

In November 1995, *Broadcasting & Cable* reported that no fewer than 150 new cable networks were to be pitched to cable system operators at the upcoming cable trade show and convention. Most of them (143) had been announced in the previous two weeks. The overwhelming majority of these, and of all cable networks, are boutique services designed to fill a narrow niche: Discovery, the History Channel, Odyssey (formerly the Faith and Values Network), the Comedy Channel. Others, such as the Home Shopping Network and Quality and Value Cable (QVC), are literally boutiques, although it is hard to imagine anyone walking into a shop given over to zirconium.

The other major category of cable networks are those that provide an alternative to going out to a movie or running down to the video store. Home Box Office (HBO) began as a channel for showing new-to-television movies, although it has recently begun to show signs of becoming a full-service channel. Showtime is also providing some original programming; American Movie Classics (AMC) remains faithful to its mission of showing old Hollywood films.

Nowadays many if not most cable systems are required to devote one channel each to public, educational, and government access. Public access refers to a channel set aside for members of the community to use on a first-come-first-served basis, at minimal cost, to produce or program their own choice of material.

The remaining channels are reserved for what many consider the future of the cable business, pay-per-view. The subscriber signs up for an individual event and is billed as much as $49.50 for access to a prizefight otherwise available only in the arena or in selected motion picture theaters, and as little as $3.95 for a first-run movie.

Taken as a whole, the more than 150 cable networks now in operation constitute a media example of the biological principle "ontogeny recapitulates phylogeny": the individual's life cycle replicates the history of the species. Feature films began as attempts to replicate the live theater; radio paid homage to both the concert hall and the theater. Television embraced *all* that had gone before—concerts, vaudeville, circuses, medicine shows, the Chautauqua Institution, political campaigns, newspapers, and documentaries. The new medium, cable, emulates network television. Somewhat paradoxically, though, as cable networks move to the center—that is, as they begin to look more and more like network television in order to increase their audiences and thus their attractiveness to advertisers—they produce more original programs. Nevertheless, the most popular programming on cable is recycled from network television. And that is true to the biological maxim, since cable owes its very being to network television, its reluctant progenitor.

Cable:
From the Waldorf to Wilkes-Barre and Beyond

As with so many earlier developments not initially seen for what they would become, there is some controversy about who actually started cable television in this country. One of the stories given the most credence is that of Martin Malarkey. Young Malarkey (that really is his name) came out of the navy at the end of World War II and returned to Wilkes-Barre, in the heart of Pennsylvania's Pocono Mountains, to join the family music store business. One of his first assignments sent him to New York, ostensibly on a buying trip to Steinway's. One also suspects that the family was rewarding him with a postwar trip to the big city, since they arranged to put him up at the Waldorf Astoria.

Malarkey was delighted with the Waldorf and its elegance, but even more with his room, especially the television set. The family firm had long been selling radios. Recently, they had been persuaded to offer television, but there had been no takers. Wilkes-Barre, though well within the range of both New York and Philadelphia stations, was surrounded by mountains. Unlike AM radio, television signals cannot jump over mountains. Instead, they follow the surface of the earth until they hit an impediment—like the Poconos—they cannot penetrate.

What interested young Malarkey was the fact that he could receive the signal in his room on a lower floor. When he looked out the window, he saw nothing but mountainlike skyscrapers. Malarkey sought out the manager to find out how they managed to get a clear signal to his room. The obliging manager took him to the roof and showed him the master antenna, explaining that wires descended from the antenna to every floor, and that each corridor carried a wire to which each room was connected.

When he got back to Wilkes-Barre, Malarkey presented his family with a marketing scheme for the unsold television sets: put up an antenna on the land they owned at the top of a hill and run it down to the store. When they did so, a crowd gathered on the sidewalk to see Uncle Milton Berle, the clear signal of the future.

The very next day a passer-by, and then another and another, stepped into the store. Each asked the same question: "How much would you charge me to hook up to your wire?" "Five dollars a month," a Malarkey replied, and an infant industry was born.

At about the same time an electrical engineer, Archer S. Taylor, was doing the same thing in a mountainous community in Oregon. Later the two pioneers would become partners in Malarkey-Taylor, a consulting firm that would be a major and longtime force in the cable industry.

The Scarcity of Abundance

Community Antenna Television (CATV), as the new cable businesses were then called, grew rapidly in what had been inaccessible regions. Mountains were not the only barriers to receiving good signals in television's paleolithic period. Signal reflections off the Atlantic Ocean caused such interference that CATV found a ready market along the Jersey Shore. Other barriers were regulatory: the FCC's 1948 freeze prohibited many communities from building their own television stations. Over the next four years dozens of those communities turned to cable to bring in distant stations. Even after the freeze was lifted, CATV continued to grow. By 1955 about 400 systems served 150,000 households.

At first the broadcasters welcomed the CATV systems as extensions of their audience. But complaints to the FCC began to mount as some cable system operators sought to bring in distant signals. In 1959 one cable system tried to bring Denver stations into Riverton, Wyoming, a town with fewer than four thousand households, where the single television station was struggling to survive. In what turned out to be its first case of regulating a cable system, the FCC refused to permit the CATV system to build a microwave antenna for this purpose.

By 1960 there were twenty-five hundred cable systems with access to four and a half million households. By the end of the 1960s some cable systems were threatening local broadcasters. An enterprising San Diego system imported all of the Los Angeles stations. The case reached the Supreme Court, which affirmed the FCC's jurisdiction over cable and supported its order stopping the importation of signals.

Today we call such practices piracy. They don't often happen in the United States anymore. A special copyright tribunal, set up in 1976, determined that cable systems would pay royalties to motion picture companies, syndicators, and stations for any distant signals they brought in.

In 1968, the FCC had issued two rules that would have a lasting impact on relations between cable and the broadcasters. One was the so-called must-carry rule, which required that a cable system carry all local stations. The second rule prevented cable operators from bringing in stations from outside the market if they were carrying a program for which a local station had paid to have exclusive rights. Both of these rules were designed to protect the local stations, particularly those with no network affiliation or with positions on the less desirable UHF frequencies. The FCC was also interested in the economic well-being of the new medium. Before 1994, stations were compelled to allow cable operators to show their programs without charge.

The Networks Have Competition

The first negative impact of the budding cable industry on the networks came from an unexpected source and as the result of a unique coincidence. In 1976 a boom in the economy brought about a rush on available network advertising capacity. The networks had no inventory left for a number of advertisers who desperately needed to reach millions of prospective customers. At the same time several very popular network series, including *All in the Family, M*A*S*H, Laverne and Shirley,* and *Happy Days,* became available for syndication. Each had been on the air long enough to have more than one hundred episodes available, and their contracts with the networks permitted the producers to sell to local stations the right to rerun them. Affiliates did not have airtime, but the independent stations did.

Throughout their early history and into the early 1970s, 90 percent of all independent stations were operating at a loss. They presented old movies and many poorly produced and unpromoted discussion programs. The 10 percent that made a profit did so by carrying major league baseball. The arrival of competitive programming and, even more welcome, the advertising dollars to buy the rights to show them presented a windfall opportunity for most independent stations. Also, cable had overcome the disadvantage most independents had suffered by being in the UHF band. Within a very few years they became valuable properties instead of tax write-offs. Over the next twenty years independents would become the major competitors to the networks. They remain so today.

Cable's impact was not really felt until it began to penetrate the cities and thus gain access to large numbers of people. At first this process was haphazard and barely noticed. Reportedly, the first cable system in New York ran a large power saw up Park Avenue in midtown Manhattan and laid its feeder cable under the sidewalk without a permit. The man in charge said that he had grown impatient waiting for the paperwork to go through, and besides, the crew had already been hired. As they approached a corner, he would simply go in search of a policeman whom he would persuade to stop traffic.

But not everyone failed to notice the new medium or to think about its implications. City governments, which granted exclusive franchises, became more sophisticated about cable operations as more and more companies entered the competition for franchises. Cable operators would promise to wire the schools, provide free service for senior citizen centers, and set up permanent remote facilities for picking up city council hearings. In such a high-stakes auction market, expectations rose to unrealistic heights. Cities demanded more and more, and franchise seekers responded in kind in the rush to wire the nation. Entire city councils were flown to distant cities to see for themselves what rival candidates were doing elsewhere. CBS, granted a waiver of the exclusion from cable system operation, joined the contest for the franchise in Alameda, California, and threw a dinner party for about one hundred community leaders. Walter Cronkite was flown in on the company plane to address the assemblage. Although the other four candidates cried foul, at least one of them had the last laugh. On the night the final decision was made, the council adopted a consensus voting system. CBS received three votes out of five but lost the election.

Although the winning company was widely believed to have been very well politically connected, no evidence of impropriety ever surfaced; CBS executives later came to believe that they were well out of what became an expensive range of promises to the city of Alameda. But in some communities around the country local politicians managed to reap personal gain from the cable franchise scramble, and more than one cable executive served time for suggesting such perquisites.

What makes cable franchises so valuable is the cash they generate. The average cable system's profit margins grew to 21 percent in 1992. But its cash flow margin was the highest in the entertainment industries, a whopping 45.5 percent. Cash flow is one of the most important inducements for investing in cable systems. Historically, subscription businesses—such as magazines and newspapers—have delivered high cash flows because a predictable number of customers pay for each new edition. Cable delivery is far more efficient in producing cash flow because the incremental costs of adding another customer are virtually nil. It is true that cable systems are very expensive to start up, as are printing presses. But the printing press's capital expenditures and the cable company's wiring costs are paid off through a fixed payment on long-term debt. Some newspapers spend several dollars to deliver a Sunday paper to a customer. A cable company pays pennies to each of its cable network suppliers for each new subscriber. The rest of the monthly subscription payment goes to a minuscule administrative cost and to the bottom line.

Cable subscriptions alone will be a $31 billion business in 2001. That figure does not include cable's other revenue streams: premium channels and pay-per-view will bring in $10 billion, while advertising will add $15 billion more. The rapid advances in digital compression will allow many systems to expand to five hundred channels without rewiring.

Wiring, of course, has been the major cost item in the cable industry. Generally accepted estimates of wiring cost run anywhere from $40,000 to $500,000 per mile, depending on the location. Stringing wires on utility poles in open countryside may run as low as $15,000; laying wires underground in some older cities can run as high as $1 million per running mile if the cable system must excavate and install a new conduit. To appreciate the magnitude of the wiring problem, one has only to think of midtown Manhattan. Wiring Forty-ninth to Fifty-ninth Streets from the East River to the Hudson required more than sixteen miles of feeder cable, all of it buried under the streets and sidewalks, with a smaller line from the feeder to each house or apartment.

More than 96 percent of American television households have cable running past their doorways. But it is easy to see why many experts believe that the remaining households, particularly those in the inner city, will probably never be wired.

The wired nation cost a staggering amount to get that way. And burdened by heavy debt loads, the operators were quickly picked up by large companies known as MSOs—multi-system operators—who could effect great economies of scale. Billing, accounting, sales, promotion, and even technical services can be centralized or outsourced. Significant repairs are routinely performed by contractors, who often bring their specialized trucks from hundreds of miles away.

Arguably, the single most significant technological event for cable system operators involved no wires at all. More than twenty-two thousand miles from the nearest American community, the communications satellite appeared on the scene, thanks to the space program, in the mid-1960s. By 1975 geostationary satellites were rotating in absolute synch with the earth, in effect remaining in the same spot twenty-four hours a day. Time, Inc., saw an opportunity. In August 1976, the president and CEO of Home Box Office, Gerald Levin, announced to the International Radio and Television Society's faculty/industry seminar that the company planned to offer new movies to cable systems throughout the country. The systems would offer the movies to their subscribers for a fee over and above the basic monthly cable subscription charge. Pay cable had been born in the form of HBO.

The economics of satellite delivery was very attractive. It did not matter how many households signed up in any particular cable system. With several thousand systems falling within a satellite's huge footprint, one hundred households here and one hundred there would soon pay for the satellite time and the motion picture studio's charges, turning a tidy profit for both the cable systems and HBO.

The profits appeared to be so tidy that for the next decade and a half most insiders believed pay cable would be the most significant sector of the cable industry. The average household was expected to have three to five pay services. Several other movie channels—Showtime, American Movie Classics, The Movie Channel—appeared, as did a number of specialized channels, such as the Arts Channel, the Entertainment Channel (which later merged to become A&E), and Bravo, all bent on becoming premium services. Of them all, the most ambitious was CBS Cable, a perfect example of how market forces were to determine the availability of quality programming from a traditional network.

CBS Cable was a pet project of William S. Paley's. The CBS founder and chairman of the board tried, in a speech delivered to an industry organization in the late 1970s, to enlist the other two networks in setting aside a block of time each week for what he called quality programming. It was an audacious idea and one that probably would have required them to come perilously close to violating the antitrust laws. It got a certain amount of press but was never taken seriously.

CBS Cable was something else again. An avowedly upscale arts channel, it was designed to be a pay channel with advertising and predominantly original programming, unlike any other cable network at that time. It opened with great élan in October 1981 and brought forth reams of praise from critics, artists, intellectuals, and a devoted, albeit small, audience.

CBS Cable seemed to everyone to be a major cultural achievement whose time had come. Timing, however, was exactly what it did not have.

In those days cable systems, still in the midst of their nationwide buildup, would run a feeder cable down the middle of the road with drop-offs to every subscriber. All the channels—broadcast, basic, and premium—were connected up and available for the new subscriber to sample. After a seemly trial period, the household would select the services it wanted and the company would send a truck and a crew to disconnect all the others. The process worked well for HBO, sports, and other popular channels. The crew would not be needed in more than three out of ten households.

But CBS Cable was, by design, a channel that appealed only to one or two in ten cable subscribers. Turning off eight or nine out of ten customers was simply too expensive for most system operators. Very few would take the service despite Herculean efforts by the promotion people. Not to worry, thought CBS: everyone in the business knew that the long-awaited addressable converter was on its way. This device would enable the system operator to throw a switch in its local headquarters and turn channels on or off in the subscriber's set without sending out a truck and crew. The Charter Oak converter was six months away; GE was close behind. Not to worry.

But the converter would not arrive for two or three long—and for CBS management, expensive—years. Not only did CBS fail to get the expected twenty-five cents or so per subscriber, but the advertisers were not eager to spend money on a service, however good, that had so few clearances from local systems. To make matters much worse, CBS management was under enormous pressure from stockholders and would soon be considered a target for a takeover. CBS Cable had cost $60 million, twice what was budgeted for the first year. CBS management thought it would not be prudent to risk as much as another $100 million in losses before the channel turned around. Besides, Paley was no longer so powerful that he could mandate waiting for CBS Cable to succeed: the board had eased him out just the month before. In September 1982, CBS announced that Paley would step down as chairman the following April. The plug was pulled on CBS Cable in December after only fourteen months of operation. No amount of entreaties, from whatever source, based on public service considerations—the provision of a unique genuine service to the viewing public, the maintenance of culture, education—could stave off the inevitable.

Cable Becomes a Player

The number of cable systems and the size of their subscriber bases were important considerations during the long, hard march down the road to 50 percent penetration, the magic number that would trigger the interest of the advertising community. There had been advertiser interest in cable from the moment it emerged, with HBO, as something other than a master antenna. But advertisers were the slowest of the marchers. In 1980 advertiser expenditure on cable totaled only $45 million. It would rise to more than ten times that amount in 1984 but would still be a pittance compared with broadcasting's advertising revenues. Cable continues to be the fastest-growing segment of the industry, but by 1999, even though cable's audience will be one-third of broadcast television's, cable advertising is projected to rise to only $9 billion, compared with broadcast television's $40 billion.

These numbers are important because advertising revenue pays for programming in this country. For purely economic reasons, it is unlikely that cable networks will ever replace television networks as the most efficient means for disseminating commercial messages to a national audience. Correspondingly, cable networks are very unlikely ever to join or replace broadcast networks as major sources of programming.

The Nielsen organization, after twelve years of study, announced in 1992 that fully 65 percent of all the viewing time in households with cable is spent watching the traditional over-the-air networks. This result confirms the long-held belief that improved reception plays the most significant role in deciding to subscribe to cable. It also explains why cable channels have found it so difficult to produce more competitive prime-time programming and why they have been forced to become highly targeted.

The Scarcity of Abundance

Economists conclude that it would take a minimum average rating of 5–6 percent for any network, over-the-air or cable, to produce and sustain programming that can compete for advertising dollars in prime time. Advertisers have been buying increasing amounts of cable network time in recent years—mostly, however, to ensure reach. Cable's audiences can provide access to groups that are underrepresented on conventional channels. Cable subscribers are a known and easily identified quantity. Broadcasters, however, complain that cable systems have been able to sell on the basis of total subscribers on all the systems carrying a cable network channel. Not every subscriber is watching that channel, even though it is available. For that matter, many cable subscribers will never watch anything on certain cable channels.

In 1995 national advertisers spent more than $30 billion on broadcasting television, ten times what they spent on basic cable networks. Total basic cable network revenues, including fees from MSOs and other cable operators, came to only $3.3 billion. In 1992, out of every dollar they took in, the cable networks spent 21 percent on marketing: letting the system operators and the public know they were out there. They spent an additional ten cents on administration and depreciation and pocketed nineteen cents as profit. That left only fifty cents for program acquisition or production.

To appreciate how little money that is in terms of supplying television entertainment to the mass audience, let's assume that there are only ten basic cable networks and each of them spends every penny of its programming budget on new programs—a total of $1.65 billion, or half their total revenue. At current average costs for prime-time programming—$1 million an hour—each of the ten cable networks, with $165 million for the twenty-three-week season, would be able to present new programming competitive with network television one hour a night. Of course, it would have no money for the other twenty-two hours of prime time, or for any other part of the broadcast day. Besides this economic reality, the fact remains that there are many more than ten basic cable networks out there.

Each of the traditional networks, ABC, CBS, and NBC, programs twenty-two hours of prime time every week. Fox's fifteen hours, WB's six, and UPN's four bring the weekly total of prime-time programming offered by broadcast television to ninety-one hours. That amounts to nearly twenty-five hundred hours of programming a year. The annual production expenditures by the broadcast networks? Three billion dollars.

The actual cost of programming is universally acknowledged to be much higher, owing to a practice known as deficit spending, sometimes by as much as one-third, by producers who are counting on syndication revenues to make their profit. From the late 1970s to 1995, the networks were barred from the syndication business. Syndication, the selling of programming to individual stations, has long been the most profitable segment of the programming industry, particularly when it involves the selling of a series that has developed a large and loyal audience during its original network run. The networks pay a substantial amount of the program development cost and buy the rights to two runs of each episode. Their contracts give them exclusive U.S. exhibition rights to a series, generally for a period of four years. After that time, the producer is free to syndicate the program to any station in the country. Some very successful recent series sell for $1 million an episode in major markets. Whoever owns the rights to syndication on a mega-hit can expect mega-returns. Bill Cosby and Oprah Winfrey, for example, both of whom own their series, have become centimillionaires several times over. Additional profit is to be made in leasing foreign syndication rights.

Obviously, cable networks cannot compete with the broadcasting networks. Yet they can and do compete with each other, as well as for public television viewers and for a small share of the total audience by appealing to narrow interests. Rich Brown, in a special report entitled "Original Cable Programming '95," which appeared in *Broadcasting & Cable*, listed all the original series on the forty-nine established cable networks. The report also focused on the top ten services, reviewing their recent programming and their strategies for the upcoming year. The results were impressive. According to Brown, "Many of the new networks are programming full lineups of original shows as they look to distinguish themselves in the increasingly crowded universe. Meanwhile, the mature cable networks continue to pour more and more dollars into their original programming."[1]

Brown cites National Cable Television Association estimates of the 1994–95 season's expenditures on original programming by basic cable as $2.4 billion, with another $1.4 billion spent by the pay services. Those figures seem to be equivalent to the broadcasting networks' figures. However, the cable figures include daytime as well as prime time. Also, there are only three full-time broadcasting networks; there are more than 150 cable networks.

For the 1995–96 season, Arts and Entertainment planned only one hundred hours of original programming, and Lifetime scheduled a monthly original made-for-cable movie. The Turner Broadcasting System (TBS), the nation's number-two cable entertainment network, committed to twenty-two hours of original programming, while the other Turner-owned network, Turner Network Television, was *reducing* the number of original movies it programmed from twelve to ten. USA Network, whose reruns of *Murder, She Wrote* made it the number-one cable network for five straight years, boasted that half of its prime-time schedule would be original material. Its entertainment division president, Rod Perth, summed up the problem and his strategy concisely: "You cannot continue to depend on the output of traditional over-the-air networks for your future."[2]

The Development Process

For the time being, even though they have joined the annual process, the basic cable networks rely on the traditional networks and the studios and their ritualized development process. That process begins in January for the fall schedules that will premiere twenty months later. Producers, writers, agents, and attorneys dust off their

Rolodexes and set about taking meetings and doing lunches with executives in the studios' production departments and the networks' entertainment divisions. Many industry professionals are fond of saying that everyone in the United States has two businesses: his or her own business, and television. Nearly everyone, it seems, has a great idea for a television show. And yet, it is not ideas that make (or break) a good television show. It is how those ideas are worked out, that is, how the potential of the show is realized.

Between the raw idea and the final television entertainment program comes development. This process may involve a number of individuals and organizations, each with its own agenda, working over a period of several years. The development process is at once spontaneous and ritualized, capricious and highly informed. That it is far from perfect is clear since fully 70 percent of all new television series fail to be renewed. At the same time that success/failure rate is better than in any other of the mass media. CBS wrote:

> The odds against success are great in almost any form of creative enterprise. The norm, in fact, is failure. So it's worth noting that television's success rate is higher than that of books, movies, records or plays.
>
> Using reasonable definitions of what constitutes a "hit" (while acknowledging that no single definition can apply equally to all creative fields), we find that for books the success rate is 0.2 percent. Movies, 5 percent. Plays, 8 percent. Records, 4 percent.[3]

At worst, development can be the bungling meddlesomeness that Merle Miller and Evan Rhodes describe so tellingly in *Only You, Dick Daring! or How to Write One Television Script and Make $50,000,000*. Others have described development as forcing a promising idea to become hopelessly entrapped in mediocrity. At its best, however, the development process can be extremely nurturing, turning a vague, well-intentioned idea into a national institution.

As Ray Timothy told it, although Grant Tinker had recently

taken over as chairman and morale at NBC was beginning to rise, the mood was tense as the network prepared for the May 1984 annual affiliates' meeting, at which they would announce the schedule for the upcoming 1984–85 season. Timothy, group executive vice president of NBC, was chairing the program committee. Composed of senior managers, including executives from the network's sales, research, and affiliate relations departments, this committee meets to review and approve the prime-time schedule for the coming season before releasing it to the affiliates, the press, and the advertising comunity.

They had good reason to be tense. NBC had been in the cellar for the previous nine seasons, many stations were refusing to carry the network's non-prime-time programs, and the affiliates were reported to be in an ugly state of mind. It didn't help that some reporters were speculating that the network might not survive the affiliates' meeting.

Despite the tension, the committee had managed to get through the whole schedule, modifying where necessary, except for Thursday at 8:00 P.M. When the choice was announced, there was a moment of stunned silence. And then the room went wild. How could anyone possibly schedule a sitcom about a sanitation worker and his family built around a standup comic whose last network show had been a dismal failure? "We don't have anything else to put there," Timothy patiently explained. But how could they accept a show without a pilot? All that had been sent in was a ten-minute clip from the star's nightclub act. Timothy pointed out that the treatment they provided was funny and tested well. Besides, the series they had planned to put in the 8:00 P.M. Thursday slot had run into trouble in development but would be ready in six weeks. Meanwhile, NBC had no choice but to place a short order for the sitcom. Still the objections continued. All of Hollywood was aware that ABC had passed on the show. For all that anyone knew, CBS had also turned it down. (It had.) Timothy reminded the affiliate representatives, as patiently as he could, that the star was a pro and would at least deliver six episodes on time, and although nobody would particularly *like* them, they would not be anything for NBC to be ashamed of. The program department would find good people to work on the show and the network would get good PR in the black community. "Besides," he repeated, "we don't have anything else we can put there."[4]

And so they all agreed. Marcy Carsey, Tom Werner, and a good production team went to work. The development process changed the leading character into the Dr. Cliff Huxtable all America would soon come to know, and *The Cosby Show* was born.

The development of virtually all sitcoms and most other television series begins with the availability of a star. Like any other presentational medium, television both makes stars and absolutely depends on them. Audiences identify with them, follow their careers, seek them out, and make a point of seeing their newest efforts. Established stars provide an enormous advantage in promoting new shows since there is little else a viewer can identify with when confronted with a series he or she has never seen. Even *60 Minutes* acknowledges the importance of its stars to the series' success. The program's legendary creator and executive producer, Don Hewlitt, was fond of saying that the program was an adventure: "People tune in to see what Mike and Morley, Leslie, Ed and Steve are up to this week."[5]

Beyond the truism that stars are promotable, their identification with a series early in the development process greatly assists the writers in shaping the characters. The quintessentially middle-class Bill Cosby could be more easily seen, and more effectively written for, playing a physician than a garbage truck worker. Even more important, the early commitment of the star makes it more likely that development can go forward on schedule and that the right performer will be available during the two months or so required to produce the pilot and during the summer and fall should the series be picked up for the season.

With a concept firmly in mind and a star in the wings, if not in the pocket, the writer, independent producer, studio development executives, agent, or packager begins shopping the project, generally starting with whichever network he or she feels closest to. How well the shopping effort goes depends on who the seller is. A major producer with a significant track record and a bankable star can get a major commitment on the phone, although it might take a lunch to work out a final deal. Bob Shanks, former ABC East Coast development head, tells of a lunch he and Michael Eisner had with David Susskind and his agent, Gary Nardino. They had talked of everything but business until Susskind casually remarked, "If I can get Katharine Hepburn, I'd like to do *The Glass Menagerie*." "If you get Hepburn, you got it," said Eisner. Susskind's track record was impressive and his professionalism unquestioned. In a handshake business, he could be trusted to approach Hepburn, Tennessee Williams, and everyone else whose cooperation was needed without damaging the network's ongoing relationships. No other details of the project needed to be specified for both sides to feel that they had a deal. Susskind knew the rules that govern the symbiosis between the networks and the creative community.

Television is not a labor-intensive industry compared with other industries or institutions, but even so, the small number of people involved in major programming decisions is still surprising. An observation of Tom Leahy, onetime executive vice president of the CBS Broadcasting Group, to whom the network and entertainment presidents reported, has been widely quoted: as a young man he believed there were only eight people in all of Hollywood and that they rotated among seven jobs.

Hollywood is a very status-conscious milieu. No one who is not a vice president—and therefore a company officer in the eyes of the law—can be considered capable of making a significant decision. The typical prime-time development decision makers include the president of a network's entertainment division, a vice president in charge of programming, development vice presidents for drama, comedy, specials, made-for-television movies, and mini-series, together with the vice presidents for current drama and comedy. Even counting a deputy for each position, the number of people involved comes to less than twenty. Fewer than one hundred people, therefore, are on the buying (network) side, even counting the emerging networks.

The number of players is also small on the selling side, historically because of the dominance of the major studios. In the 1996–97 season, the six majors (Disney, Fox, Paramount, Sony, Warner Brothers, and Universal/MCA) provided 45 percent of all network prime-time programming in the announced schedule for the fall. The three networks, with eight hours of news programming, the two hours of *Monday Night Football*, and five and a half hours of their own entertainment production, supplied 18 percent. Six independent producers accounted for 15 percent of prime-time programming, and all other independents 12 percent. There are eighty-five hundred members of the Writers Guild of America–West, the union with which all the major studios and the networks have a contract, but fewer than four hundred writers are responsible for most of what is seen on prime time in the course of a season.

Of all the parties that might buy programming, the traditional networks remain the most attractive customers, owing to the five thousand hours of original programming they consume each year. Prime time alone requires nearly twenty-five hundred hours. Because of the audience available in prime time, a conservative estimate would be that a single rating point difference in a network's overall prime-time audience—that is to say, the whole evening, every night of the week, all year long—can affect revenues for the year by $112 million. Because numbers of that magnitude generate intense competition, the networks are continually in search of fresh product. Their need drives the creative community and sets the calendar for all other possible program users.

Although development goes on all the time, it begins in earnest after the January wake-up calls, reaching its peak in April and May. A typical project goes through six critical stages. After the initial idea stage and the shopping stage, the next two stages are making the development deal and preparing the sample script.

The Scarcity of Abundance

Only a small number of projects get past these stages to reach the most critical stages: pilot commitment, then acceptance or rejection for the upcoming season.

Alan Wagner, a former head of programming at CBS, estimates that he and his associates were presented with about six thousand ideas a year, many of them over breakfast, coffee, lunch, or dinner with the other networks. The ideas come from a variety of sources, most of them within a few miles of Sunset Boulevard. Some are generated by network executives, some by the major studios, others by stars and their agents, still others by independent producers, writers, and packagers. Partly because of Hollywood insularity and arrogance, and partly because the networks fear lawsuits from rejected nonprofessionals, the more than twenty thousand unsolicited manuscripts submitted by the public are routinely returned unread. According to Wagner, about two thousand program ideas are seriously considered in a given year. Of these, sample scripts are commissioned for as many as two hundred. From those, a limited number of fully produced programs—seldom more than twenty—are ordered.

One tension-filled night in April, a senior network executive makes a series of phone calls. Executives from the other networks do the same within days. Each call bears one of three messages: the show has been "picked up" and will be on the fall schedule; the show will not appear in the fall but will be held in reserve as a possible second-season replacement; the network is "passing"—the show is rejected. After those calls are made, the press is alerted and a series of screenings for the advertising community are arranged for the end of the month. Finally the networks can show off their wares to the affiliates.

For many years the nearly weeklong affiliates' meeting followed a set routine. The affiliates were booked—at network expense—at the posh Century Plaza Hotel in Beverly Hills, a glassy postwar tower on the Avenue of the Stars with a crew of car parkers who scurry about in contrast to the hotel's legendary doormen, who are mysteriously, but resplendently, dressed in seventeenth-century yeoman-of-the-guards costumes. From the moment the affiliates entered the door, they received cosseting, deference, and pampering. Flowers and fruit and individual notes waited in their rooms. Mementos—leather suitcases, crystal, neckties, scarves for the ladies, golf jackets, all embossed or emblazoned with the network's logo or the promotional slogan of the season—were liberally dispensed throughout the week. Bountiful breakfasts were served with only another packet of information, but luncheons and dinners were special. Each luncheon—most often held among the wading pools in the garden—had a theme, usually built around one of the ongoing hit shows, the news broadcasts, or the network's sports schedule. Stars of the shows and amusing buskers either sat at decorated booths or mingled during the reception. Dinners, held at Chasen's or another legendary Hollywood restaurant, were lavish. Sometimes gourmet picnic baskets were provided in the boxes at the Hollywood Bowl—followed, of course, by a concert under the stars.

Between meals, the affiliates went down an escalator, crossed under the Avenue of the Stars, entered the Schubert Theater, and sank into the most comfortable theater seats in the Western world to listen to the network's promotion plans and watch the pilots. The last morning was devoted to a closed meeting of the affiliates' organization, followed by a confrontation with network executives. The tone varied from smug mutual congratulation (the network remained in first place last year) to exuberance (the network had miraculously solved its problems and is out of the cellar, heading, most assuredly, toward first place), to outright nastiness (the idiots running the network are running it into the ground; the pinko newscasters are disrespectful to the President, the American way, and family values; the skinflint new management wants to diminish compensation; the network is *still* in the cellar).

The culmination of the week was the annual black-tie banquet with a parade of stars limoed in to make their entrances during the reception. The dinner itself was preceded by the introduction of as many as one hundred stars and featured players taking their individual bows and being escorted from the stage to one of the tables to join the affiliates and their network hosts. Every station manager and spouse could go home with autographs, pictures, and dinner-table conversation about at least two or three of the fabled performers, as well as a breathless description of the spectacular floor show.

A week later a second network would repeat the ritual, and then finally the third. At one point during the 1980s, PBS, on a much lower—virtually ascetic—scale followed the big three into the Century Plaza to meet with the management of its affiliated public stations.

In recent years, with new managements and constrained budgets, the networks have scaled back their affiliates' meetings somewhat, and the venue is no longer confined to the Century Plaza and the Schubert. But the process is essentially the same.

Once the season's schedule is set and the affiliates have been motivated to promote it heavily and effectively, the attention of most of the network executives turns to the "up-front" market. Sometime in June or July the major advertisers, which need a certain number of advertising impressions in order for their products to build or maintain market share, begin the negotiation process. Meanwhile, the new productions are turned over to current drama or comedy executives to nourish and monitor, and the development staffs are free to concentrate on the season that will begin fifteen months later. Seven out of ten of the new shows will not survive the season.

American network television will remain the fundamental source of new entertainment programming for the foreseeable future. Only the networks can aggregate sufficient audiences to provide the exposure that advertisers need. Similarly, the aggregated advertiser expenditures on network television, estimated to reach more than $14 billion in 1997, represent the only likely source of funds large enough to underwrite more than two thousand hours of original programming every year.

Moreover, cable networks will continue to rely on previously aired network programs for much of their schedules—in part because of several important differences between cable networks and broadcast networks. For one thing, cable networks are not entirely dependent on advertising, as broadcast networks are. They have two sources of revenue—advertising and a portion of the cable operator's fees.

The cable industry comprises two distinct businesses. One is the cash-rich distribution business, the system operators and increasingly large multi-system operators that have wired the nation and now maintain the wires and buy the rights to carry the cable networks. The second business is that of the cable networks themselves. Interestingly, the nation's two largest MSOs, Time Warner and Tele-Communications, Inc. (TCI), have made considerable investments in developing and operating networks. Time Warner owns Cinemax and HBO outright. It also holds majority interests in Court TV and Comedy Central, as well as 49 percent in E! Entertainment Network. TCI owns 90 percent of Encore, 60 percent of Mac-Neil/Lehrer Productions, 49 percent of the Odyssey Channel, more than a 30 percent interest in Court TV, the Discovery Channel, and the Learning Channel, and 18.5 percent of the Family Channel.

For some time the myth has been widely accepted that cable will force the networks out of business. To be sure, the drop in revenues for the big three as a result of the drop in audience share from 98 percent to 63 percent has given rise to a spate of low-budget reality shows. Yet 63 percent is still a significant number. Imagine the celebration in Detroit if the Big Three car companies had a 63 percent share of their market. Surely, no one would even suggest that they were about to go out of business.

One fundamental difference, however, between the automobile companies and the networks illuminates the importance of the latter in the larger entertainment industry. Only one customer can enjoy an automobile as a new product. The second customer inevitably gets diminished value—at best, a used car, at worst, a lemon. But a television program is not worn out after its first or even its second run. Many shows have a rich and often seemingly endless life in syndication, both domestic and foreign. The reverse side of the coin is that those markets depend on off-network productions. Howard Stringer, while still president of the CBS Broadcast Group, described one of his worst nightmares: "100 channels each with a one rating. . . . No mass audience for which to create."[6] He might just as well have said that there would be no mass audience *by which* to create.

In addition to the role their programming plays in sustaining this country's seventh most important export, commercial networks play a major role, disproportionate to their gross, in the domestic economy. The FCC inquiry into network advertising practices led by the economists Stanley Besen and Thomas Krattenmaker revealed that 534 companies can make use of network television's advertising efficiencies. These are the only companies with mass consumer products that are equally attractive in all climates, and a national distribution system to get them to market. Yet these five hundred or so companies place $13 billion in advertising, generating revenues probably in excess of $200 billion.

There is arguably a national interest in maintaining the networks' efficiency as a means of generating commerce. But the FCC has been wary of networks historically, dating back through the era of the "chain-broadcasting" rules to the beginning of broadcasting. The regulators have always been seriously concerned over the prospect and the reality of network dominance. In addition, the Communications Act of 1934 mandates that the FCC encourage, stimulate, and support the emergence and development of new media. This mandate worked to the networks' benefit when FM radio and television were being developed. The networks had an advantage in obtaining licenses for the new media on the grounds that they had the expertise, the vision, and the wherewithal to underwrite new media during the development years.

For at least the last twenty-five years, regulatory attitudes and actions have seemed to favor the new media to an ever greater extent, sparking network complaints. The networks have also complained about being precluded from entry into most new media businesses. Similarly, a consent decree stemming from a 1972 Justice Department antitrust suit precluded the networks from producing more than an hour and a half of the twenty-three hours of prime time each week, while the FCC's so-called fin-syn—financial interest and syndication—rules made it illegal for the networks to hold a financial interest in what others produced for their prime-time programming and kept them out of the syndication business. Finally, the prime-time access rule shrank prime time itself by 12.5 percent on every night except Sunday (see chapter 5).

These regulatory changes were perceived by the networks as particularly onerous during a period when (1) independent stations became more important, largely as a result of their success in buying up attractive series that had built audience loyalty and awareness on the networks; (2) cable, which had grown initially by carrying network programs at no cost, now was becoming a competitor for advertising dollars; and (3) Fox, given special dispensation to grow into a competitor, was also permitted co-ownership with a motion picture studio.

Yet, although the restrictions on the networks may have encouraged the growth of the cable and independent stations, there was no corresponding development of five hundred channels' worth of original programming, for a number of reasons. The net financial effect of the FCC regulations, as we have seen, has been less revenue for the networks as audience share dropped to two-thirds of what it once was while production costs have risen steeply. The networks will remain, however, the primary source of new programming. With the restrictions lifted, the broadcast networks are now permitted to have financial interests in the programming they carry and once more to produce programming.

Besides the fact that cable networks do not have the revenue flow to produce even a fraction of what the broadcast networks do, there is another reason that any no other source of programming is likely to emerge: the principle of relative constancy. Over the decades since

The Scarcity of Abundance

World War II, the share of gross domestic product (GDP) available to support *all* media products has remained remarkably constant. In 1996 the average American spent $512.05 on media—books, magazines, newspapers, movie tickets, CDs, videocassette rentals, cable, and television. Not only does the percentage of GDP Americans spend on media products stay constant, but so does the time they expend. That fact probably shouldn't surprise us: there are, after all, only twenty-four hours in a day, and no immediate prospect of change.

(5)

Where the Action Is
Television News

FOR NEARLY FOUR DECADES the polls have reminded the American public that it gets most of its news from television. What they have not told us is that during that period television news has changed—not only in form but, more important by far, in substance. Even so, most of us need little reminding. We know as well as the news producers that "if it bleeds, it leads."

Crime news, delivered in excruciating detail, has nosed out all but the most sensational news from elsewhere on the planet. We have all seen the reduction of political news—unless it involves scandalous personal behavior—to a horse race. The coverage of issues is left to PBS, ideological radio, and academic journals. In April 1997, eight universities released the results of a study of news broadcasts in New York, Los Angeles, Chicago, Miami, Indianapolis, Syracuse, Austin, and Eugene, Oregon, showing that coverage of blood and mayhem exceeded coverage of government, education, and race relations combined by a factor of two to one.

What should be covered in a newscast? For that matter, what is news anyway? What should it be? We may never satisfactorily answer these questions. Joseph Pulitzer, the legendary turn-of-the-century media baron, defined news for the new managing editor of his *New York World* as

> what is original, distinctive, dramatic, romantic, thrilling, unique, curious, quaint, humorous, odd, apt to be talked about without shocking good taste or lowering the general tone, good tone, and above all without impairing the confidence of the people in the truth of the stories or the character of the paper for reliability and scrupulous cleanliness.[1]

Sam Zelman, vice president and executive producer of Cable News Network (CNN), looked at the question from an entirely different perspective: "News is what's important because of its impact on society; it's what people need to know and what they want to know."[2]

Most thoughtful journalists would vigorously underline Zelman's first clause. But virtually all journalists would agree that the relative emphasis on what people *need* to know and what they *want* to know makes all the difference. As Martin Mayer put it in *Making News*, "All news items are necessarily in competition with all other news items, and the decision on what is 'news' today is a function of the intensity of competition."[3]

For about fifteen years after the surveys first began to reveal the primacy of television as a source of news, the news that respondents were referring to was the news gathered, edited, and presented by CBS, NBC, and ABC at 7:00 P.M. on the East and West Coasts, and at 6:00 P.M. in the Midwest. These three news organizations were recognized throughout the world for their resources, credibility, and ubiquity. When major news was breaking, the network news chiefs preempted entertainment programming.

That kind of journalism has virtually disappeared, but not because CNN and the other twenty-four-hour news services are now available. Giving the public what it wants to see and hear, not what it needs to know—the philosophy of marketing—is what brought an end to the dominance of the three network news services. Driven by technology, the change was encouraged by misregulation, and it continues to have serious consequences for the American public.

The Consultants Come to Town

For a number of years the industry failed to realize what was happening. Imagine, therefore, how astonished the movers and shakers must have been when they opened their copies of *Broadcasting* in 1971 to find an ad headlined, "It's News." The first paragraph read: "The things you've been hearing from various researchers and consultants are true. It's news, your station's news that makes the difference between being first and out of the running in your market."[4]

The statement was an affront to the received wisdom of the network television age. But it could not be dismissed out of hand. After all, the ad had been placed by McHugh & Hoffman, Inc., the first consulting company that specialized in interpreting and applying social science research findings in order to develop strategies to improve station performance—that is, get larger ratings and beat out the competition. Although McHugh & Hoffman had been around for less than nine years, its clients included all three networks, almost all of the leading group-owned stations, and many independents.

But if the initial statement was astonishing, the rest of the first paragraph soon came to be considered epiphanic:

Local television news develops a warm, trusting and dependent relationship between the audience and the station that is essential to success, and it does it on a daily basis. The feeling that people have about the number one news station overflows into almost all the other areas of its programming. It gives you first chance at the audience for entertainment as well as informational programming. If you doubt this, just check how many stations are number one in total day share that don't lead in news. Very few, and almost none are in key markets.

The games had begun: the era of local news was soon in full flower, and the voice of the consultant was heard in the land. The most obvious effect was the development of the proprietary formats with their sophisticated graphics, distinctive news features, and heavily promoted names, *Action News, Eyewitness News,* and so on. The *Eyewitness* format, the most successful, was devised by Al Primo when he was news director at ABC-owned WXYZ-TV in Detroit and later at the ABC flagship station, WABC-TV in New York. He ascribed the success of the format to several simple but essential principles.

Chief among these was having "the reporters perceived as people telling the viewers about the stories they had covered in a way that viewers could identify with the story and empathize with the people involved, by writing the story so that the details were what the man-in-the-street could recognize." Primo's second law was every bit as important: "develop[ing] rapport among members of the team so that their interaction [will] not be perceived as contrived." The harbinger of "happy talk."

Other secrets to the format's success, according to Primo, included varying the order so that a sports or weather story led off the broadcast when such a story was "what people would be most interested in that night." He also advocated heavy use of the newly developed ENG—electronic news gathering—equipment, the first portable video cameras. This equipment added "credibility," he contended, as did having a shot of the reporter involved in the action. Primo also advocated heavy use of "supers" (superimposed names) in the lower third of the screen, "so the guy at the end of the bar, who can't hear, can identify the newscaster."[5] He might also have added that supers increased name recognition of anchors and reporters.

The format was used most successfully at WFIL-TV in Philadelphia, the nation's fourth-largest television market. The station, an ABC affiliate, was owned by Walter Annenberg's Triangle Publications. Being an affiliate of ABC, the butt of industry jokes, took a certain amount of resignation at that time. It would be at least ten years before the network's news was taken seriously, and its prime-time schedule had been in third place since the network was established. In the local market, the CBS-owned station had the legendary John Facenda, for several decades the best-known and most trusted newsman in the area. Using Primo's methods and some of his own, the talented Ron Tindiglia, producer of the 11:00 P.M. news broadcast while still an undergraduate at Temple, turned the market upside down. His broadcast, then the early news, and finally the entire station became number one in the market. Indeed, WFIL-TV became the most successful local station in the country. It reached and held an unprecedented 50 percent share of audience, even when the network was in third place.

What effect did WFIL's success have on the industry? Predictably, it was not long before the importance of news to a station's overall ratings led industry leaders to think about the potential profitability of local news. Soon not only was local news seen as much more profitable than had been supposed, but it was seen as a profit center. Advertising research indicated that products advertised on news broadcasts enjoyed a halo effect—greater credibility among audience members—and news began to garner higher advertising rates. Local news became increasingly sought after by sponsors that viewed it as good for their image and thus for profits.

Meanwhile, network news remained, for at least a few years, a loss leader. In fact, network news still does not make a profit. In 1993, for example, the three network news departments spent between $1.1 billion and $1.15 billion. Since these costs were hardly offset by the $200–$230 million profits *60 Minutes*, *20/20*, and *Dateline* brought in, the pressures to reduce costs are increasingly severe. The bottom line for TV news is no longer providing accurate, relevant, and significant information. The bottom line for television news has *become* the bottom line.

The profitability of local stations was aided greatly by another development in the late 1970s—the hegemony of network news was broken. One-hour local news broadcasts, even profitable ones, require more material than thirty-minute newscasts. Increasing the number of camera crews is expensive; not only did each require several hundred thousand dollars' worth of equipment, but each crew required at least three expensive professionals at that time. The effort to reduce the number of crews while remaining competitive forced stations to incorporate national and international news into their hourlong early news broadcasts. At first they could rely on the regular feeds from AP and UPI and the daily afternoon feeds of the network news divisions to affiliates. The networks, however, imposed an embargo on footage until after the network evening broadcasts. Thus, the only material they fed to affiliates consisted of follow-ups, reruns of the previous day's network broadcasts, and stories they had rejected as too inconsequential.

As competition in local news stiffened, that system for acquiring material was no longer satisfactory. The stations began to explore the possibility of sharing news footage with other stations. Group-owned stations used satellite time to share footage of the stories that might have more than local interest. Westinghouse's KDKA, for example, shared its footage of the 1979 Six Mile Island nuclear plant accident with Group W stations and about one hundred other stations. These stations formed the basis for Newsfeed, a Westinghouse-operated nationwide service. A station in whose area an event of regional, statewide, or national interest was taking place would feed its story to all members. With access to news from around the country, local news broadcasts became both competitive with the networks and much more attractive to advertisers.

Ironically, having stolen the national news franchise from the networks, local stations soon abandoned it. Except for national stories that feature celebrity and/or salaciousness, there is precious little national news on any local station. National and international news have been reduced to a thirty-second roundup, generally read over a slide bearing an imposing title, such as "Today Around the World," that pretends to attest to the local broadcaster's diligence in carrying out its journalistic mandate and maintaining close watch on developing news wherever it may occur.

Changing the Definition of News

The local stations changed their attitude toward national and international news because of a fundamental change in the definition of news—or, more precisely, the process by which news is defined.

The FCC has long considered news dissemination an important function of radio and television stations. Indeed, particularly during the regulatory era, its license renewal applications required stations to state the number of minutes of news and public affairs they aired in a randomly selected composite week. In the 1970s and early 1980s, if the news numbers did not meet or exceed a specified percentage of the station's broadcast day, a full audit of all of the station's activities would be triggered. The commission offered the following program definitions:

News programs include reports dealing with current local, national, and international events, including weather and stock market reports; and when an integral part of a news program, commentary, analysis, and sport news.

Public affairs programs are programs dealing with local, national, and international issues or problems, including, but not limited to, talks, commentaries, discussions, speeches, editorials, political programs, documentaries, mini-documentaries, panels, roundtables and vignettes, and extended coverage of public events or proceedings, such as local council meetings, Congressional hearings, and the like.[6]

Although in other contexts the FCC does address the question of what "issues or problems" rise to the level of acceptance, the commission, mindful of First Amendment law, does not attempt to specify which of the myriad local, national, or international "events" on a given day qualify as news. For this definition, you must look elsewhere.

There are several classic definitions of news. In *A History of News*, Mitchell Stephens, having commented on the overtly political cast to earlier newspapers, makes the case that "the elaborate mechanisms for its collection and distribution created in the last two centuries have made it easier to see news as a substance independent of moralizing and polemic." Rather, with the caveat that "shared values and selective perceptions continue to taint the supply of news," he uses the following as a working definition for discussing news in our times:

> *New information about a subject of some public interest that is shared with some portion of the public.* (Historical data usually lacks the freshness to qualify as news; art, for the most part, does not offer that layer of compelling information; government intelligence is reserved for private use; chitchat often is of only personal interest—though in smaller communities, with smaller publics, reports on family or friends often are newsworthy.)[7]

This definition reminds us that the news is inescapably bound by time and place.

For most of the twentieth century, most of the world journalism was practiced exactly as it had been for the previous three centuries. News was handed down by fiat from the autocratic rulers. As when the divine right of kings was unquestioned, in many countries the news serves to support the regime and advance its policies. A modification of that model prevailed in the former Soviet Union, where mass media were used to unify the Communist Party and the state. Television, radio, and newspapers all served propaganda and agitation ends.

In democratic societies, one of two other models prevails: the libertarian and the trusteeship models. The libertarian model traces its lineage to the Enlightenment and the work of John Milton, John Locke, and John Stuart Mill. Often identified with an insistence on the rights of man and a reliance on the free marketplace of ideas, it has been recognized as a guiding principle of Western civilization for the last two hundred years. Yet even its supporters agree that it fails to provide rigorous and stable standards that would make clear to all citizens—including those in charge of day-to-day mass media operations—the differences between liberty and its abuse.

William Peter Hamilton, writing in the *Wall Street Journal*, spoke for the publisher's view of his responsibility under the libertarian model: "A newspaper is a private enterprise owing nothing whatever to the public, which grants it no franchise. It is therefore affected with no public interest. It is emphatically the property of the owner, who is selling a manufactured product at his own risk."[8]

The trusteeship model holds that the owner, in exchange for the use of the public's airwaves, serves as the guardian of the public interest. This was supposed to be the operating principle for all of broadcasting. With respect to network news as it developed before and after World War II and subsequent decades, the trusteeship model was clearly that. William S. Paley, Richard Salant, and Frank Stanton at CBS, Donald McGannon at Westinghouse, Robert Kintner and Grant Tinker at NBC, Elmer Lower and Elton Rule at ABC, Daniel B. Burke and Thomas S. Murphy at Capital Cities, and a host of other broadcasters spoke often and convincingly of their responsibility to the public. Along with a number of publishers, these media leaders seemed to acknowledge and accept the six functions assigned to them by a democratic society: providing information, discussion, and debate on public affairs; attempting to enlighten the public, thus making it more capable of self-government; serving as watchdogs over government activities, thus safeguarding the rights of the individual; providing entertainment; serving the economy by bringing together the buyers and sellers of goods and services through environments welcoming to advertising; and maintaining their own financial independence and thus presumably staying free from the undue pressures of special interests.

As competition has stiffened in the television industry—first at the stations during the 1970s, later at the network level—the task of defining news appears to have been delegated by default to the consultants who were selecting and critiquing reporters. Platoons of consultants, armed with three-pack monitors that enabled them to hole up in hotel rooms and watch three affiliates at the same time, fanned out across the country in search of fresh and promising talent. They would identify and watch—sometimes for as long as ten years—a promising but not yet seasoned young talent, who would move from small to medium markets until finally he or she was deemed ready for one of the nation's largest stations, the big time. Increasingly this system of cultivating broadcast journalists by moving them from small markets to larger ones, and hoping they would learn the job on the air, replaced newspapers and wire services as the primary means to identify young people with a nose for news and a flair for reporting. Indeed, a number of the best television reporters now in their fifties were recruited in just this fashion.

But the highly competitive marketplace of the 1970s, preoccupied by the bottom line, decided that this system simply wasn't good enough. What was needed was a scientific evaluation of what difference a newly hired reporter might make to a station's performance (its ratings). Thus arose the mystery, the magic, and the mischief of the "Q."

Industry social scientists are wont to say that we know more about people's television watching than about any other aspect of American life. However immodest, perhaps even grandiose, this claim may be, it is hardly surprising, since far more is at stake in the results of audience research than the revenues of one mass medium. So long as television remains the most efficient way for advertisers to reach a mass audience, the health of the economy as a whole is directly tied to audience research.

As local news became more and more competitive, in terms of ratings as well as prestige, the consultants refined the process of selecting on-air talent. The most successful of these efforts was that of a firm in Port Washington, New York, Marketing Evaluations, which began developing qualitative rankings of on-air journalists and entertainment series performers. Audience members are questioned as to their "awareness" of, and "degree of enthusiasm" for, a newsperson or performer. The percentage of viewers who can identify a particular newsperson results in a "familiarity" or "FAM" score. The "Q" score for an individual is arrived at by dividing the number of viewers who describe him or her as "one of my favorites" by his or her FAM score. At the height of his exposure in the mid-1970s, Walter Cronkite's FAM score was 92, and his Q score was 33. The late Harry Reasoner, then an ABC anchorman, was the next-highest-scoring newsperson, with a FAM of 82 and a Q of 29. (By comparison, during the same period the top-scoring comedians were Bob Hope, with a 93 FAM and a 48 Q, and Carol Burnett, with a 96 FAM and a 38 Q.)

Although the person credited with devising the Q score reportedly said that "many creative people have been helped rather than hurt in their careers by this service,"[9] a large number of first-rate journalists trace their dismissal from a station or network to an unsatisfactory or merely unimpressive Q score or similar ranking. Even as you read this, it is likely that somewhere in the United States someone is being shown a photograph and asked, "Do you recognize this person? If so, on what channel do you see him or her? Now, on a scale of one to five . . . "

Q scores would have been meaningless before news, like every other element of television, came under the imperative to maximize the return from every single minute of airtime. The culprit is neither the broadcast journalists nor even the beleaguered executives of the broadcasting companies. But the results are clear: no longer do any of the other functions of news matter. In the interest of shareholder profitability, the deciding factor in any news judgment, whether about personnel or subject matter, is the immediate gratification of the audience.

Dan Rather, in the 1993 keynote address to the Radio and Television News Directors Association, summed up broadcast journalism in our era:

> They've got us putting more and more fuzz and wuzz on the air, cop-shop stuff so as to compete, not with other news programs, but with entertainment programs (including those posing as news programs) for dead bodies, mayhem, and lurid tales.
>
> They tell us international news doesn't get ratings, doesn't sell, and, besides, it's too expensive. "Foreign news" is considered an expletive best deleted in most local stations' newsrooms and has fallen from favor even among networks.
>
> Thoughtfully written analysis is out, "live-pops" are in. Hire lookers, not writers. Do powder-puff, not probing, interviews. Stay away from controversial subjects. Kiss ass, move with the mass, and for heaven and the rating's sake don't make anyone mad—certainly not anybody that you're covering, and especially not the mayor, the governor, the senator, the President or Vice-President or *anybody* in a position of power. Make nice, not news. This has become the new mantra. These have become the new Rules. The post-Murrow generation of owners and managers have made them so.[10]

How did these industry leaders come to act as they do? And why now?

Deregulation spelled the end of a vision. The privileged position of news could not be sustained, and the repeal of the anti-trafficking rule was the harbinger of things to come. Before 1982 the FCC required that an owner not sell a station before at least one license renewal period had passed—at that time, three years. The rule was intended to foster stability and develop a sense of connection between the station and the community it served. Once the rule was rescinded, stations changed hands far more rapidly than ever before.

Spurred by the inevitable rise in sale prices and eager to avoid the tax penalties that threatened the third generation of owners, stations that had been closely held by the families of their founders came onto the market. As we pointed out in chapter 4, during the go-go eighties, many new owners took on enormous debt loads at very high interest rates.

Moreover, when the Wall Street financial analysts learned that the limitations on the number of stations a single company could hold were to be removed, the trade became even brisker. Even the networks were in play. During a nineteen-month period from March 1985 to September 1986, all three commercial networks—and therefore the stations they owned and operated as well—changed hands. With the exception of Capital Cities, which took over ABC, the new managements did not come from broadcasting and their top executives were not accustomed to doing business with "the public interest" in mind.

The public interest, as we pointed out in chapter 1, is often an amorphous concept. The commercial networks had paid lip service to it at all times, and given exemplary service to it on many occasions. In fact, a case can be made that ABC News owed much of its credibility, and perhaps even its very existence, to one single opportunity to act in the public interest.

During the 1970s the hearing-impaired community, increasingly frustrated with television, was making certain that television stations and networks knew how they felt. One strategy available to deaf groups in that consumer activist period was threatening to challenge station licenses at renewal time by claiming that the lack of on-air captioning or signing denied them their right to enjoy the public airwaves. Broadcasters pointed out that captioning was very expensive and, given the technology of the era, distracting to the hearing, who made up the vast majority of the audience.

The hearing-impaired were particularly disturbed at being unable to benefit from what had become the primary source of news for the American public. The discussion had gone on for several years, with little or no movement on either side, when a Boston group came up with an innovative and seemingly effective idea. After the FCC approved a captioning device in 1976, the group spoke to public television stations, particularly WGBH-TV, which promised to cooperate; the group also obtained funding, prospective staff, and technology, and it drew up realistic plans for accomplishing the project.

The plan was to tape the evening news, write and insert captions, and replay the program later that night on PBS stations. Neither CBS nor NBC was interested. But the group found a champion in Leonard Goldenson, the founder and chairman of ABC. Goldenson stipulated that the broadcasts could not go on the air until after the affiliates' late news broadcasts were completed and that written approval had to be received on a market-by-market basis. The captioned news would appear only in markets where the affiliate gave permission. The WGBH-TV Caption Center would have to negotiate with the unions with respect to residuals arising from the retransmission.

It was a win-win-win situation, and the deaf community was delighted. The benefits of the project, however, went far beyond meeting their needs. In the pre-VCR days, commuters and other people who had to work late had never been able to watch a network news broadcast. Now they could do so—and they developed a taste for ABC News.

What was most important was the reaction in Washington. For the first time government news makers could see a network news broadcast nearly every night. The payoff was immediate. ABC had always had trouble booking guests for its Sunday public affairs discussions and other broadcasts. Now official Washington was volunteering to come on its programs. Arguably, ABC's newfound cachet with significant public figures gave the network more credibility in the eyes of the print press and other broadcast journalists. An electronic good deed provided one of the launch platforms for ABC News in its efforts to attain a position of parity with the two established news services.

Commodification Threatens the News Bureaus

Broadcasters, however much they have sought to maximize profits, at least understand that news serves a unifying national purpose. To the minds of investors, news is no different from any other item up for sale. A dramatic example of its commodification followed almost immediately after the three networks changed hands. In 1986, shortly after he took control of the company, Laurence Tisch went on a tour of CBS News' bureaus throughout Europe. Within a year, three bureaus had been closed and staffs had been reduced in at least four others.

Why do we think these closures were so important? News bureaus have a significance far beyond their actual utility. Their very existence speaks to the professional commitment of the parent news organization. News gathering, as opposed to news accumulation from the wire services and press releases, is an expensive business. Its two most costly components are investigative units, which may spend six months developing a story, and news bureaus, which may spend six months waiting for a story to develop. Yet every major news organization, in the days when news gathering was held to be important, maintained both investigative units at home and bureaus abroad.

Each bureau was required to file a certain number of background or color stories each week, the vast majority of which never made the nightly news. After being discarded by the signature broadcast, the stories were released to the news feed for affiliates, the late late-night broadcasts (2:30–6:00 A.M.), or the early-morning broadcasts (pre-6:30 A.M.). Some were sold off to international syndication. For example, the BBC's New York bureau recently conducted an interview that the BBC carried domestically and on the BBC World News Service. That news service, in turn, sold it to ABC News. ABC aired it sometime after 2:30 A.M. Such sales offset some of a bureau's costs: in this case, the BBC's New York bureau benefited.

Bureaus cannot, however, underwrite all of their costs, nor were they expected to historically. Bureaus provide an ongoing surveillance system in a place where significant news events may occur at any time. The reporters spend time finding their way around, cultivating local sources, and thinking through what may be needed when a story breaks. When that happens, they are indispensable. In the post-bureau-closing era, stringers, local technicians, and freelance camera reporters may be on call, but the bulk of the activity on a major breaking story from abroad is covered—if that is the term— by a frequent-flyer anchorperson who jets in after the story has made all the wire services.

Contrast that with the experience of NBC News in Berlin in 1989. About a year earlier, Bill Wheatley, vice president of NBC News and the head of its foreign desk, began to perceive that someday the political structure in East Germany might change. He called together his assistants in New York and, in a conference call with the bureau chief in the Berlin bureau, posed the question: What would NBC News do on the night the Berlin Wall came down?

It was a challenging exercise. Over the next six months the bureau identified the probable locations of events, scouted out camera positions, anticipated logistical problems, came up with possible components of the story, and prepared essential backgrounders and a list of historical figures, scholars, and so on, who should be interviewed. All of Wheatley's colleagues addressed the problem seriously, plans were drawn up, and a report was filed. And shelved. No one thought anything more about it. In late October and early November 1989, however, Eastern Europe was a news source again. Demonstrations against the East German government had been held in Leipzig and Dresden. The NBC West Berlin bureau sent people into East Germany with super-8 film cameras for surreptitious filming.

On Tuesday, November 7, the government of the German Democratic Republic resigned. Under the network's frequent-flying-anchor protocol, Tom Brokaw was sent to Berlin that night after presenting the story on *The NBC Nightly News*. The next day there was to be a press conference at 11:00 A.M. in the East Berlin sector. It did not seem too promising; a minor official was to make an announcement. But Brokaw, appropriately, suggested that he had nothing else on and would be in Berlin anyway. Why not cover the story himself? At the very least, he would get another look at East Berlin.

Brokaw showed up the following morning, certainly the only American television anchor. At the end of a dry and otherwise inconsequential report, the spokesperson, almost offhandedly, mentioned that all restrictions on travel to and from West Berlin were canceled, effective immediately. Brokaw, good reporter that he is, cornered the spokesperson and "determined the significance" of the statement. Meanwhile, the dream scenario had been taken down from the shelf and dusted off. A remote truck had been positioned by the Brandenburg Gate and forty-five technicians, correspondents, producers, and directors from eight NBC European bureaus had converged on Berlin. NBC went live at 1:20 P.M., Eastern Standard Time, and again four times during the afternoon.

That evening, unique among American networks, *The NBC Nightly News* presented Brokaw reporting live from the very best vantage point in West Berlin. The next day the first two East Berliners to test the decree were seen coming up on the top of the wall, where they paused to take in the enormity of what they had just done. Soon West Berliners joined them in a dance of celebration, and together they began the process of tearing down that symbolic barrier after twenty-eight years of containment. NBC had scored a global scoop.

But not even world-class journalists like Bill Wheatley and Tom Brokaw, backed up by a world-class organization like NBC News, could have done it without the aid of a bureau staffed with seasoned professionals who had been on-site long enough to know the area and its people.

Yet another example is the triumphant reporting of CNN during the Persian Gulf War. CNN had been the brainchild of Ted Turner, the dynamic America's Cup winner who made a small regional outdoor advertising company into an international communications company. Turner took control of an Atlanta UHF independent television station in 1969 and parlayed it into the world's first "superstation," which was snapped up by cable systems throughout the South and West that were easily reached by a microwave relay system Turner owned. The local cable systems were attracted by the station's programming: it featured the sports teams Turner had acquired. Thus, WTBS, as Turner renamed it, became the first de facto cable network. In 1980 his Cable News Network (CNN), the first 24-hour television news operation in the world, began operations on 172 cable systems throughout the country. Several other news operations were watching CNN carefully to see whether a cable-delivered 24-hour system would provide airtime for stories shot and edited but preempted for their own network news services by more pressing news. A year after CNN started, two of them acted. Westinghouse and ABC, co-venturing as Satellite News Channels, opened not one but two channels; Turner countered with his own second channel, CNN Headline News. Already experienced in cable distribution and able to take advantage of the cost savings in owning a portion of the distribution system, Turner had an additional competitive advantage. Georgia is a right-to-work state. Citing start-up costs, among other factors, Westinghouse and ABC shut down their operation in October 1983.

Subsequently, Turner's operations have grown. He purchased MGM, Hanna-Barbera, and Castlerock Films. Before being acquired by Time Warner, Turner Broadcasting Systems owned and operated seven domestic and four international networks, including CNN International.

Committed to programming twenty-four hours with news, and needing to catch up with the fifty to sixty years of brand-name recognition the traditional American networks had, CNN opened a number of foreign bureaus. When the Persian Gulf War was imminent, CNN sent Peter Arnett, a career foreign war correspondent, to bolster the bureau in Beirut. With the skills he brought, the knowledge of Baghdad his colleagues had developed, and the all-important presence provided by the bureau and the wired Iraqi government offices, CNN would have found itself at the very least in a preferred position vis-à-vis the competition. What clinched its advantage was its pre-science in leasing dedicated phone lines in Baghdad to ensure getting the news out. Arnett's planning paid off. CNN had the best coverage on the first night and the only coverage from Baghdad throughout most of the war. On the first night, CNN, which normally received less than a one-point rating, increased its audience more than tenfold.

Beyond the obvious advantage the presence of a bureau provides when a major story breaks, the regard in which it is held says much about a network's seriousness of purpose. Foreign news is not as easy to comprehend or relate to as news from the community. The per-haps apocryphal calculus at the *London Times* used to be that one British death was more newsworthy than those of ten Frenchmen, fifty Germans, or a thousand victims in India. And deaths are far eas-ier for an audience to deal with than trade deficits.

Critics have long noted that political news has been reduced to analysis of the relative standing of the candidates in the poll du jour. The candidates themselves, through their spin doctors and political consultants, have become willing participants in this process, con-fining their commercials to ad hominem attacks and failing, for the most part, to engage in serious discussion of the pressing problems of the day. They are not entirely to blame, however, for how politi-cal news has evolved. It all seems to be part of the dumbing-down of America. Anti-intellectualism has always been a leitmotif in American life, but recently the media, largely because of their insis-tence that news is what the audience wants to see rather than what they need to know, have played a central role in perpetuating that climate.

One example is emblematic. When Rupert Murdoch bought *TV Guide* from Walter Annenberg's Triangle Publications, the magazine had the largest weekly circulation of any in the United States, sixteen million copies. Among all U.S. magazines, it was second only to *Reader's Digest,* which had a monthly circulation of seventeen million copies. Observers might have thought that Murdoch was taking over a highly successful venture with a secure and very lucrative future.

TV Guide was secure enough perhaps, but hardly lucrative enough for its new owner. This did not surprise anyone who has watched Murdoch's career. Again and again, as he takes over existing media, Murdoch has called for increased circulation and reshaped the product to ensure it.

If Murdoch were alone in this practice it would be bad enough. But dumbing-down is spreading throughout American culture. The film critic Peter Lapote has written of the studio executives who reflexively call for reduction of dialogue in movie scenes without even bothering to read what the scene is about. In the last year or two, the word *mother,* connoting as it does a precise biological relationship, is almost never heard in anything but an R-rated cable broadcast. Newscasters have been counseled to use *mom* in every instance, whether or not the term is appropriate. Newsradio 88, a Westinghouse/CBS all-news AM station in New York City, has similarly decreed apparently that only the words *dad, cop, grand,* and *guy*—and never the words they stand for—are to be used.

These are not merely niceties of nomenclature: the tabloidization of terms leads inevitably to the trivialization of the news itself. Not only must news be given in words that even an airhead can understand, the consultants insist, but it is improper to suggest that issues of moment are ever at stake. "I'm just happy that the anchors sound like they are comfortable with each other," the station's consultant responded when asked about the language and its function.[11]

The paradigm is clear: the audience will select whom and what they wish to watch. We have always known and accepted that determining fact with respect to entertainment programming. But are we sure we wish to structure informational programming—news and public affairs—in the same way?

Can Broadcast Journalism Survive?

None of the concerns we are expressing here would be of any consequence to the media were it not for the fact that they continue to employ thousands of dedicated professionals eager to uphold the proud tradition of the ABC, CBS, and NBC news organizations. The accomplishments of those organizations and many others, including local station news departments, are manifest. They made television news the national hearth. At critical moments—the Cuban Missile Crisis, the Kennedy assassination, Watergate—the shared experience and images they made available to all had a unifying and healing effect.

So much has changed in the intervening years that we can never go back to those simpler media times. The paradigm of a family united around the television hearth has given way to the paradigm of individual access. The multi-set household has become a middle-class commonplace, cable has increased programming choices exponentially, and channel-surfing is now normal viewing behavior (except, of course, on Superbowl Sunday).

There have been changes in television journalism as well. When the three traditional networks reigned supreme, their news division presidents literally were the gatekeepers for breaking news. Newsboys could cry "Extra," and newspapers could print special editions to cover breaking stories, but television executives had the power to cut off entertainment programming to bring breaking news to the attention of the American public. During the Vietnam War, Fred W. Friendly, the president of CBS News, who once referred to himself as the Hand on the Big Switch, found that power to be far from absolute when the affiliates complained too loudly about lost revenue. When the news judgment of Friendly and his staff was ignored in deference to the affiliates, he created a major firestorm and resigned as a matter of principle. Nowadays the notion of three networks carrying live coverage of a Senate committee hearing would not even be considered. We have the Cable-Satellite Public Affairs Network (C-SPAN) funded by the cable industry and specifically set up for such purposes. And if C-SPAN is too busy, there is

Where the Action Is

C-SPAN 2. To say nothing of the twenty-four-hour all-news cable channels, Fox's FX, NBC's CNBC, and MSNBC. There is talk of a Bloomberg all-news channel with an emphasis on business and economic news, similar to CNBC. CBS's cable channel, *Eye on People,* a Monday through Friday evening *60 Minutes* spin-off, entered the news and information field in early 1997. And of course there is CNN.

As if cable, with its unlimited airtime, were not enough to reduce the broadcast networks' influence, there are also the independent stations in major markets, most of which have found a profitable niche by counterprogramming the networks' 10:00–11:00 P.M. entertainment. Many Fox affiliates, and the independent stations signed up with the nascent WB and UPN networks, have been building their news operations for a decade or more with considerable success.

Ironically, the independents have succeeded in capturing what the network news departments coveted for more than twenty years: an hourlong nightly news broadcast (albeit devoted mostly to local news).

The possibility of one-hour network news programs had long been a leitmotif of any serious discussion of the state of television. Richard Salant, the president of CBS News for sixteen years, had made it his unrelenting—though unsuccessful—mission: to increase the *CBS Evening News* broadcast from thirty minutes to an hour. As late as 1990, when asked in an interview for *Television Quarterly,* "If you were the czar of a network, are there certain things you would like to do that have never been done before?" Walter Cronkite answered without hesitation:

> I would certainly try the hour news in prime time. I think I'd tell the affiliates that I'm simply going to do it just like we did going into a half hour. We would never have had a half hour if we had to wait for the affiliates to approve it. And I think going to an hour could be done by a courageous network . . . 10 to 11 broadcast news.[12]

At about the same time Andy Rooney resurrected an idea he had floated in a newspaper column ten years earlier. The column had taken the form of an open letter to CBS Chairman William S. Paley. Why not, Rooney asked, make use of the *60 Minutes* brand name, producers, and correspondents and convert the broadcast into a half-hour to follow *The CBS Evening News*? Paley did not reply. When Rooney made the same suggestion to Larry Tisch a decade later, he got a response. Tisch rejected the idea and in no uncertain terms objected to Rooney's advancing it.

The dream of a sixty-minute news broadcast was not confined to CBS. Each of the commercial network news divisions had been working toward the same goal, but none had managed to achieve it. How could that be? With every journalist, every media critic, and many network executives in favor of the idea, why didn't it happen? What put an end to their dream?

Nothing more nor less than another unintended consequence of misregulation.

The coup de grâce to the dream of a one-hour prime-time news broadcast on the three commercial networks was PTAR—the prime-time access rule. One exception to the ruling that stations in the top fifty markets could not carry more than three hours a night of network programming was that they could carry thirty minutes of network news during access time, provided it ran adjacent to an hour of locally programmed news. Since an hour of network news would run counter to the primary purposes of PTAR—reducing network dominance and providing a prime-time window for independent productions—it is doubtful that the FCC would have made an exception for a 7:00–8:00 P.M. news. And no affiliate would sit still for a full hour of network news after 8:00.

This was dramatically demonstrated a few years into the rule. ABC News had made the commitment to change its poor third-place standing in public and industry esteem. Plans had been drawn up for a forty-five-minute evening news broadcast. In 1976 the network was so sure that the new format would happen that the trade bible, *Broadcasting* magazine, reported that the question "seemed likely to dominate" all three networks' affiliate conferences. Frederick Pierce,

ABC-TV Division president, declared it was "inevitable."[13] "Never," said the affiliates.

Increasing competition from independent stations—which could counterprogram with former network hits—not only prevented ABC from going forward with its forty-five-minute newscast but prompted affiliates from all three networks to resist proposals for 6:00–7:00 or 6:30–7:30 P.M. (Eastern Standard Time) network newscasts because local news, a key profit center, would have to move to earlier and far less desirable time or face stiff competition from independent stations from 7:00 to 8:00.

ABC's news plans had to wait until the Iranian hostage crisis came along in 1979. *Nightline* is a fixture of late-night programming now, but it came into being as a day-by-day countdown until the hostage crisis came to an end in 1981. By that time the broadcast was so well established that the network retained it in its present form. Since then, some observers have come to regard the combination of Peter Jennings and Ted Koppel as one news broadcast interrupted by entertainment, which is precisely what Roone Arledge, president of ABC News, foresaw. Because *Nightline* often treats issues relevant to the news of the moment and frequently picks up on the day's top news story, it can easily be seen as a delayed extension of *The ABC Evening News with Peter Jennings.*

However accurate that observation, there has actually been a one-hour daily network news broadcast in prime time since 1976, PBS's *MacNeil/Lehrer Newshour,* now *The Newshour with Jim Lehrer.* PBS was not subject to the prime-time access rule, nor is it constrained by the commercial imperatives that dictate the scheduling of the commercial networks and their affiliates.

It would be a gross oversimplification to blame the prime-time access rule for the state of broadcast news in this country today. But what if there had been no PTAR? What difference might a tradition of competitive one-hour news broadcasts have made in American political, social, and cultural discourse over the last twenty years? How much news was the American public actually getting from the commercial networks? Walter Cronkite once pasted the script for a typical network evening news broadcast onto the front page of the next day's *New York Times*. It covered less than half of the page.

Marvin Kalb, the longtime network diplomatic correspondent who now heads the Joan Shorenstein Barone Center for the Press, Politics, and Public Policy at Harvard, was asked in a fall 1996 NPR interview about the future of network news. Both he and Marlene Saunders of PBS agreed that it is unlikely that all three networks will continue to have an evening news broadcast. A more important question is, What will national news broadcasts look like in the future? What about the content issue?

A recent *Congressional Quarterly* analysis revealed that more airtime was spent on the O. J. Simpson trial than on the 1994 elections. Two years earlier the story of Amy Fisher and Joey Buttafuoco overshadowed the 1992 election in the New York print tabloids. Each of the three networks did a docudrama on the little nymphet who shot the wife of her lover. Phil Donahue got the highest ratings in the history of his series when he presented two separate hours on the Buttafuocos and their lawyers. O. J. Simpson, Joey Buttafuoco, Amy Fisher, the Bobbitts, the Menendez brothers, Tonya Harding and Nancy Kerrigan—under Stephen Mitchell's definition of news, these people would all have fit into the "chitchat" category.

The Canadian media guru Marshall MacLuhan prophesied that television would transform the world into a global village. Was MacLuhan closer to the mark than we thought? Is it possible that we are in the global village and all news has been reduced to what can be gossiped about over the electronic back fence? It is easy, in 1997, to imagine the worst. Global media mega-mergers, helped immeasurably by the misguided deregulation of our era, threaten to reduce the number of news organizations in the United States to a handful. Little wonder that E. B. White tried to warn us that in the final analysis a civilization is judged by its television.

(6)

Kinderfeindlichkeit
The Plight of Children and Children's Television

I N 1969 THE ANNUAL CONVENTION of the National Association of Educational Broadcasters (NAEB) was held during the second week of November at the Shoreham Hotel in Washington, D.C. For the first time the meeting coincided with a major broadcasting event, and an educational broadcasting event at that. Throughout Tuesday and Wednesday there had been much talk among the attendees about the event and its implications for the field. On Thursday, November 10, a special hall with about four hundred seats had been set up with television monitors. The room soon filled up and many stood around the edges of the room and four or five deep at the open double doorway, eager to see the much heralded (some said ballyhooed) premiere broadcast of the most expensive, most talked about, most anticipated educational broadcast of all time.

Down the Tube

The monitors were turned on, with the sound muted, four or five minutes before 9:00 A.M. The audience grew quiet and expectant. The sound came on, the call letters of the Washington station WETA appeared, and audiences in the eastern and central time zones, including the room in the Shoreham Hotel, heard for the first time the now familiar

> *Sunny day*
> *Sweepin' the clouds away*
> *On my way to where the air is sweet*
> *Can you tell me how to get*
> *How to get to Sesame Street.*

The regular characters appeared and were identified, the mythical street and the broadcast began to take shape, and the middle-aged audience—there wasn't a single child in the room—settled in. Soon some became increasingly uneasy. As professional producers and directors, they knew how to count a house and assess an audience's response, watching for the moment when they ceased to be individuals and allowed themselves to come together in a communal experience of comprehension, empathy, or delight. At the Shoreham Hotel, something was wrong. This audience was far from cohesive: it was very divided. Some individuals, even some groups of individuals, were enjoying the broadcast and themselves, commenting on the unexpected, appreciating a pedagogic point, even laughing. But many were retreating further and further into their jackets and into themselves. Their arms and legs were crossed, their chins down, their faces fixed.

At 10:00 the broadcast came to an end, the lights came on, and the monitors were turned off. A smattering of applause, some of it spirited, did not last long. An officer of the NAEB mounted the dais and began the discussion. Several members were already lined up at the floor mikes.

A number of those in the room were astounded. No one would

have expected unanimity of approval for the premiere of a broadcast series as complex and ambitious as *Sesame Street*. But the criticism kept coming, mounting in intensity. One man's veins seemed about to burst as he fairly shouted into the mike, "Education is not supposed to be pleasurable. It's supposed to be hard work!" Another man vilified the manner in which the letters of the alphabet and the numbers 1 to 10 were presented. "They look like commercials, popped in that way, and short, and looking like advertisements for the number 3." These reactions were particularly distressing to one of the authors of this book, George Dessart, who was there that morning. He had been a consultant in the early phase of the series' planning, and the idea that numbers and letters could best be taught by producing and scheduling them like commercials had been his principal contribution to the series.

He should not have been surprised. *Sesame Street* was predestined to generate controversy. A Boston University professor of education, Frank Garfunkel, carried on the attack on the teaching methodology in the pages of the *Boston Globe*. He characterized *Sesame Street*'s educational methods as "rote memorization" that would "put a noose" around children and make it impossible for them ever to "engage in sustained and developed thought."[1] The *Globe* also printed a detailed response from Harvard's Gerald S. Lesser, one of the early consultants and the research psychologist who drew up the original educational plan for the series.

Another early complaint appeared in *Childhood Education*. The director of an experimental program for nursery through third-grade children at the State University College at Fredonia, New York, had a somewhat different complaint. The program should have hired teachers to replicate what they did in nursery school and kindergarten: "Why debase the art form of teaching with phony pedagogy, vulgar sideshows, bad acting, and layers of smoke and fog to clog the eager minds of small children?"[2] Martin Mayer, writing in the early 1970s, made an interesting observation: "Perhaps the most remarkable thing about *Sesame Street* is the fact that few schoolmen take it very seriously. It is by any standard the largest educational experiment ever."[3]

Meanwhile, of course, the intended audience was paying no attention to the programs' critics but supporting the judgment of the programs' champions. Within the first two years, analyses of the Nielsen ratings showed that eight million children were watching every week, and six million saw *Sesame Street* as often as three times a week.

The Constancy of Concern

No matter how large the audience was for *Sesame Street,* it was bound to create controversy. Children's programming has always been troubling to adults, for many reasons. Thomas S. Rogers, then senior counsel of the Telecommunications, Consumer Protection, and Finance Subcommittee of the House of Representatives (he is now executive vice president of NBC, Inc., and president of NBC Cable), understated the condition of children's programming when he wrote in 1988 that it was "the area where the greatest number of public policy makers in Washington agree that broadcasters as a whole have not lived up to their responsibilities as broadcasters."[4]

Clearly something very similar can be said as of this writing. Though the debate seems, for the moment, to have shifted its focus from children's programs to what else children might possibly see or hear, there appears to be a growing consensus that the V chip cannot be relied on to clean up television, as well as fervent (though less widespread) support for a form of Internet censorship. What does not change, however, is the constancy of debate about television and children.

Ellen Wartella, a leading researcher in the area of children and television who served as a consultant to both the FCC and the Federal Trade Commission in the 1970s, has developed a theory as to why this debate never ends:

[T]he ongoing debates about television's influence on children (and earlier debates about film and radio's influence) are part of the way that our society negotiates the introduction of communication technologies. Many of the same issues are now being discussed about children's use of video cassettes and of computers. Indeed, debates about the impact of communication media on children may serve to deflect wider public concern about who controls and creates media in the society. When such control issues are not subject to debate— and by 1953, American television was fully entrenched as a large commercial system—children's issues may be debated instead.[5]

Even those who have difficulty with Wartella's theory would have to agree that the introduction of every popular medium in this country has been attended by grave concern over its potential dangers and by intense conflict over who will control it so that those dangers will bring no harm to the most vulnerable among us. The link with the most vulnerable, children, is remarkable. Indeed, the earliest court case in the United States against a media product thought to be improper, *A Book Entitled Memoirs of a Woman of Pleasure* (Fanny Hill) by John Cleland, was brought in 1821 in Massachusetts, during the same decade in which that state became the first to establish mandatory public schooling. Many states passed their first laws against obscenity in the 1820s and 1830s. A federal law was passed in 1842, but no one was prosecuted under it until after the Civil War. After several years of intense lobbying in Congress, the president of New York City's Society for the Suppression of Vice, Anthony Comstock, single-handedly managed to get a sweeping anti-obscenity law passed.

After books, the next medium to come under scrutiny was the next to appear: the film. The first narrative moving picture, *The Great Train Robbery,* was released in 1903; by 1907 there were editorial attacks on the nickelodeons, theaters where admission cost five cents. "Wholly vicious," a *Chicago Tribune* editorial shouted. Films appealed to "the lowest passions of childhood," and no one under eighteen should be admitted.[6]

Radio, the next emerging mass medium, also experienced criticism. "Parents have become aware of a puzzling change in the behavior of their children. They are bewildered by a host of new problems, and find themselves unprepared, frightened, resentful, helpless," one researcher exclaimed.[7] As early as 1931 a Senate resolution expressed deep disappointment in what radio seemed to have become.

In the 1940s the psychiatrist Frederick Wertheim attacked the comic books for their depictions and seeming approval of unrestrained violence. Later he expanded the theme of his *Seduction of the Innocents* to focus on television.

In January 1951, the body count began. The NAEB, financed by the Ford Foundation, set up groups of viewers in several cities to monitor violence. The New York City group announced that 2,970 "acts or threats" of violence could be seen on television in one week. More than 17 per hour were reported during children's viewing periods.

The contents of periodicals were studied more systematically. Wartella found that until April 1949, only 14 articles about children and television appeared in *The Reader's Guide to Periodical Literature*. Within the next four years the number had reached 135. That same year, 1953, a young graduate student at Columbia University's Bureau of Applied Social Research, Joseph Klapper (later the head of CBS's intramural social research unit), combined content analysis with interviews of opinion leaders who had an interest in the subject area. Wartella points out that the concerns of the public today "have changed . . . little from Klapper's three major findings in the working paper he prepared four decades ago."[8]

The first was what he called "time and crime" issues. What these boil down to is parental and educator concerns that children spend too much *time* with television and that too much of what they *see* involves violence. The second theme Klapper identified came from the statements of everyone he interviewed and from 35 percent of the articles: children's television should be "better," and programs "more educational." Finally, there were the long-term concerns. Would the viewing of adult conflicts make children suspicious of adult "deceitfulness"? Would they attempt to emulate adults at too early an age? Would children become too passive as a result of the "passivity" involved in watching television?

Perhaps Wartella's most interesting observation is that the public's concerns about children and television are not consistent but intermittent. Similarly, we would point out that broadcasters' interest in children's programming has also waxed and waned. There was great interest and activity in the 1950s, very little in the 1960s, renewed interest and activity in the 1970s, little interest in the next fifteen years, and considerable concern in the mid-1990s. The reasons for this fluctuation all seem, to our surprise, related.

Children's Television in the Golden Age

If the decade of the 1950s was a golden age of television, it was also a sterling age for children's programs. During television's first decade, programming was everything. There were no shelves of old programs to reuse, nor did television have the technology to make use of film libraries. Nor was there videotape to make reruns possible. Every program had to be live. These factors made television even more voracious in its use of material than it is in today's multi-channel environment. Prime-time programmers converted the few radio formats they could make visual, but they relied primarily on theatrical talent and material to develop the new medium. Inevitably, the golden age was dominated by vaudevillians and the legitimate theater, but even children's programs made it on to the air in the early evening.

Among the first on the air were ABC's *Teenage Book Club,* at 8:00 P.M. on Fridays, and *The Lone Ranger,* a radio serial that became one of the first film series made for television. In 1949 the DuMont Network—its stations were later bought by Metromedia and survive as

Fox O and Os—premiered *Captain Video and His Video Rangers,* "one of the low-budget wonders of television history and one of the most popular children's programs" of its day. It appeared Monday through Friday, 7:00–7:30 P.M. "The Guardian of the Safety of the World," as Captain Video described himself, offered all manner of premiums—space helmets and decoding rings, for example—and also offered advice to "the rangers at home" on "tolerance, fair play and personal integrity."[9]

Peggy Charren, the founder of Action for Children's Television (ACT), looks back with fondness to children's programming in the 1950s. When asked why so much of it was good for children, Charren quickly replies, "That's simple. The stations needed to sell sets."[10] Joan Ganz Cooney, the driving force behind *Sesame Street,* completely agrees. "Buying a set for your children was the perfect rationalization."[11]

As more and more children pressured their parents to buy sets, and more and more parents acceded, more children's programs appeared. Like the golden age's serious dramas for adults, children's programs of the 1950s attracted many of the most promising writers and performers of the era. Paul Tripp, the author of *Tubby the Tuba,* created, wrote, and played the title role in CBS's *Mr. I Magination* on Sunday evenings. Tripp wore a candy-striped engineer's uniform as he drove the show's regulars to Imaginationland, with station stops at Ambitionville, Inventorsville, Seaport City, and I Wish I Were Town. The show was distinctive for encouraging viewers to send in letters describing what they wished would happen. Their fantasies became the subjects of many of the program's sketches.

On Saturday evenings, NBC presented *Watch Mr. Wizard.* Mr. Wizard would show a neighbor's child how to do simple scientific experiments using common household items. "Gee, Mr. Wizard," the child would inevitably exclaim at the denouement of the experiment.

Watch Mr. Wizard was originally produced in Chicago but moved to New York in 1955. Chicago was also the birthplace, and longtime origination venue, of the legendary *Kukla, Fran, and Ollie.* Fran was played by the actress and singer Fran Allison. The other characters were all Kuklipolitans, the creations of Burr Tillstrom, a Chicago puppeteer, who had created Kukla in 1936. By the time they reached television, their number included the carefree and outgoing Oliver J. Dragon, with one prominent tooth; the mailman, Fletcher Robert; Madame Ophelia Ogelpuss, who never let anyone forget she had been an opera star; Beulah Witch, a student of electronics who patrolled the coaxial cable on a jet-propelled broomstick; and several other equally whimsical regulars.

One of the most remarkable features of this highly successful and highly regarded program was that it was never scripted. It was also always broadcast live, with the characters on both sides of the proscenium reacting to each other in the most natural and completely spontaneous fashion. Later, in the 1970s, the program would do a season on PBS and yet another for the syndication market.

While the products of NBC's Chicago School, as it came to be called, were feeding that network, CBS found a source of children's programming in its nearby Philadelphia affiliate, later to be an O and O, WCAU-TV. *Big Top* appeared on Saturdays, 7:00–7:30 P.M., in its first season (1950–51). The next year it ran for a full hour but was moved to Saturday afternoon at 1:00, where it remained for seven years. The original venue, the Convention Hall in Camden, New Jersey, burned down; *Big Top* then moved back across the river to a National Guard armory in West Philadelphia.

The show was set up like a small one-ring circus. Each week viewers saw a mustachioed, top-hatted ringmaster, a brass band, a strong man, a pretty girl to ride the occasional elephant, two resident clowns (one of which was Ed McMahon), and six better-than-average circus acts. What set *Big Top* apart from other circuses, on television or off, was the merchandising and producing genius of its originator, Charles Vanda, who put the spectacle together on a budget that would have delighted any cost accountant.

Every circus opens with a parade. *Big Top*'s opened with a high school twirler at fifteen dollars a week, followed by banners proclaiming the show's title and saluting its sponsor, Sealtest, and its milk and ice cream products. The banners were carried by the uniformed roustabouts who would later set up and strike the various acts. The roustabouts marched with great élan: officers and NCOs of the armory's cadre, they ensured that a proprietary security force would keep an eye on the show's equipment during the week. The commercial performers, a stable of circus look-alikes, also joined the parade. But what really swelled the parade were troops of Scouts—one each of Brownies, Cubs, Boy Scouts, and Girl Scouts—carrying balloons with the name of the sponsor. The show maintained a waiting list for troops, which came from as far away as Miami or New Orleans at their own expense. Other Scout troops, having waited about eighteen months for tickets, made up the perennially packed audience.

Vanda's chef d'oeuvre was an hour-and-a-half children's program that appeared live, five afternoons a week, on CBS. The story often told of its inception may have been apocryphal, but it caught the spirit of the man and of the young writers, directors, and producers who flocked to the new medium and to the innovative learning ground Charley Vanda provided.

At one point, Vanda, who was also vice president for programming at WCAU-TV, produced nineteen hours of programming a week on the network. One was the Peabody Award winner *What in the World*, later adapted by the BBC.

Vanda was scrupulous in attending the meeting of CBS producers held each week in New York and presided over by Oscar Katz, then the chief programmer. He was probably not the most popular producer among his New York peers, but with his track record, his production capacity, and his showmanship, he could command Katz's attention and respect at the weekly get-together. At one such session, according to the story, Katz was lamenting the lack of excitement in what the medium now calls the early fringe daypart, roughly from the end of school to 6:00 P.M. He reminded the producers of their own childhoods, when they would wait all week to go down to the local movie house and, for a dime, spend Saturday afternoon watching the serials. What the serials represented, Katz mused, was the very thing that was missing on CBS in the weekday afternoon schedule: the excitement, the action.

Vanda leapt to the challenge. They had been thinking the same thing in Philadelphia, he told the assembled producers. "You know we just moved into our new studio building, there on the outskirts of the city. And we have woods behind us. If you look out over that rolling land, you could almost imagine you were out West. Well, we've put together our own cowboy serial, an hour and a half a day." Katz was now on the edge of his chair. He suggested they set up a closed-circuit line from Philadelphia the very next day. Vanda urged that they be given a chance to fix some problems that had come up and offered to feed the show in a few weeks.

Katz agreed, and the meeting soon ended. On his way out to another meeting, Vanda had a secretary call his office to arrange a midnight meeting with his entire program department. At dinner Vanda excused himself to send a wire to a friend who had been in the B unit at Republic Pictures, producing cowboy serials.

When he got back to Philadelphia that night, what Vanda saw was a very tense staff. They were all there, and they seemed to be fearing the worst. They could not have been more surprised by what he had to say: "We go on the air six weeks from tomorrow with a brand-new show. We're going to need to convert studio 2 into the interior of a bar. And we need to build a Western town out behind the building. We're going to have to make a deal with a riding stable, find some old wagons . . . "

Six weeks later they were on the line. Shortly thereafter, television's first and only live Western, *Action in the Afternoon,* went onto the CBS schedule. The series continued during 1953 and 1954, Monday through Friday, for nearly 350 episodes, rain or shine, hot weather or cold. Like its producer, the show was in many ways emblematic of television in the golden age: opportunistic, flexible,

Down the Tube

improvisational, and resourceful. But the days of live television were numbered.

Television Invents Saturday Morning

The year 1955 marked a clear demarcation in children's programming. Two developments signaled a change in thinking about the genre and about children themselves. The implications of the first were less immediately discernible, but very clear in retrospect. NBC, in moving *Kukla, Fran, and Ollie* to New York, was clearly consolidating its children's programming in New York and thus preparing for a more aggressive move into the daypart. CBS bought the rights to the entire library of *Terrytoons*. Many local stations had already purchased the rights to black-and-white cartoons originally produced as movie theater curtain-raisers for primarily adult audiences. A station would rent a clown costume, a cowboy outfit, or a pith helmet and jungle gear, then draft an announcer to serve as host for a half-hour children's program. Three or four cartoons might be shown. In between, Cowboy Bill would strum a guitar, Buffie the Clown would advise caution in crossing the streets, or Explorer Bob would advocate drinking milk, sometimes even bringing in a guest expert—from the local milk company—to drive home the point.

When 168 *Popeye* cartoons hit their markets, Bill and Buffie and Bob were nearly all knocked off the air. What astonished many station programmers was that children wanted to see these cartoons again and again; clearly, cartoons might be infinitely cheaper in the long run than programming that relied on live performers. The 1,100 *Terrytoons* represented only the first step toward a goal that all three networks were pursuing: developing less expensive ways to produce cartoons than the traditional full animation devised by Disney, Warner, and other studios to serve the market for theatrical releases. Crusader Rabbit was the first made-for-television cartoon character. Building on the techniques pioneered in such films as *Mr.*

162

Magoo and *Gerald McBoing Boing*, 19 five-minute *Crusader Rabbit* cartoons were produced for $1,500 apiece. More and more studios opened to cater to the networks' Saturday morning schedules. It was not long before all the live performers were replaced with a three-hour block of cartoons.

One significant exception was *Captain Kangaroo*, which made its debut on CBS in 1955. Appearing Monday through Friday, the program was targeted to the preschool subset of the baby boomer generation. A young Bob Keeshan played the avuncular Captain, assisted by Mr. Green Jeans and Bunny Rabbit. The program, warm and supportive, became an instant favorite of the boomers and their young mothers, who rose up en masse to petition the network to reconsider the cancellation of the series at the end of its first year because it had not attracted sponsor interest. Armed with forty thousand letters from the mobilized mothers of America, the network sales force marched down Madison Avenue and quickly enlisted enough advertisers to keep the program on the air. It long outlasted the baby boom and became a fixture on CBS for thirty years.

The second and pivotal development in children's television in 1955 was the awakening of significant sponsor interest in the children's daypart. While neither NBC's nor CBS's actions represented, in and of themselves, a major shift in how children's television was perceived, ABC's actions clearly did. In October 1954, ABC, in a collaboration rich in meaning forty years later, premiered Disney's first foray into television, *Disneyland*; this show was remarkable because it represented the first time a major Hollywood studio had deigned to produce a series for television. The series became the ABC network's first hit. Both of the other networks had tried but failed to snare Walt Disney: among other things, they balked at his terms, which reportedly included $90,000 per episode (perhaps the highest cost per program at that time) and a $500,000 investment in a revolutionary idea, a theme park. As the world soon learned, Disneyland was successful as both a program and a theme park, and ABC made money on both.

One year later, in the fall of 1955, Disney permitted the first use in any other medium of its oldest asset, the epynomic *Mickey Mouse Club*. Convinced of the power of the Disney name and the talent it could command—a three-episode mini-series with *Disneyland* had launched the Davy Crockett craze, including the song that was still number one on the charts—ABC guaranteed advertisers that they would have access to 90 percent of the nation's television sets. This seemed a risky guarantee considering that ABC was scheduling the program from 5:00 to 6:00 P.M., Monday to Friday, a time period during which the local affiliates could refuse to carry the program. ABC sought twenty sponsors, each of which would pay $500,000 for one-quarter sponsorship, once a week. Three commercials would appear during a sponsor's weekly segment. Moreover, the network would sell advertising only on a fifty-two-week, noncancelable basis. The gamble was to pay off: *The Mickey Mouse Club* owned its time period, and the show's advertising strategy forever changed children's television.

One of the first advertisers to agree to ABC's terms was a small toy company in Hawthorne, California. At the time Mattel's annual sales were only $4 million. The largest toy company, Marx, grossed $50 million in 1954. Total sales of toys in the United States that year came to less than $1 billion. Of that amount, the entire toy industry spent less than one-tenth of 1 percent on advertising. Louis Marx, the founder of the company that bore his name, claimed in a *Time* magazine cover story that he had spent $312 for advertising the previous year. He believed that advertising was ineffective for toys. It had never sold toys, and it never could.

Elliot and Ruth Handler, the founders of Mattel, thought otherwise, and they literally bet their business on the premise that television advertising was the wave of the future. The first filmed toy commercial went on the air soon after *The Mickey Mouse Club* made its first appearance in November 1955. The commercial was for a new product, the Burp Gun, an automatic cap-firing machine gun that sold for four dollars. The commercial pictured a small boy stalking elephants. The plants in his living room were augmented with rear screen projections of his quarry in the African rain forest, while the voice of his father talked about the product, its safety features, and its price. Although the commercial was ostensibly addressed to adults, it carried strong child appeal. Most notably, it clearly introduced the company's strongly visual logo for the benefit of pre-readers, with the reinforcing voice-over, "You can tell it's Mattel, it's swell."

When the Christmas toy season opened the Monday after Thanksgiving, it was clear that the Burp Gun was in demand. Mattel reported that it could not open the factory doors because they were blocked by sacks of mail orders that morning. Stores sold out faster than the plant could ship in reorders. Everyone seemed to want one, even President Eisenhower, who wrote to Mattel's advertising agency to ask for help in finding one for his grandson. One million were sold, and who knows how many more could have been. Mattel doubled its annual sales volume.

The nature of the toy business had been changed, as had the nature of children's television. Retailers began to make decisions based on their assessment of the drawing power of the commercials and the size of the manufacturer's advertising budget. Today the toy industry puts out two kinds of toys, "television items" and "standards" (balls, anonymous wagons and tricycles, stuffed but unfranchised animals). After the success of the Burp Gun, Mattel and its agency, Carson/Roberts, "began thinking of toys in an entirely different way. We began to see toys as concepts that could be depicted or demonstrated in television commercials," as Cy Schneider put it.[12] Schneider was the account executive for the Burp Gun and would become president of the agency after more than a quarter-century of writing and producing children's commercials.

That kind of thinking would ultimately lead Mattel to become a giant in the toy industry—and the world's largest manufacturer of "women's" clothing. Within three years after its first television commercials aired, Mattel had become the industry leader in toy guns and toy musical instruments, both of which appealed primarily to boys. It needed a toy for girls and found it in the least likely place. A doll named Lili, based on a playgirl character in a cartoon in *Das Bild*, a German tabloid, had been merchandised to adult men through bars and tobacconists in Germany. The Handlers saw the Lili doll and realized that it could be a three-dimensional version of the paper doll. They tested the concept with children and their parents. Schneider reports that "almost 100 percent of the mothers literally hated the doll and felt it was too mature for their little girls. Most said they would never buy it. Almost 100 percent of the girls, shown the doll independent of their mothers, said they loved the doll and definitely wanted to own it."[13]

Schneider describes how they "positioned" the new toy: Mattel bought the rights to Lili and renamed her Barbie. Carson/Roberts was assigned to merchandise the new line: "The Barbie doll gave growing girls an opportunity to make a short fantasy leap to becoming a teenager and wearing pretty clothes. This factor was the key to the doll's appeal."[14]

Barbie became an instant best-seller among the target audience, four- to eight-year-olds. When her wedding gown proved to be the most popular outfit, it became obvious that a bridegroom was necessary, and Ken was created. Barbie and Ken, their associates, and their clothes and possessions brought in more than $1 billion over the next thirty years. During that time the toy business grew to more than $12 billion in the United States, and its advertising budgets, which are almost exclusively devoted to television, ran to more than $300 million. Most of this growth came about directly as a result of the techniques Mattel adopted in 1955.

"That is what really spelled the end of children's programming in this country," Peggy Charren insists. "When Mattel came out with Barbie Dolls and advertised them all over children's television, that was the end of any kind of hope for quality programming."[15]

The Adults Step In

Charren may not have been the first to realize why the quality of children's programming had deteriorated, but she certainly was the first to take effective action to change that situation. What prompted her to do so was very simple: "Inadequate day care," she explains.

> If there had been decent daycare available and I didn't have to stay at home with those two little children and see what they were watching on television and what the broadcasters were doing, I would have opened a children's book shop. And who knows what would have happened?[16]

What did happen is that in 1968 Charren convened a meeting in her living room in Newton, Massachusetts, a suburb of Boston, to discuss children's television. The group included neighbors, PTA members, teachers, and others who had expressed interest in the topic. A committee of four women, including Peggy Charren, spent the next few months drawing up "a reasonable set of guidelines for children's TV."[17] Since that winter evening in 1968, the organization, Action for Children's Television (ACT), was to become a national organization with between 15,000 and 20,000 members at its peak, and a budget that reportedly reached somewhere between $300,000 and $400,000.

If ACT has not become a recognized name in every television household, it has certainly become a household name in every television executive's office. It has also become a name to reckon with on Capitol Hill. In 1970 ACT filed a petition with the FCC to ban all commercials from children's television. It also filed a petition with the Federal Trade Commission, which has jurisdiction over truth in advertising on television, to ban the advertising of toys and a subsequent petition to ban the advertising to children of anything edible. The next step was to file a complaint against three pharmaceutical companies for advertising vitamins directly to children.

Obviously, not all the petitions ACT filed then or subsequently succeeded. But the organization managed to accomplish a great deal. The initial filings did bring about hearings. Even before the hearings took place, the drug manufacturers voluntarily agreed to stop the practice of advertising to children. By 1973 ACT pressure had become so pronounced that the National Association of Broadcasters modified *The Television Code*, the industry's self-regulatory standard to which the networks and most affiliates adhered. Under "Audience Sensibilities: Children," the code was revised to read:

> The broadcaster and the advertiser should exercise special caution with the content and presentation of television commercials placed in or near programs designed for children. Exploitation of children should be avoided. Commercials directed to children should in no way mislead as to the product's performance and usefulness.

To anyone familiar with children's programs in the 1950s and 1960s, the most astonishing change ACT brought about in the code was the following: "No children's program personality or cartoon character shall be utilized to deliver commercial messages within or adjacent to the programs in which such a personality or cartoon character regularly appears."[18] Characters were also prohibited from delivering lead-ins that might imply an endorsement.

Peggy Charren and her associates achieved another of their primary goals. Commercials in time periods during which "programs initially designed primarily for children under 12 years of age are scheduled" would be limited to nine minutes and thirty seconds per hour on Saturday and Sunday and twelve minutes per hour on weekdays.[19] This was a major victory for the pro-children activists.

The entire code, however, would be revoked in 1980 as a result of a consent decree. Ironically, the Justice Department brought suit against the NAB claiming that its limitations on commercial time, whether during children's or any other programming, were in restraint of trade.

Nevertheless, ACT's pressure not only kept undesirable material *off* the air but resulted in the broadcasters putting highly commendable programming *on* the air. Critics, including Charren, were not surprised and pointed out that this was the broadcasters' characteristic response to pressure. Charren says, "Again and again and again, if the FCC merely suggested that they might be moving in any kind of direction that might possibly force the broadcasters to do something, they found ways to do it."[20]

In 1971 CBS responded to the perceived threat by setting up a unique and highly acclaimed project to provide news to children. The CBS News producer Joel Heller was put in charge of a twenty-person unit dedicated to children's programs. They came up with a short program concept, *In the News*, to provide clarifying background material to make issues of the moment come alive for children. Later they produced *Thirty Minutes*, a children's news magazine similar to the Sunday night staple for adults. The unit also developed a number of specials, notably on the election process.

ACT, the National PTA, and the American Academy of Pediatrics were delighted. They were also pleased to note that NBC had demonstrated a commitment to children's television by elevating George Heinemann, the original producer of the Chicago School's *Ding Dong School,* to vice president for children's programs—a network first. Heinemann, who garnered more Peabody Awards than any other producer to this day, came up with *Take a Giant Step, Go,* and *NBC Children's Theater.* ABC followed suit, granting stripes to Squire Rushnell, who oversaw the *ABC Afterschool Specials.* Saturday morning in the 1970s began to blossom with pro-social series. Emblematic was CBS's *Fat Albert and the Cosby Kids,* a charming cartoon series that marked Bill Cosby's first venture into producing for television and was overseen by a panel of no fewer than eleven psychologists, educators, and sociologists to assure that no *anti*social messages intruded.

Suddenly, though, the threat to the networks was over.

Deregulation was already under way in several industries—long-distance trucking and the airlines, for example—but it did not affect broadcasting until the Reagan administration. Mark S. Fowler was a deregulatory president's choice for chairman of the FCC; he was also ideologically committed to reducing the role of government in virtually every area. Recalling the shock Fowler delivered to the industry by declaring that TV was nothing more than "a toaster with pictures," Charren says that she was not surprised by what happened next:

> And of course the instant that Fowler came in and talked about the toaster, that was the end of all of those programs. CBS went from fourteen to three to zero in the *Specials,* and the *In the News* broadcasts disappeared, and Joel Heller was assigned to other things, and the unit was disbanded.[21]

We have attempted to make plain our belief that the electronic media are at their best when a reasonable degree of thoughtfully devised regulation is in place to ensure that the public interest is being served. But it would be an oversimplification to defend that belief by asserting that deregulation was responsible for all the evils that have threatened or befallen children's television throughout most of its history. Much more was at work. Deregulation, to be sure, is one of the cyclical phenomena in American history. But cyclical theory also reveals that from the mid-1960s through the early 1980s, not only children's television was being assailed but all other children's concerns as well. Children themselves were in thrall to a societal animus. German scholars refer to it as *Kinderfeindlichkeit,* literally, a condition of pervasive hostility toward children. We have no word for it in English, but we have experienced it again and again.

William Strauss and Neil Howe, in their seminal study of the fifteen generations born in what is now the United States from 1584 to the present, describe the childhood years of the generation following the baby boomers, roughly from the mid-1960s to the mid-1980s, as "an era of unremitting hostility toward children."[22] They rest their argument on a variety of factors affecting virtually all areas of American life. The murder rate of children under four more than doubled. We began to hear about increasing numbers of runaways and about children being abandoned. The term "throwaway kids" appeared. Landlords refused to rent apartments to families with children. Fully 25 percent of all rental units in the United States had "no children" clauses in their leases, a 50 percent increase over the preceding postwar years. Income tax rates were raised significantly for families with children, while childless couples' rates remained constant. Child poverty increased, while the poverty rate for adults and elders fell. California's Proposition 13 and other tax revolts throughout the country led to cuts, often severe ones, in school budgets. As a consequence, public-school teachers lost purchasing power for seven years in a row.

G-rated films fell from 41 percent to only 13 percent of the film industry's output; Disney cartoonists were laid off. Even more significant was the picture of children—actually the attitude of adults toward children—portrayed and fostered by the film industry. In the 1950s, Strauss and Howe point out, films like Disney's *Shaggy Dog* presented "bright, well-meaning kids whom adults respected, kids any filmgoers knew would grow up to be interesting people."[23] Contrast these, they suggest, with what followed in the wake of the 1968 film *Rosemary's Baby,* in which the father sells the unborn child to a witches' coven. Nine or more film hits of the 1970s featured demonized children— *The Exorcist I* and *II, Omen I, II,* and *III, Damien, It's Alive, It Lives Again, Demon Seed.* Other films (*Taxi Driver, Paper Moon, Carrie,* and *Willy Wonka and the Chocolate Factory*) portrayed children as prostitutes, hucksters, arsonists, or impossibly spoiled.

In the mid-1980s, Strauss and Howe report, "many of these trends began stabilizing—and in some cases, turned around." The 1980s saw a run of films "featuring tots audiences felt like bundling in their arms and protecting."[24] *Raising Arizona* was followed by *Three Men and a Baby* and *Parenthood.*

The period of *Kinderfeindlichkeit* will not be the last in Western history if cycle theorists like Strauss and Howe, Arthur Schlesinger, Arthur Schlesinger Jr., Auguste Comte, José Ortega y Gasset, and others are correct. Nor does it appear to have been the first. But what made the 1970s unique is that its children were the first such generation to grow up with television on the scene. It is little wonder that children's television commodified children, or that children were exploited. And little wonder that even the best of commercial broadcasters needed to be prodded by Peggy Charren.

In fact, there is no issue related to children's television that ACT has not raised and addressed. Similarly, there has been no regulatory, legislative, or judicial activity in the field that Charren and her colleagues did not initiate. As early as 1970, scarcely more than two years after that first meeting in Newton, FCC Chairman Dean Burch declared:

> Let me acknowledge the powerful influence of ACT on the prevailing climate of opinion. . . . ACT has gone to the core issue. They are asking, in effect, whether a commercially based broadcasting system is capable of serving up quality programming for an audience so sensitive and malleable as children.[25]

By 1980 ACT appeared to be on the threshold of success with one of its most bitterly contested initiatives. The incumbent FCC chairman, Charles Ferris, was reportedly disposed to approve ACT's proposal that each station provide one hour of children's programming each day. This would have gone far beyond the requirements of an earlier ACT achievement, the FCC's 1974 *Children's Television Report and Policy Statement,* which stipulated only that stations provide a "reasonable amount" of programs "designed for children and intended to educate and inform, not simply to entertain."[26] The chairman of the FCC, however, serves at the pleasure of the president; President Carter was defeated, and in came President Reagan's choice, Mark Fowler—who, of course, would have none of it.

On December 22, 1983, the FCC ended the process that had begun in 1970. The *Report and Order* of 1983 made it clear that no age-specific programming would be required, nor would there be any requirements respecting the time of day programs were to be presented or how many hours per week would be appropriate. It also indicated that general or "family" programs, not just programs designed for children, might be considered in assessing whether children were getting the "special programming attention" licensees were required to provide. ACT filed an appeal with the U.S. Court of Appeals for the District of Columbia. The appeal was denied.

Another of ACT's longtime concerns was the so-called program-length commercial, long frowned upon by the FCC. The commission's reasoning was that a program on how to use a sewing machine, sponsored by a sewing machine manufacturer, might be scheduled on the basis of its certain revenue and not on its program value. Thus, the audience might be deprived of some other broadcast in that time period that might be more clearly in the public interest. In the present age of the infomercial and shop-at-home channels, the question may seem positively quaint.

To be sure, toys based on characters in books or movies had been around for a long time. But when ABC ran a cartoon series entitled *Hot Wheels*, Charren and her associates brought it to the attention of the FCC. The series, they pointed out, was made by and for Mattel, and it featured a line of Mattel toys, Hot Wheels cars. After an investigation, the FCC wrote to ABC expressing its disapproval but took no further action.

Program-length commercials remained a hot issue with the children's television public interest groups for the better part of the decade. No one minded the licensing of toys or clothing based on characters children had already become familiar with and attached to through television programs, but programs based on toys seemed unfair.

Meanwhile, ACT was going far beyond the program-length commercial issue. Evelyn Kaye, a onetime president of ACT, made the group's larger agenda clear:

For some reason, while we don't allow teachers to sell products to children in schools, we accept selling to children on television. If a salesman rang our doorbell and said, "Hi . . . I'd like to come into your living room and show your four-year-old a few toys while you go on cooking in the kitchen . . . ," as responsible adults we'd slam the door in his face. We know that most four-year-olds couldn't cope with a fast-talking toy salesman. Yet this happens every day in our living rooms through television and not only do we allow them on adult programs, but we allow them on programs specifically designed for children which reach very young audiences.[27]

Virtually any executive in commercial television, whether at the station or network level, would reply with something like what Cy Schneider, discussing ACT, said in *Children's Television:*

What these people fail to realize is that commercial television, even for children, is just another business. It is a business that makes its money by helping sell products, a valuable stimulator for gross national product which in turn helps to create jobs and greases the wheels of our economy.

. . . If commercial television cannot move the goods, it cannot be in business. Just because commercial television devotes many hours to the special audience of children doesn't change the fundamental point of view one iota.[28]

Clearly, ACT was aiming for the very heart of commercial television's business. But it was doing far more. It was directly assailing the industry's perception of its child audience and its function.

For the most part, the industry had long regarded children as fungible, as "one size fits all." The older children control the set, broadcasters thought in the days when one set per household was the rule, and the younger children watch what the older ones choose. But that's all right, because everyone knows that younger children always want to see what the older ones are up to. And for

God's sake, the industry seemed to be saying, don't forget that they are out of school on Saturday mornings. They don't want to learn; they deserve to enjoy themselves.

Early in his career, George Dessart wrote a thirty-minute weekly children's program designed as a commercial vehicle and built around an irrepressible clown who was unaware of his own limitations and constantly running headlong into reality. When the massive Picasso retrospective came to the Philadelphia Museum, Dessart brought in an armful of prints and built a program around the clown's efforts to paint his own Picassos. The script worked, the cast played it fully, and the two hundred or so children in the studio audience that Saturday morning responded with delight. When George was called into the program director's office the following Monday morning, he had every reason to suppose he was about to be congratulated. Instead, for forty-five minutes he was forced to defend the program, unsuccessfully, against charges of indulging his own taste at the expense of the audience. Picasso, he was told, was totally beyond the comprehension of five- to ten-year-olds.

Two weeks later Dessart was again summoned to the program director's office—this time for an apology. It seems that the program director had been driving past the museum with his own five-year-old, who begged to be taken there. She wanted to see the Picassos, she told him. Questioned as to why, she said she had seen the paintings on the program and liked them. "Picasso wants to see both sides of the lady at once. Or maybe the top and the bottom of a table." Thoroughly convinced, the program director gave the program carte blanche. The clown went on to explore the intricacies of simple mechanics, mathematical models, and archaeology. The program, *Carney*, soon took its place as the most popular Saturday morning program in the market, and perhaps the only one in the country to successfully compete head to head with the Popeye cartoons.

The point is that all too often commercial broadcasters, when they think about children's programs at all, tend to operate on the basis of some unexamined assumptions. The most persistent—and the most sinister, since it has permitted the abandonment of the genre to trivialization—is the assumption that children want only to be diverted. So convinced, otherwise good people have had no compunctions in making the decisions that have led to completely commercialized children's programming—which demands, in turn, that the audience be maximized, minute by minute. Only then, the logic of the marketplace insists, can full sponsorship be achieved.

Of course, the commercialization of children's programming would not matter too much if the most basic assumption underlying Saturday morning programming were valid: that television for children is just a relatively benign way of occupying their time. The reductio ad absurdum is that they would watch anything on the screen.

That assumption is flawed in three respects. First, children do not start watching television to be diverted or to pass time; that is cultivated behavior. Second, there are verifiably distinct patterns of television use and comprehension at different ages. Third, reducing television to chewing gum for the eyes is a shameful waste of a valuable national resource. This lesson should come home to us with epiphanic clarity as we see our children fall further and further behind their counterparts elsewhere in other parts of the world.

The psychologist Jerome Bruner pointed out that "the single most characteristic thing about human beings is that they learn. Learning is so deeply ingrained in man that it is almost involuntary."[29] John Holt remarked, "A young child has no stronger desire than to make sense of the world, to move freely in it, to do the things that he sees bigger people doing."[30] Young children want to watch television because they see older children and adults doing so. Children's television has been criticized for nearly a half-century for so seldom capitalizing on that simple insight. Yet many have observed with the pediatrician Richard Granger that "as a nation, we have acted as though no body of knowledge about the developmental needs and pitfalls of childhood existed."[31] Once again, the medium is seen as part of the zeitgeist in which it must operate.

In an age of *Kinderfeindlichkeit,* that is only one reason the net-works have so resisted the cries for age-specific programming. They also believe that such programming would, as one CBS executive was fond of saying, "balkanize the schedule." *Captain Kangaroo* proved the point: CBS had no hope of developing a viable morning news broadcast as long as the viewer was forced at 8:00 to go to NBC or ABC. That limitation, as much as diminishing audiences, was why the Captain was shuttled off to introducing films on Saturday shortly after Mark Fowler appeared on the scene.

The ABC *Afterschool Specials* and their cloned counterparts on the other networks were remarkably good examples of programs designed for a small sliver of the audience, the pre- and early teen. They were tolerated only because they were occasional. So too were the Dr. Seuss and Peanuts cartoons in the 8:00 P.M. slot, though they also attracted a family audience. As for Saturday morning, however, the networks resisted stubbornly.

ACT was nothing if not persistent. Finally, in 1990, the Children's Television Act returned to the congressional agenda. The industry, Peggy Charren reports, tried to get the definition of the age limit for children's programs changed from ages two through twelve to two through seventeen "so they could program for the fifteen- to thirty-year-olds."[32]

The act was signed into law with age twelve as the upper limit. It also eliminated the 1984 language that had permitted stations to use the existence of public television or cable programming for children in their markets as an excuse to not include children's programs in their own schedules. The limitations on commercials were reinstated, and, significantly, a question was added to the license renewal application asking that stations specify all the children's programs they had carried during the previous license term. They were also asked to declare what educational objectives their children's programs met.

In October 1992, a group of organizations, including the Center for Media Education and the Georgetown University Law Center, presented the FCC (and the press) with an analysis of the shows named as children's programming by the fifty-eight stations whose licenses were up for renewal. Such series as *The Jetsons, The Flintstones,* and *Leave It to Beaver* were produced, so they claimed, for educational purposes. An episode of *Buck O'Hare* in which "Gooddoer Buck fights off the evil toads from aboard his ship" was cited to demonstrate that "issues of social consciousness and responsibility are central themes of the program." A Cincinnati station included *Hard Copy, CNN Headline News,* and a local newscast that aired after midnight. A Fort Smith, Arkansas, station simply listed all of its local news broadcasts as meeting the FCC children's programming requirement.

Quite apart from the cynicism and disdain for the legitimate concerns of Congress and the FCC that these lists convey, to say nothing of a total disregard for the children, they do underscore the importance of age-specific programming. If children of all ages watch these programs, what do they make of them? One study has shown that children from ages six to sixteen believe that about half of all real-life American families live like the families they see in situation comedies. What do two- to four-year-olds make of *Hard Copy*? What do the prereaders, the four- to five-year-olds, get out of *CNN Headline News*? We know that children cannot differentiate commercials from programs, most of the time, until they are seven or eight. What do the six- and seven-year-old I-Can-Reads think about *The Jetsons*? Parents and teachers understand that children from two to fifteen are the most diverse age group there is. They know that you have to deal with perhaps as many as six different language (and thus understanding) competency groups in different ways. Besides the three groups already mentioned, there are also the middle-aged children—the nine- to ten-year-olds, the preteens, and the young teens. Think about that list of "programs designed primarily for children" submitted by the errant stations, and about what our own children, or we ourselves, would make of the programs listed. Would they really teach us about social responsibility?

CTW on the Way to Sesame Street

So far only one television entity has consistently and effectively shown that it truly understands the problem and that it is genuinely concerned. Whatever the zeitgeist—when children were out of fashion as well as when they were in—the Children's Television Workshop (CTW) has been there. *Sesame Street* was by every criterion a success in its first season. "Within a few months, the now familiar animated numbers and letters and problem-solving games were being viewed enthusiastically by more than 50 percent of the program's potential audience—by an estimated 7 million children," a staff report noted.[33] The Yankelovitch firm, specialists in audience research, confirmed the numbers. The Educational Testing Service conducted a massive summary study concentrating on educational achievements. Part of the study was based on the reactions of a panel of teachers. Although they split on whether *Sesame Street* should be presented in the classroom during school hours, the teachers all admired the show for its appropriateness and effectiveness in teaching young children. They singled out the Muppets for special praise and thought that the teaching of numbers and letters was particularly effective.

More important, the study showed that children in "ghetto communities, middle-class suburbs and isolated rural areas all benefited." "Children who watched *Sesame Street* achieved many of the stated goals in letters, numbers and forms and they gained appreciably in their skill in sorting and classifying."[34]

The series has attracted a remarkable amount of press attention and garnered a Peabody, sixty-seven Emmys, and about two dozen other awards. What accounts for such unprecedented success? Richard Polsky, a CTW senior research assistant, in his definitive *Getting to Sesame Street: Origins of the Children's Television Workshop,* is very precise: "The success of 'Sesame Street' was due primarily to three things: (1) talented personnel, (2) careful planning, and (3) money."[35]

The series was particularly fortunate that heading the list of the talented were the policy advocates who commissioned the initial feasibility studies, engaged the interest of like-minded and well-positioned change agents in government and the private foundation sector, and had the discernment to latch onto a young, energetic, and phenomenally talented documentary producer, Joan Ganz Cooney.

Sometime in 1966, Lloyd Morrisett, then vice president of the Carnegie Corporation, had come upon his two young children sitting before the television set staring at a test pattern and waiting for whatever would come on. He waited to see what it might be. When he saw what came on, he was appalled. He had thought of television as a remarkable learning tool; surely there could be something better for children than what his were reduced to watching. Soon after, at a dinner party given by the Cooneys, Morrisett, his hostess, and Lewis Freedman, director of programming at WNDT, New York's educational television station (soon to be renamed WNET), got into a discussion on the teaching capabilities of television. Unbeknownst to Cooney and Freedman, Carnegie was already thinking about what it could do to improve the prospects of the nation's preschool-age children. Morrisett set up a meeting with the two at Carnegie to explore how television might serve that population.

Several meetings later, Cooney was commissioned to do a feasibility study for a program to air on WNET. On the basis of that study, Morrisett sought other funding sources. CBS, NBC, Time-Life Broadcasting, Westinghouse, and other commercial entities expressed interest in the idea but declined to provide funds. So too, at first, did the Ford Foundation. It asked to be kept informed and ultimately did become a major funding source. Two small foundations, the Learning Resources Institute and the John and Mary R. Markle Foundation, also pledged support. A longtime friend of Morrisett's, Harold Howe, was at that time the U.S. commissioner of education. He took on the task of mobilizing federal support and assigned his assistant, Louis Hausman, who had come out of commercial television, to serve as a financial and operational consultant.

"His historical role," Joan Cooney said, was to tell Howe "that the Office of Education must give the project enough money so that, once and for all, we can see what really can be done."[36]

The meticulous planning process was under way. Cooney consulted more than two dozen psychological, developmental, and educational experts throughout the country. She and Morrisett and Hausman assembled a group of television professionals to meet with them and the other key planners, Freedman and Gerald Lesser, a research psychologist from Harvard. The group was given the feasibility study and a list of topics to address, including the kind of production unit needed, the best outside sources of production material (such as animation), the amount of lead time required, the amount of time before the production could be evaluated, and the probable costs involved in the experimental phase, in preproduction, and for the first season's programs. The industry professionals were George Dessart, George Heinemann, Oscar Katz (then with General Artists Corporation), Mark Goodson of the game show production firm Goodson-Todman, and Stuart Sucherman from public television. The group strongly urged the creation of an autonomous production entity.

In March 1968, two years after the Cooney dinner party, the Carnegie Corporation, the Ford Foundation, and the U.S. Office of Education announced the formation of a not-for-profit corporation, the Children's Television Workshop, to stimulate the intellectual and cultural growth of children—particularly those from disadvantaged backgrounds. The press release also promised that "television professionals will work in partnership with educators, psychologists and other child development specialists to fuse education and entertainment into taped programs that will interest, engage, and instruct four and five year olds."[37]

A budget of $8.191 million was assembled to fund the next two years. This period would include nineteen to twenty months of further planning and a first season of twenty-six weeks. The Department of Health, Education and Welfare would contribute $4 million, and Carnegie and Ford would each put up $1.5 million.

Down the Tube

Eight million dollars (it would require at least $30 million today) seemed at first an enormous sum for an experiment in preschool education. But the cost of educating the nation's four- and five-year-old children in a school setting at that time would have been $2.5 *billion*. After the first year's test results came in, few doubted that the sum was a bargain. The budget for the 1970–71 season was $6 million.

Within the first five years, CTW had mounted a second series, *The Electric Company*, designed for second-, third-, and fourth-graders. *3–2–1 Contact, Square One TV*, and *Ghostwriter* followed. Each of the series found an audience, yet none became the big hit that *Sesame Street* was and still is.

Sesame Street, celebrating its thirtieth season in 1998, is going stronger than ever. An audience of 20 million American children tune in every day to watch Big Bird, Bert and Ernie, and Oscar the Grouch. Countless millions of other children in 130 countries, through 17 coproductions or through packages of inserts, watch versions of *Sesame Street*. CTW has built considerable financial support through licensing toys, games, educational materials, a theme park, and the recently opened *Sesame Street* stores in malls throughout the country.

At one such store we watched young mothers with strollers, seemingly as delighted as their children were to see their favorite characters on socks and baseball caps. Two fourteen- or fifteen-year-old boys came in, playing word games with each other: "This is brought to you by the letter *B*," we overheard. "How about this shirt?" They both seemed to answer, "Brought to you by the letter *T*." Four or five teenage girls flocked in, as un-self-conscious in their delight as the matrons of their mothers' generation. One could not help marveling at how fresh the program remains. When asked about it, Joan Cooney remarked simply:

Sesame Street started in the *Laugh-In* environment. When TV slowed down in the seventies, so did we. We not only watch the

American scene, but television as well. The zeitgeist changes. If children's programming doesn't keep up, the children will not watch.

If commercial television had done *Sesame Street,* they would have stayed with it for a season or two and then dropped it.[38]

Children's Television Workshop's current plans call for a commercial cable channel. Cooney refers to it as an "educational interstitial channel." CTW plans to acquire foreign programming and to recycle its series that public stations are no longer carrying, such as *3-2-1-Contact, Square One TV,* and *Ghostwriter.*

CTW's future, like its past, will be determined by the meticulous planning, adequacy of funding, and, most especially, talent that have marked its operation from the very beginning. Today Cooney and the brilliant staff she assembled are icons. The late David Connell, the former *Captain Kangaroo* executive producer who was coaxed back to television, proved to be the perfect choice for that job on *Sesame Street.* The late Joe Raposo, who had studied with Walter Piston at Harvard and Nadia Boulanger in Paris, left a far more lucrative career as a conductor and composer on and off Broadway to turn out, sometimes in twenty minutes, the lyrics and music. Before his untimely death, Jim Henson, creator of the Muppets, went on to do feature films and created one of the few triumphs of the prime-time access rule, *The Muppet Show.*

That half-hour early-evening entry appeared not on public television but on commercial network affiliates. It catapulted Kermit the Frog, Miss Piggy, and other Henson creatures into stardom and at the time was the most widely seen show in the world. Dominant in the time period in every market, *The Muppet Show* became a weekly family ritual in millions of households—as well as a weekly press event as major celebrities besieged the producers for a place on the list of future guests, often signing up a year in advance. It also, sadly, became an egregious example of the unanticipated results of regulation.

The Communications Act requires that candidates for federal

office be granted "reasonable access" to television airtime. Since the so-called prime-time access daypart represented the only prime time controlled by local affiliate stations, communications attorneys throughout the country were advising their clients that candidates for federal office should be accommodated in that choice time period, advice that many station managers did not like to receive since political announcements must, by law, be offered for sale at the lowest rate. The law also specifies that if *any* candidate for a public office is permitted to purchase time, *all* candidates for that office must given the same opportunity. Moreover, the law states that political announcements may not be censored.

Having opened access time to candidates for Congress in the 1976 elections, Channel 2 in New York found itself with no choice but to air a commercial for a Right to Life Party candidate for Congress. No manner of explanation could possibly assuage the anger and shock, whatever their views on the issue, of parents whose children witnessed, with no warning, shots of aborted fetuses. We submit that given the significance of the abortion issue and the importance of candidates being able to express their views on such issues, surely a society with any real concern for children could have found a more satisfactory resolution than a visual and emotional assault on unsuspecting child viewers as young as three.

That incident represented the convergence of the three conditions under which children's television has labored for the last forty years. The first and most obvious is *Kinderfeindlichkeit*. In 1976, and for nearly twenty years before, children simply had not been considered important.

The second condition was the logical consequence of the imperatives of the American system of commercial broadcasting. We have tried to convey our admiration for the genuine accomplishments of commercial broadcasting, including its achievements in children's programming. Most commercial broadcasters are skilled professionals committed to the medium and possessed of a high degree of personal integrity. "When we entered this business, we were going into a priesthood," one major network executive said of his cohort, which includes both of us.[39] But as we can attest, the imperatives of commercialism are relentless. The increasing demands of stockholders for returns markedly above those available throughout the economy in general force audiences to be maximized, as we discussed in chapter 3. The same pressures were reflected in the comment of an early network executive responsible for Saturday morning cartoons: "You can't have an involved story line [specifically] for five-year-olds."[40] He pointed out that the networks sought to reach the entire population of four- to fifteen-year-olds. At a time when children were not considered in need of special consideration, networks subjected children's television to the same criteria they apply to adult programs.

The third condition is closely allied to the second, and once again a product of timing. The broadcasting framework set up in the laissez-faire 1920s and early 1930s established a marketplace system with few checks and balances, especially with respect to children. It relied on a relatively impotent Federal Communications Commission armed with only the vaguest of standards, the elusive public interest standard. "It is meaningless," Peggy Charren says. "I would be perfectly happy to see the public interest standard go up in smoke."[41]

Many believe it has already done so.

(7)

World Television
The Privatization
of the Global Village

FOR MORE THAN FORTY YEARS the international television market has been dominated by the United States, in part because of the tremendous impact Hollywood films have had on audiences throughout the world since the end of World War I. During the four years of that conflict most European film studios were shut down entirely. After the war the backlog of American silent films got a three- or four-year head start in the market over the revived European studios' productions. Also contributing to the universal acceptance of American cinema productions was their producers' experience in reaching diverse audiences of immigrants, the primary market for the silent films of the period. Directors became skilled at conveying meaning to members of twenty or more cultural groups simultaneously, thus ensuring the films' later viability throughout the European market and beyond. During the Roaring Twenties, when the film industry moved from New York to the West Coast, the glamour and mystique of Hollywood was cultivated and merchandised throughout much of the world.

By the time filmed and taped television came along, millions of potential viewers were familiar with American popular culture. And the nation with three networks, each on the air for nearly twelve hours a day, seemed to be able to produce an endless supply of product.

By the mid-1990s, media products—feature films, television, books, and music—had become the seventh-largest export of the United States. In 1994 the growing importance of the internationalization of television came up informally at a meeting of the executive committee of the International Council of the National Academy of Television Arts and Sciences. Among the seven people present were Thomas Rogers, executive vice president of NBC, Howard Stringer, then president of the CBS Broadcast Group, and Herb Granath, president of the ABC Cable and International Broadcast Group. Stringer commented, and the group agreed, that "every major executive in the industry has to have international as one of his three top concerns."[1]

What are the implications of that assessment for the future of television? And more important, what changes now under way may change the nature of the marketplace and the relative ranking of its players? To answer those questions, we must first understand the differences between "international television," "multinational television," and "global television."

The economist Richard Parker of Harvard's Kennedy School of Government identifies international television as the first of three stages; properly applied, it refers to the simple export of programming (overwhelmingly from the United States) that prevailed into the 1980s and continues to this day.

Down the Tube

Multinational television embraces what used to be referred to as coproduction—the exchange, almost exclusively by major U.S. studios and networks, of production expertise and the cachet of American stars for on-location expenses, each partner receiving rights to distribute the product in its country. In effect, under this arrangement a foreign production company or network would provide location, underwrite travel and living expenses, arrange significant tax breaks, or even pay a sum of money to an American production company. The host-country industry would get jobs, and the host broadcaster would acquire promotable programming with internationally famous stars. The mini-series *Marco Polo,* which ran on NBC in 1982, may have provided the model: representatives of Chinese and Italian television, the American sponsor, and the latter's advertising agency and public relations firm traveled from location to location and were frequently on the set. In 1989 there were nearly four hundred such projects under way, sixty-one of them in the United States. By 1992 European television was spending more on multinational programming than on imports.

In contrast, the 1990s have seen the development of global television, which, according to Parker, is "an expansive multinationalism that promises to make all, or at least a great portion of the planet's audience available to a set of individual broadcasters."[2]

Global television can be viewed as an outgrowth of global marketing. Just as consumer tastes—in popular music, for instance—have converged across cultural and geographical lines, broadcasters believe that television will also, as it becomes increasingly privatized, succeed in finding a worldwide audience. The result will be additional eyeballs for advertisers and more profits for broadcasters. Rupert Murdoch sees the situation somewhat differently. In an interview for *World Business,* he said: "We're not going global because we want to or because of any megalomania, but because it's really necessary. The costs are so enormous today that you really need to have worldwide revenues to cover them."[3]

Government and Public Systems

In the 1970s most European broadcasters were public service broadcasters, many of them modeled on the BBC. The *UNESCO Statistical Yearbook, 1982* analyzed the television systems in 131 countries. Sixteen percent had primarily private and commercial systems. Twenty-two percent had systems operated, like the BBC, by public corporations. Fully 48 percent had only government-operated systems. The television systems of the remaining 14 percent combined two or more of these options.

When Americans think of government-operated systems—assuming that we don't fall into the error Leonard Maill mentioned of thinking the BBC is a "government" network—we generally think of the former Soviet Union, Cuba, or the People's Republic of China. All of these are government-operated systems that fulfill the ideological purpose of controlling the flow of information in what the government considers the best interests of the people and often in the name of the revolution against a previous oppressor. Other governments, particularly among the developing nations, have other reasons for establishing government-operated systems. Algeria, for example, when it first became independent in 1962, faced a number of problems; among the most pressing was the teacher shortage in the public schools. Virtually all of the teachers had been French, and after independence, most of them chose to return to their homeland. Faced with a critical problem in maintaining the school system, the new government turned to television to fill the gap. Television proved a most effective means of educating children, as it has been in other places where educational resources were critically scarce. A number of developing countries have gone this route for the same reason.

Still others have chosen government-operated systems to promote national development and cultural identity. Many developing countries see government-operated television as a powerful and effi-

cient tool not only to educate and inform but to motivate and indoc-
trinate. Similarly, in this age when nationality is often redefined along
linguistic or cultural lines rather than in terms of governance, cultural identity has become a significant concern of governments and
even of nongovernment public systems. For example, Britain has
made efforts to provide programming, some twenty-two hours a
week, in Welsh through the government-overseen commercial Channel Four.

Indeed, even Canada, with its combination system based on the
BBC model, has established a quota on programs from abroad (read,
the United States). The quota applies both to the public corporation–operated Canadian Broadcasting Corporation (CBC) and to
the network of private stations, Television Network, Ltd. (CTV).
The initial impetus for imposing a quota was spillover—signals from
nearby American stations, a phenomenon particularly vexing when
bordering countries share the same language. By the time the CBC
began television broadcasting, there were already 140,000 sets cus-
tomarily tuned to American stations across the border. Similarly,
cable in Canada has long depended on American programming from
both cable networks and state-side stations and their networks.
Canadian officials, concerned about the cross-border flow of advertising as well, have even gone so far as to delete commercials from
American programs, a practice that incurred lawsuits by American
advertisers and threats by the American government.

Although Canada might justify its concern in terms of protecting
its own media industries, there is a far deeper interest at stake.
Canada's land mass is larger than that of the United States, but its
population is smaller and most Canadian population centers are hud-
dled just north of the border. Cultural identity has always been an
issue in Canada, as it is in many smaller developed nations as well as
undeveloped nations. In 1979 the Canadian government commissioned a study on telecommunications development; the resulting
Clyne Committee Report made an adamant case for taking strong
measures against U.S. dominance in television:

Canadian sovereignty in the next generation will depend heavily upon telecommunications. If we wish to have an independent culture then we will have to continue to express it through radio and television. If we wish to control our economy, then we will require a sophisticated telecommunications sector developed and owned in Canada to meet specific Canadian requirements. To ensure our Canadian identity and independence we must ensure an adequate measure of control over data banks, transborder data flows and the content of information services available in Canada.[4]

Program quotas have been imposed in many parts of Europe and are mandated by the European Economic Community, although they are often criticized as ineffective. For developing countries the problem is even more acute. Costa Rica, for example, watched its children play revolutionaries and counter-revolutionaries rather than cops and robbers when the Sandinista radio stations in neighboring Nicaragua increased their power.

For those countries still trying to define their nationhood, government-owned television is especially attractive when economic conditions make privately owned television unlikely and the level of political development would not foster the comparatively sophisticated public corporation. Today more than 160 countries have systems that include some form of government-supported monopoly system—none of which, Parker emphasizes, have gone out of business despite the rush to privatization that began in the late 1970s and continues today throughout Europe and most of the developed world. Government-owned stations by definition are closely controlled by the government. Governments do not surrender that control easily.

What happened in Europe in the 1970s and early 1980s was not unlike what happened in the United States. Because of this country's preeminent position in the entertainment industries and, at that time, in the emerging global economy, it first came to light here that financial markets had discovered the media. Ultimately, however, every broadcaster, from the BBC in the United Kingdom to public service broadcasters in Europe and the United States, as well as commercial broadcasters everywhere, would be affected.

The Role of Regulation

Political scientists, economists, and media watchers may differ on the details, but all agree on the significance of certain historical trends. As Parker points out, the public may not have become aware of the latest trend until the Reagan-Thatcher era, but it actually began in the late 1960s with a report on the FCC commissioned by the Nixon administration and prepared by Eugene Rostow. Once again, a regulatory cycle, the one established in the 1920s, was about to give way to a deregulatory cycle, which is only now coming to an end.

Deregulation never takes place in only one industry; during the Carter and subsequent administrations, significant deregulation was initiated in telecommunications, transportation, and banking as well as in broadcasting and cable. Nor does deregulation take place in a vacuum. Phillips identifies ten economic policy issues in the cyclical pattern of economic change, several of which were to affect public service broadcasters in many countries.

There arose on both sides of the Atlantic a movement, led by entrepreneurs and free-market advocates, calling for access to television ownership and thus to the considerable profits to be realized in exploiting the spectrum. Many factors fueled the fire. A generation of family ownership of newspapers and broadcasting stations was about to come to an end; heirs with disparate objectives, little emotional connection with the family business, and good tax lawyers found that selling off assets was a highly desirable option. Moreover, cable penetration in the United States had largely removed the disadvantage under which independent stations had labored: being relegated, for the most part, to the UHF portion of the spectrum. These developments coincided with an excess of advertising demand, notably in 1976, that could not be accommodated by networks and affiliates. The independent stations were also being offered a bonanza in programming: popular series such as *All in the Family, M*A*S*H, Happy Days,* and *Laverne and Shirley* were coming to market, and the affiliates in the top fifty markets were prevented from showing them in any desirable time periods. The antitrust division of the Justice Department was on hiatus, barriers to mergers and acquisitions were being relaxed, and there seemed to be no end to the money available for financing them.

In this country the return on equity for newspapers is generally as high as or higher than the average for the manufacturing industries. The average return—the precise amount is known only for publicly held corporations—was 16 percent in 1976 and consistently more than 25 percent in the 1980s. Profit margins for broadcasting stations, which have a greater proportion of fixed costs than newspapers, were even higher—for affiliates they typically exceeded 40 percent.

In the United States and Europe in the early 1980s, government policy stood in the way of entrepreneurs and investors eager to share broadcasting profits. In this country many prospective owners were discouraged by the limitation on the number of radio and television licenses any single owner could hold and by the anti-trafficking rules, which prevented a station owner from selling before at least one license term had been completed. By 1987 both of these strictures had been abolished. In Europe the principal barrier to entrepreneurs was seen to be monopoly.

Since the late 1950s offshore pirate radio stations, some on ships, some on artificial islands built as World War II forts, and some backed by heavy U.S. investment, have plagued established broadcasters. A number of broadcasters, including New Zealand's and Israel's radio systems, Sweden's Sveriges Radio, and the BBC, adjusted their broadcast schedules to compete with these illegal stations and their popular music formats. Piracy in Italy, however, provided the most theatrical and extensive challenge of all.

Italian broadcasting had long been under the monopoly control of Radiotelevisione Italiana (RAI), a corporation in which 99 percent of the stock was owned by the government. Acknowledged for the high quality of its product, RAI had nevertheless begun to be a target of consumer dissatisfaction. It procrastinated until 1977 before converting to color, and although it was required by law to be politically impartial, it had long been seen as an arm of the ruling Christian Democratic Party; its management had become dominated by party appointees.

As early as the 1960s, entrepreneurs in France, Yugoslavia, Switzerland, and Monaco began to target audiences in northern Italy. In 1971 Tele Biella, an illegal cable system, appeared in a small northern Italian town. Systems began to appear in other communities. "It is difficult to convey to a foreign reader the enthusiasm which greeted these first experiments in cable television in Italy," Fabio Cavazza, an Italian journalist, would later write. "The desire to demolish RAI's monopoly [was] like a latter-day Bastille."[5]

After years of legal battles, the Italian Parliament retained RAI's monopoly of *national* services while permitting private cable systems and broadcast stations to operate *locally*. Only RAI could operate a network, however, a ruling that was upheld on two occasions by the Constitutional Court.

Cable systems and stations sprang up almost immediately. As many as 2,000 radio stations and 450 television stations were estimated to be operating at one time. As they scrambled to find programming sources, the stations developed a number of ways to circumvent the "live interconnect, *hard* network" prohibitions.

No one was more successful in this climate than Silvio Berlusconi, a prominent contractor who had developed several noted planned communities in Milan. In 1978 he entered the communications field when he installed a cable system in his Milano2, "an urban environment" for ten thousand residents. In 1980 he launched Canale5, Italy's first private national network—despite RAI's monopoly—by setting up an elaborate plane and motorbike delivery system to distribute tapes to affiliated local stations throughout Italy for simultaneous broadcast. The law was not broken, and Berlusconi was established as a major media figure. Soon he controlled three networks in Italy and was launching the first private network in France. As the owner of Fininvest, Europe's second-largest media conglomerate and Italy's third-largest private company, which comprises more than 150 companies, Berlusconi was reported to be the richest man in Italy.

Later Berlusconi became prime minister of Italy, a post he would hold for only eight months. During his tenure he attempted to exert control over RAI as well as over his own three private networks, an act that quickened his departure from government. Under investigation for antitrust and other alleged illegal practices, Berlusconi was forced to sell off many of his interests, including a large minority of his shares in Fininvest, which continues to operate in Italy and elsewhere in Europe.

Rupert Murdoch, the Australian-British-American publisher and owner of Fox, is another media entrepreneur who attempted to enter a monopoly market, in this case, the United Kingdom. By 1991 his Sky Channel had absorbed its competitor, British Satellite Broadcasting, and was being beamed down by two satellites to the United Kingdom. Murdoch had bought Sky—a minuscule operation then known as Satellite Television, plc.—in 1981.

It was nearly a fatal mistake. The effort to assemble and deliver a menu of light entertainment, feature films, music, and sports would prove to be extraordinarily difficult and lengthy. Sky was losing a reported $3 million a week and Murdoch's short-term debt mounted to such an extent that in December 1990, 145 banks in several countries had to be persuaded at the eleventh hour not to demand immediate payment, which would have bankrupted the entire Murdoch empire. It was a good move on the banks' part. By 1994, BSkyB alone was estimated to be worth $20 billion.

Throughout, he did not lose his vision of a popular-culture-based system attracting new, young viewers, as R. I. Davis put it, "drawn by News Corp.'s intuitive understanding of the universal language of sports, sensationalism, and celebrity." In August 1989, for example, he gave vent to his antipathy toward the BBC and British television in general when he was invited to address the prestigious Edinburgh Television Festival: "Much of what is claimed to be quality television is no more than the parading of the prejudices and interests of like-minded people who control it." As for the BBC, its programs "are often obsessed with class, dominated by anti-commercial attitudes and with a tendency to hark back to the past."[6]

Notwithstanding Murdoch's views, the BBC was holding its own. BBC1's 1990 share of audience, 37.9 percent, was the largest share garnered by the four channels, private and public, and BBC2 held its respectable 10.2 percent.

The BBC was not alone among public broadcasters in maintaining its audience. Indeed, other countries with combined public and private systems—Japan, France, Germany, and Italy—have all shown the same pattern. The public system tends to be watched more than the private competitor.

Nonetheless, there had been a substantial change in content since the private channels came on line. Entertainment programs represented 54 percent of the schedule in 1988 for all Western European public broadcasters, which were trying to respond to the competition from private broadcasters. In 1991 the figure for entertainment and sport was higher than it had ever been, 54 percent for BBC1 and 42 percent for BBC2. The balance, 47 percent on BBC1 and 61 percent on BBC2, was devoted to such program types as documentaries, current affairs, news, and education. BBC2, for example, devoted 22 percent of the total broadcast day to education, while the senior channel devoted only 3 percent. Conversely, news, documentaries, and current affairs occupied fully 34 percent of the BBC1 day, and 29 percent of BBC2's.

The Beginning of a New Era—STAR TV

Before globalization, the focus of the international television businesses had been almost exclusively on the transatlantic exchanges. At that time Jeremy Tunstal could correctly entitle his study of world television *The Media Are American*. To be sure, the United Kingdom provided programming to PBS, and an occasional syndication success—*Benny Hill*, for example—would make the crossing. Other series were, as the term in the trade had it, formatted. *All in the Family* and *Sanford and Son* were Americanizations of the formats of popular British shows, for the rights to which American producers paid royalties. *Three's Company* began life in Australia and was formatted for both the United States and the United Kingdom. The set, characters, and scripts were duplicated faithfully; only the slang was different.

The bulk of the traffic, however, was from the United States. As one executive put it at the time, "This business is about as 'global' as a one-way New York–to–London plane ticket is a trip around the world."[7] More than 70 percent of the export business was from the United States to Europe, with the more than 170 other countries accounting for 25 percent.

All this would soon change, with three new streams of business developing that ultimately dwarfed everything that had gone before. What technology would be involved in this change? Where would it happen? Who would emerge to capitalize on it?

The technology was the same that had launched the cable business in the United States, the geostationary satellite. The changes, however, would be as dramatic as anything in the history of television, and the change agents nothing if not surprising. First on the scene would be the Satellite Television Asian Region Limited, STAR TV.

From the outset, STAR TV was the stuff of which legends are made. Consider the following characters and events. In the early 1980s, WESTAR 6, one of a series of communications satellites, was launched from an American spacecraft, destined to take up its assigned position at longitude 91 degrees west, there to remain in geostationary orbit serving the needs of American television for the next decade or so. It soon became apparent that the launch had gone wrong. WESTAR never made it into its assigned orbit but wandered off into an area of space where it was totally useless. In 1985, as a demonstration of its usefulness to the communications industries, NASA retrieved the errant bird and brought it to earth. And there it remained until it came to the attention of Michael Johnson. A native of New York City and the son of a schoolteacher and a city official, Johnson had studied filmmaking at New York University and become a freelance documentarian. A commission took him to Africa, where he remained for the next fourteen years, making nature films and political and feature documentaries. Somewhere along the way he wound up owning a lucrative game farm in Botswana.

Johnson was intrigued by the possibilities suggested by the idle satellite. He considered how valuable an available satellite might prove to be now that the orbits for the Pacific Rim had all been assigned and agreed to by the international agencies and nations involved. He arranged to buy the satellite from Lloyd's of London, which had insured its launch. Johnson then moved to Hong Kong and set about finding enough money to put the satellite into orbit and launch a direct broadcast service. Inevitably, his search led him to Li Ka-shing.

Li Ka-shing was then a major source of financing for any number of ventures. Through his investments in Cheung Kong, a holding company, and his personal investments, he had significant positions in container ports, utilities, real estate, and mobile phone franchises. He owned 49 percent of 60 Broad Street, a major new building in Manhattan, 46 percent of Husky Oil in Calgary, drugstores and supermarkets in China, Hong Kong, and Singapore, and he had joint ventures with Leached and with Procter & Gamble in China. He also owned 100 percent of the largest property development project ever attempted in North America, Pacific Place in Vancouver. Li Ka-shing is the richest man in Hong Kong. He is also a folk hero throughout Southeast Asia.

Li Ka-shing was born and grew up in southern China. When he was twelve, his schoolteacher father arranged to send him to a school in Hong Kong. Two years later he was forced to withdraw in order to support his mother and younger brothers when his father died. Li sold plastic watchbands and toys, sixteen hours a day, seven days a week. By the time he was twenty, he was general manager of the company. When the rent on the factory was raised, Li bought the building and began the real estate and investment career that would make him a billionaire.

The satellite idea was appealing. Li set up a budget of $300 million of his own money, bought the operation—retaining Johnson as a consultant—and persuaded Deng Xiaoping to use a Long March III rocket to launch the bird, now rechristened AsiaSat-I and ready to take up its position in the eastern longitudes. The launch would not have been possible had not President Bush waived the sanctions against China that were put into place after the Tiananmen Square massacre, prohibiting the transfer of high-tech equipment—like secondhand satellites.

All told, it had cost Li $120 million to this point, a bargain in any part of the world. He had given the Beijing regime's CITIC (China International Trust and Investment Corporation) a one-third share. Cable and Wireless, a Hong Kong company, was also brought into the deal. Li retained the rest and ten of the satellite's transponders. The consortium would lease out space on the remaining transponders to various Asian governments for local television and telephone use.

Almost immediately after the April 1990 launch, Li began to put together the Satellite Television Asia Region (STAR) service. He offered MTV shares of stock in Hutchvision, the new company that would operate the service. He also paid MTV $2 million in advance for two thousand 30-second spots on MTV Asia, a version of the music video channel tailored to the region.

By the time STAR TV made its debut, in December 1991, five channels were in place. Hutchvision offered the same incentives MTV Asia had been offered. In addition to MTV, a sports channel and a Chinese channel programming in Mandarin were available on the service.

Because of STAR TV's orbital position, its footprint reaches from Egypt to Vladivostok, from Murmansk to Jakarta. It covers at least thirty-eight countries, including China, all of the Indian subcontinent, much of what had been the Soviet Union, and every place in between. More than 2.6 billion people lived within the footprint.

Obviously, those 2.6 billion potential viewers include many of the world's poorest people, the vast majority of whom have scant access, if any, to television receivers, let alone CATV, SMATV, or their own dishes. But that did not daunt the STAR TV management: they were more than willing to settle for a small portion of the potential. Said Adrian Mounter, the first president and CEO of STAR TV: "Within the top five percent of the total population in that footprint, we have identified an internationalist, English speaking audience with similar tastes and sophisticated interests, an audience which cuts across all national and cultural boundaries."[8]

That was STAR TV's initial target audience, the top 5 percent of the footprint population—130 million people. There is little likelihood that anyone could manage to attract an audience of this size, particularly given the diversity of the populations it encompasses. But even if only 10 percent of the target audience became regular viewers, they would amount to an audience-in-being larger than that of the Fox Network, and several times larger than CNN's audience, even on the first night of the Gulf War, when it obtained its highest ratings ever. Even more significant, as Gary Brown, executive media director in the Hong Kong office of the American advertising agency Leo Burnett's, told the *International Herald Tribune*:

Whether it succeeds or fails, STAR TV is changing the nature of broadcasting in Asia. We have only just seen the start of the proliferation of new channels. The biggest problem that the broadcast industry in Asia will face in the coming years is finding enough programming to fill up all of the hours.

Brown acknowledged that many had been skeptical of the grandiosity of STAR TV and the claims of its executives and proponents, but that "initial skepticism . . . is now being overcome as the realization of STAR TV's long-term potential increases."[9]

STAR TV's "long-term potential" was dramatically apparent in the results of two surveys. The first, commissioned by STAR TV and conducted by Frank Small and Associates, surveyed ten of the thirty-eight countries during December 1992 and January 1993. According to the report, "6,380,180 households validated receiving STAR TV" in India, Taiwan, Israel, Hong Kong, the Philippines, the United Arab Emirates, Pakistan, Indonesia, Thailand, and Kuwait.[10]

In the second survey, China's State Statistical Bureau reported that 4.8 million homes were able to receive STAR TV in China. Yet another survey result reported 200,000 Saudi Arabian homes. The total, STAR TV says, came to "11,360,180 households (more than 45 million people)," as of February 8, 1993—a "203 percent increase" since the previous survey eight months earlier.[11]

What was most surprising was STAR TV's penetration in India—more than 1.2 million households ("and continuing to grow fast," according to the *International Herald Tribune*), a total second only to that claimed for China.[12]

The reports were silent on how many people actually watched the service, with what frequency, and for how long, but there is anecdotal evidence that the introduction of comparatively extensive new television options in areas of the world where only one governmental service has been available has usually been met with widespread sampling and initial general acceptance. STAR channel schedules were printed in 240 newspapers, and 800,000 copies of "hotel and consumer television guides" were distributed in 9 countries. A fax-on-demand service that provided program information at an average cost to the user of $1.65 per minute drew nearly 40,000 new requests per month.

Perhaps the most telling, and astonishing, evidence came from India. In parts of India there is a booming trade in modified trash-can covers, which local hustlers have found can serve as makeshift "Taros," household reception dishes. Also, although cable television is illegal (under the Indian Telegraphs Act of 1885), more than 11,500 makeshift cable systems with 100,000 subscribers are operated by other neighborhood entrepreneurs. The unauthorized cable system operators, "dish wallahs," first appeared in Bombay, where English is widely used. A densely populated city, Bombay is often referred to as "Bollywood," since it has been the center of the Indian film industry.

Many of the dish wallahs had been operating video rental stores, but their business was meager since a VCR costs more in India than the average yearly salary. To the wallahs and their customers, STAR TV was a blessing from the sky. But not everyone was thrilled. "Cable has killed the cinema theater industry," Katy Merchant, a vice president of the Indian Market Research Bureau, told the *Los Angeles Times*.[13] Nonetheless, cable appears to have reached India to stay. "We cannot prevent the phenomenon, so we might as well legalize it," says S. G. Pitroda, chairman of the Telecom Commission.[14]

By 1993 STAR TV reported that there were more than forty thousand cable systems "whose primary business is relaying STAR TV to their customers."[15] Several thousand of them were in Taiwan, STAR TV's third-largest source of audience, where a scenario similar to India's—legalizing illegal cable—is being played out.

The rapid growth of the free-to-air service's audience was reflected in the growth of advertising. In STAR TV's first two years the most popular regularly scheduled programs and special events—such as grand-slam tennis—were consistently sold out. More than two hundred advertisers whose products included automobiles, consumer electronics, and package goods were using STAR TV to reach the growing Asian consumer market. Some appeared to be using it to reach the broad market: the forty-five advertisers on MTV Asia include Garden jeans, Nike, Levi Strauss, and Bajaj Motors Indian-made motorcycles. Polygram Records alone placed $500,000 of advertising on the music channel.

Other advertisers were using STAR to target hard-to-reach markets. Taiwan seeks to discourage liquor advertising in its media by limiting a liquor advertiser's campaign to only twelve months—too short, the advertisers say, to establish a brand. Hennessy and United Distillers got around the limit by using STAR to reach Taiwan audiences. For Procter & Gamble, among others, the satellite-delivered service was a vehicle for getting feminine hygiene products into India, where ads for such products are banned.

Most significant may be reports in the *Far Eastern Economic Review* that, based on the Chinese government's figures, "several companies willing to spend 'oodles' on ads for the Chinese market may now opt to direct some of their budgets toward StarTV."[16]

Detailed financial information on any privately owned media company is not readily available, and Li Ka-shing's holding company, Hutchinson/Whampoa operation was no exception, but the *International Herald Tribune* reported STAR TV's claims that advertising commitments for its first two years would generate "at least $132 million, more than the $100 million it has spent on programming."[17]

A model such as the pan-Asian service targeting a monied elite would make no sense anywhere else in the world. But given the sheer number of persons gathered under the footprint of the STAR TV satellite, the notion of concentrating on the 5 percent who have the money—130–135 million, an audience nearly as large as two-thirds of the entire U.S. population, rich and poor and in between—apparently seemed feasible and attractive to many international adventurers. Li Ka-shing was actually running ahead of his projections.

But whether or not his elegant strategy would actually have worked, we will never know.

Li Ka-shing became impatient. As early as September 1992, he informed his son, Richard Li, STAR TV's CEO, that the family was pulling out of broadcasting. The short-term prospects were slim, and the long-term prospects nowhere near as attractive as in other businesses. While continuing to release enthusiastic reports to the press, the Satellite Television Asia Region management team adopted a new strategy. They would go digital before any other service in the world and offer a direct-to-home pay service to the same target audience. The cost of making this change, $300 million, would be raised by seeking a partner to take a minority interest in the company.

When one bank assessed the company's worth at $400 million, Goldman Sachs was retained to reassess. It came up with a figure nearer to $1 billion. Eight executives spent three months putting together a spectacular road show. "To create [it] cost $3 million and it was worth every penny. We worked and worked on those numbers to give STAR-TV the most dazzling prospects," a member of the team told *ASIA, INC.*[18] Joint-venture deals were worked out with Disney, 20th Century-Fox, the Discovery Channel, and others. Negotiations were opened with Pearson, the British media giant.

In June 1993, Rupert Murdoch announced that he would buy a 22 percent interest in TVB, the Hong Kong cable system, from its owner, Sir Run Run Shaw. This would have given Murdoch access to Sir Run Run's library of Chinese films and television, said to be the largest in the world. Richard Li swung into action. The Hong Kong government, the journalists' association, and, most important, the People's Republic of China, all raised objections.

Richard Li called up Murdoch, told him he was heading to London to sign with Pearson, and asked whether Murdoch would like to talk. Murdoch made a News Corp plane available to fly Li and a Goldman Sachs executive to Corsica, where they talked on Murdoch's yacht. At the end of the meeting, they had a handshake deal. Murdoch paid $525 million in cash and stock for a 63.6 percent interest in STAR TV. On July 26, 1993, it was announced that Rupert Murdoch had taken control of the service. Two years later he would pay $346 million for the remaining shares.

Almost before the ink was dry on the initial contract, Murdoch

sent in Sam Chisholm, a veteran of the News Corp UK satellite operation, BSkyB, to trim costs. Sixteen percent of the 740 staffers were
released. The new owners also looked carefully at the numbers and
found them to be not what they had thought. Craig Erlich, a Hong
Kong banker and former STAR TV employee, is reported to have
said, "He didn't do any due diligence."[19]

Whatever the condition of a new operation might be, Murdoch,
characteristically, has followed his early newspaper instincts. With the
possible exception of *The Australian*, his goal has always been firmly
fixed on one thing—circulation. In his words, "We want to put our
programming everywhere and distribute everybody's product
around the world. We want to reach into every corner of the
earth."[20] He need not have added that his vision does not encompass
narrowly focused audiences. Rupert Murdoch never settled for 5
percent of any potential audience: he wants it all.

In January 1994, Garey Davey was appointed CEO of Satellite
Television Asia Region. His mission was to convert the pan-Asian
service into a provider of digital, country-specific satellite channels.
The launching of STAR's own sophisticated satellite, AsiaSat-2, gave
it thirty channels and a sufficient number of transponders to provide
service to several core markets. Initially, STAR is concentrating on
India, Indonesia, and China. In 1996 it announced plans for JskyB, a
digital Japanese service. As with all its services, the primary fare will
be music, sports, movies, and entertainment programming in the target audiences' own languages. By January 1997, STAR had set up
co-ventures with ESPN; with NBC to supply CNBC and MSNBC
Asia; with Viva to provide programming in Tagalog; and with Zee
TV, a Hindi-language television network. It has also replaced MTV
by developing partnerships with Sony, EMI, BMG, and Warner
Music.

All of this activity has been expensive. Murdoch admitted losses
of $80 million in 1995 and a probable loss of $100 million in 1996.
He predicted a break-even in 1997, but at least one brokerage
watcher of News Corp, Terry Povey of the London firm James Capel

& Company, estimates that Murdoch will lose as much as $2 billion (excluding the Japanese channel) before a payback at the turn of the century.

The biggest prize in STAR TV's footprint is China, but so far that has eluded Murdoch. In an effort to please the Chinese leadership—and build up his own international news operation—the BBC World Service, always a thorn in Deng Xiaoping's side, was soon taken off STAR. Unaccountably, however, Murdoch was to incur the wrath of Beijing with a 1993 London speech in which he made the correct but impolitic statement that "advances in the technology of telecommunications have proved an unambiguous threat to totalitarian regimes."[21] Davey has "worked pretty hard" on STAR's relations with China,[22] and STAR has entered into a number of coproductions with Central China Television (CCTV), the government-operated television system. STAR movies are distributed in Beijing hotels, and STAR has sports production facilities in Tianjin.

Despite Murdoch's extensive efforts to curry favor with Chinese leaders, they have refused him unrestricted access to their billions of potential viewers. Partly as a result of the London speech, the Chinese have been attempting to develop cable—a massive and enormously expensive alternative. Meanwhile, STAR TV continues to lose money. Most observers believe, however, that eventually the economics of satellite transmission will be inescapable and China's unparalleled market will be opened to global television.

Northeast Across the Equator: The Second Stream

Not too long after the Soviet Union dissolved, many Muscovites who prided themselves on being in step with the times began to refer to their dachas as *fazendas*. Even as television has popularized icons such as Nike across borders, oceans, and cultures, so too has it managed to transport slang from one nation into the vernacular of another. *Fazenda* is a term used by characters in the most popular broadcast in Moscow, a novella produced and distributed by Brazil's dominant network, TeveGlobo.

TeveGlobo, a commercial network that enjoys a 75 percent share of audience in Brazil, had long been distributing its novellas—180-episode Latin adaptations of the soap-opera format—in Mexico, Venezuela, and Argentina, the three other major population centers in Latin America. TeveGlobo has also achieved great success in other parts of the world. The star of one series won the Chinese equivalent of the Emmy for best actress. She cannot walk on the streets of Shanghai or Beijing without drawing an unmanageable crowd. Vacationing cast members of another novella found that they could not walk on the streets of Rome. Romans refused to believe the actors could not speak Italian since they saw—and believed they heard—the cast speak to them in Italian every day. Dubbing, particularly into other romance languages, has been brought to a high art in TeveGlobo's thirty years. With international aspirations, the Brazilian network realized from the beginning that it could not make money by relying on its only language partner, a very much underdeveloped Portugal.

Nor did it rely solely on dubbing. In 1992 TeveGlobo began offering its interactive program, *Voce Dicide* (*You Decide/Do the Right Thing*), in English for formatting. In its first year the program proved to be competitive in Sweden and in twenty-nine other countries. In its second season the BBC purchased the format rights.

One of the chief reasons TeveGlobo has been able to syndicate its programs so broadly is that they are superbly well done. Like the BBC and the Japanese public system, NHK, and unlike the U.S. networks, TeveGlobo has always combined production and distribution. The Brazilian network, with forty-three hundred hours a year, is the world's largest producer. Three novellas, each an hour long, are produced every day in addition to children's programs, animation, variety, and mini-series.

TeveGlobo is the creature of its owner, Roberto Marinho, who, at the age of twenty-three, inherited *O Globo* only three weeks after its first edition appeared. He built *O Globo* into one of the country's most influential newspapers, and in 1939 he founded Globo Radio. After considerable testing, he started TV Globo in 1965.

Marinho was considered foolhardy when he made that decision in his sixties. But his timing appeared to be nearly perfect. Color television was about to arrive in Brazil, and the public's interest in the medium grew exponentially. So too did Globo. It ran its first novella in 1969, and others followed. As one commentator put it, "Soon . . . it was a case of Globo and the rest."[23] Ever since, Globo's share has been consistently in the 70s, and sometimes as high as 98 percent. In 1995 three Brazilian networks carried the same coverage of an international soccer match played by the Brazilian team. Globo's share was 34 percent; the other networks had 7 and 6 percent, respectively.

With the same initiative he displayed in his sixties, Marinho celebrated Globo's thirtieth anniversary when he was more than ninety years old himself by beginning to build the world's largest television studio facilities, the Centro de Producas de Jacarepagua (PROJAC), on the outskirts of Rio de Janeiro. Now nearing completion, it has nine major studios, four of them more than thirty-two hundred square feet. Each of the four is part of a complete production module, with scene shops, storage, dressing rooms, offices, and post-production editing facilities. Thus, the three daily novellas will have their own buildings, with a fourth available for mini-series or even another novella.

With PROJAC, its more than four thousand professionals, its five hundred contract actors, and its thirty-year domestic and twenty-year international track record, TeveGlobo will be a global production player well into the next century.

Two incidents reported during the 1996 Russian elections speak to both the popularity of the Brazilian novellas and the unintended consequences of global television. Many of Europe's most influential newspapers, among them the *Guardian,* the *Sunday Times* of London, and *Le Figaro,* picked up a report from a Russian government propaganda paper that one of the most popular stars of a TeveGlobo novella then playing in Moscow and elsewhere in Russia had come out in favor of Yeltsin's candidacy. Both TeveGlobo and the star denied the story. Later it was reliably reported that a special extra-long episode of *Mulheres de Areie (Secrets of the Desert)* was rescheduled to play on election day, thus, presumably, dissuading many urban Russians from leaving their homes to go to the polls.

From Tierra del Fuego to the Canadian Border: The Third Stream

The third change in the flow of electronic mass media products may be the most surprising of all. In many ways reminiscent of the 1950s, this stream is at the same time largely satellite-delivered. And like STAR TV, its earliest development was improbable.

Mario Kreutzberger is the son of Jewish parents who fled Nazi Germany and settled in Chile. As an adult, he adopted the stage name of Don Francisco and began his show business career in Santiago. In 1961 Kreutzberger, having watched and absorbed the variety and game shows on North American television, debuted his own program, *Sabado Gigante*. Today it is listed in the *Guinness Book of Records* as the longest-running series in television history without a single repeat. The aptly named *Gigantic Saturday*—210 minutes—has the largest weekly audience in the Western Hemisphere, more than eighty million persons.

After more than twenty-five years of production in Santiago for an all-Chilean audience, Don Francisco was persuaded by Univision to tape a month's worth of programming at a time in Miami; he has now done so for the last ten years. From Miami the shows are carried by satellite to stations in the United States and eighteen Spanish-speaking countries in Central and South America.

The programs consist of an eclectic selection of segments tested and perfected by such performer-hosts as Johnny Carson, Ed Sullivan, and Art Linkletter, as well as ideas from *Good Morning America* and *The Today Show,* with some game shows thrown in. The studio audience plays a significant role, even to the extent of singing along with the commercial jingles.

One typical Saturday included a segment very much like *The Dating Game* in which a Mexican medical student interviewed three attractive young ladies from Chile, Puerto Rico, and Venezuela. There was a *Talent Scout* segment with competing couples from New York, Los Angeles, Mexico, and Chile. Children from ages five to seven gave advice to a child who had written in that he did not like his stepfather. The children reflected the pan-Americanism that distinguishes *Sabado Gigante:* they came from Florida, New Jersey, Cuba, Mexico, and Uruguay. Yet another segment reported on folk festivals in Spain. There was a report on Placido Domingo being honored in Los Angeles. Another showed a woman with AIDS marrying a Mexican man in California and trying to rebuild her life. Hispanic performers who are in town drop in to perform, and contests award cash prizes. Through it all, Don Francisco remains avuncular and smiling. Occasionally there will be something on homelessness or child-raising or other personal and interpersonal problems.

When Univision moved its headquarters to Miami in 1986 within months of the Mexican network Telemundo, which opened its facilities less then three miles away, Miami was already a major financial center for Latin American and Caribbean trade. Fifteen major U.S. banks had established their Latin American operations there, as had companies like Du Pont. A *Washington Post* study declared Miami to be the capital of an economic and cultural region looking southward to include Venezuela as well as the islands between.

With the relocation of the two most important Spanish-language networks in the Americas, Miami became the center of Latin American show business, *la farándula. El Show de Jaime Bayly,* an hour-long interview show that had been a fixture in Lima, Peru, moved to Miami in 1995, along with Channel Sur, the cable network that carried it throughout much of South America. MTV Latino located in Miami to be near the Latin American headquarters of the two largest record companies, WEA and Sony. Performers from Placido Domingo to Julio Iglesias and "El Puma"—José Luis Rodriguez, the Venezuelan novella and recording superstar—now live in the Miami vicinity and are followed by South American paparazzi as they frequent the restaurants and nightclubs that have become the mandatory scene for the men and women of *la farándula*. More important, the vast Spanish-speaking population on both American continents is being transformed into a pan-American market, united in the iconography and values of popular culture. As *la farándula* continues to mimic an earlier Hollywood, *Sabado Gigante*'s audience of eighty million may be only a hint of the potential of the south-north stream.

What Lies Ahead?

It is difficult for anyone interested in television not to be somewhat in awe of the sheer audacity of those who put together STAR TV—but such ventures are frightening to those who care about where the medium is likely to go.

By the year 2000, Asia will encompass two-thirds of the world's population and most of its largest cities; the number of households with an annual income of $30,000 or more will have increased by 50 percent to a total of 51 million. Asian per-capita GNP will double by 2000. Asia now has more than 240 million TV households, up 70 percent in five years. There is no reason to suppose that advertisers will not stand in line to exploit this emerging market. T. Burke McKinney, senior vice president and director of marketing for Coca-Cola Japan, speaks of the opportunity at least one American firm sees: "Our world is changing so rapidly in terms of communications that you have to be at the forefront. You've got to take some risk. We believe our advertisements work in virtually every language."[24]

It is also difficult to believe that public television will survive in many of the countries whose government-controlled systems are like India's lethargic Doordarshan. At the very least, as John Ure, a communications research associate at Hong Kong University, observed, "STAR is serving as a pioneer in challenging the regulatory restrictions that bind Asia hand and foot in terms of the free flow of information."[25]

Beyond these considerations, a number of questions arise. Before Murdoch changed STAR TV's strategy, the questions focused on the use of the English language. What are the consequences, scholars asked, of introducing a predominantly English-language system into nations already marked by huge discrepancies between the haves and the have-nots? The question is not really moot. In January 1997, Murdoch concluded deals with ESPN and with NBC to carry both CNBC and MSNBC. Not only are the NBC services in English, the ESPN channel, which lends itself to indigenous-language voice-overs, presents American sports and American advertising.

The question may become particularly significant when, as is planned, STAR TV augments its basic free-to-air service with "premium" (read pay) channels. Will there be an even greater widening of the intellectual, cultural, and linguistic gaps that already exist between classes in Asia? And what might the consequences of that be? Some linguists have remarked on the alienation of German intellectuals from the political struggles in the first half of this century as a result of the difference between "scientific German" and the speech of the rest of the populace; they believe that alienation may have played a role in the rise of National Socialism. Could there be any such effect in the context of pan-Asian broadcasting? What are the implications for cultural survival in many of the areas under the AsiaSat footprint? Quite aside from concern about the effects of STAR TV on the populace, what will be its effect on public television in its coverage area?

The implications of STAR TV, with its menu of international sports, American films, teenage rock and rap subculture, and multinational commercials, are staggering to contemplate, even if impossible to foresee accurately. Richard Li, Hutchvision's chairman, told *Asahi Shimbun:* "I believe that the reality of the so-called global village is still just a dream. However, I do believe that by linking at least three billion people an 'Asian Village' is possible. STAR TV is the first step toward this."[26]

Meanwhile, the international television community in the United States continues to develop new market opportunities. All four networks have begun or are planning Spanish-language news services for both radio and television. Like the entertainment community in *la farándula,* they understand the enormous leverage a North American base can provide in marketing southward.

Similarly, international syndication of television from the United States will continue. But meanwhile, the rest of the world is busily defining its own preferences, priorities, and opportunities. The overseas Chinese market is recognized as one of the top five world markets. Many overseas Chinese live in the United States, and Chinese-language television is available on cable in every market with a substantial Chinese concentration.

We believe that the three models of contemporary international television detailed in this chapter are the models that will prevail in the next century. Yet even the STAR model is being modified to acknowledge that reaching people in their own language is the key to building audience support for American and other English-language schedules in a competitive market. That fact should serve to underline the viability of the TeveGlobo and *la farándula* models. We may well see a sharp decline in this country's seventh-largest export.

(8)

The Underfunded Afterthought
Public Television

WITHIN TWELVE YEARS after the first broadcasting license was issued in this country, what Eric Barnouw terms a "nationwide broadcasting system financed by advertising" had already become established. Under this system, "the salesman [was] the trustee of the public interest, with minimal supervision by a commission."[1]

Perhaps if Congress had seriously considered what kind of broadcasting system this country should have, its members would have agreed with Secretary of Commerce Herbert Hoover, who, you may recall, believed that broadcasting was entirely too sensitive to turn over to advertising: "It is inconceivable that we should allow so great a possibility for service to be drowned in advertising chatter."[2] But turn it over they did. And public radio and later public television, then called educational television, became mere appendages. Precisely the opposite would happen in the United Kingdom, which, like most other industrial nations, made certain that public television was well established before permitting commercial television to operate.

At the very outset of American broadcasting, as we have seen, universities sought licenses, in many cases to experiment with the physics of the spectrum or the engineering of radio, but in some cases to explore the potential of using radio, and later television, to extend the reach of their educational services. Then as now the popular press was captivated by the prospect of radio providing high school diplomas or even college degrees to the shut-in or the geographically isolated. At their peak, more than two hundred educational radio stations were on the air.

By 1934, however, most had fallen victim to the economy, to interference from other stations, or simply to disillusion with the medium. Nevertheless, hope was rekindled when Congress began to respond to Roosevelt's request for telecommunications reform. Educators, churches, organized labor, and farm groups had even managed to attract the support of two powerful senators, New York's Robert Wagner and West Virginia's Henry Hatfield. When the bill that would become the Communications Act of 1934 came to the floor of the Senate, they offered a revolutionary amendment: all licenses would be revoked and reallocated, with 25 percent to be assigned to "educational, agricultural, labor, cooperative and similar non–profit making associations." The amendment also addressed the chronic poverty of the educational stations by permitting them to sell enough of their airtime "as will make the station[s] self-supporting."[3]

The debate was drawn. *Broadcasting* magazine, then as now the trade journal of record, sneered at "self-seeking reformers," while Senator Hatfield denounced the commercial "pollution of the air."[4] The argument was lengthy and fierce, but the amendment failed. Educational stations continued to languish during the Depression even as commercial broadcasting flourished.

Educational Television

By the time television arrived on the scene, commercial broadcasting was, for all practical purposes, the only model around. None of the stations operating before World War II or in the first three postwar years were educational. As we pointed out in chapter 1, the prospect of television had excited the entire country. In an effort to respond quickly to the public's demand, more than one hundred television licenses were issued early in 1948—all of them for commercial stations. Fortunately for public television's future, before the FCC gave away all the frequencies it realized it had made a mistake: its plan would limit most cities to only one or two stations, commercial or noncommercial. The commission declared a freeze on further allocations while it reexamined the situation.

The freeze might have had no impact on educational television (ETV) were it not for serendipity. In 1948 Frieda Barkin Hennock was confirmed as the first woman to serve on the Federal Communications Commission. Fourteen years after the defeat of the Wagner-Hatfield Amendment to the 1934 Communications Act, Hennock raised the issue again. During the next four years, in league with educators, she advocated for educational television within the commission and toured the country on its behalf. *Broadcasting* declared her ideas "illogical, if not illegal."[5]

When the freeze was lifted in 1952, the FCC announced a new allocation table assigning 2,000 additional stations to more than 1,300 communities. Largely thanks to Frieda Hennock's personal involvement, 242 of the 2,000 were reserved for ETV.

ETV, like its radio counterpart, started up in colleges and universities. The nation's first such television station was the University of Houston's KUHT, which came on the air in 1953. Houston, a relatively young university, had been planning an ambitious building program. When the FCC announced the reservation of channels for education, the university reasoned that lecture halls would soon be a thing of the past and put money into a station to produce and distribute televised lectures that students could view in dorms, their homes, or special viewing rooms. *Broadcasting* magazine headlined a report on the station, "Houston U Sees TV Educational Station Saving $10,000,000 in Buildings."[6]

Exactly one year later, while noting that many of the reserved frequencies were not yet being used, a *Broadcasting* editorial commented: "One day the FCC must take another look at the Communications Act in relations to these socialistic reservations."[7]

Twenty-four ETV stations were on the air by 1956. Several of the most successful, however, were not established and operated by educational institutions but were so-called community stations. As the term implies, they were put together by groups of citizens convinced that television held great promise for education and culture. The first community station, WQED–Pittsburgh, went on the air in 1954. It was followed within a few months by KQED–San Francisco and KCET–St. Louis, also community stations. Boston's WGBH-TV, which began broadcasting in February 1955, was the creature of a consortium of no fewer than fourteen, including several of the nation's most prestigious institutions. WGBH's mission statement captures its early vision:

> The purpose of the corporation, is to promote, through broadcasting or other means, the general education of the public by offering programs that inform, stimulate and entertain, so that persons of all ages, origins and beliefs may be encouraged, in an atmosphere of artistic freedom, to learn and appreciate the history, the sciences, the humanities, the fine arts, the practical arts, the music, the politics, the economics, and other significant aspects of the world they live in, and thereby to enrich and improve their own lives.

The going was not easy for these pioneer community stations. One year after going on the air, KQED's community board, discouraged by mounting debt and with little help in sight, was narrowly dissuaded from closing the operation down. What ultimately saved the station was an on-air auction of donated merchandise. The auction became an annual event at KQED, and a public television fund-raising tradition was born.

The second major development in educational television at that time also involved serendipity. The Ford Foundation, the nation's largest foundation with assets at that time larger than those of all other American foundations combined, took an interest in television. Henry Ford, whose name was synonymous with mass production, somewhat ingenuous peace crusades, opposition to both world wars, and paternalistic labor policies, died in 1948, at which time the block of stock he had placed in his foundation was worth more than $500 million. Since Ford's wife and his only son, Edsel, had already died, the oversight of the foundation fell to Ford's daughter-in-law, Eleanor Clay Ford. She wisely recruited Paul Hoffman, who had administered the Marshall Plan. Hoffman, in turn, hired Scott Fletcher as executive director. Together they and the board articulated policies supportive of world peace, democratic government, economic well-being, education, and the scientific study of mankind. Under that rubric, the board could easily try to improve American television, and it promptly set out to do so.

The Ford Foundation's first effort involved commercial television. Fletcher set up the Ford Foundation Television Workshop to produce *Omnibus*, arguably the most outstanding as well as the longest-running cultural program on commercial network television. With Alistair Cooke as its host, *Omnibus* made its debut on CBS late on a Sunday afternoon in October 1952 and ran for ninety commercial-free minutes: Ford had underwritten the entire production, and few advertisers at that time were interested in Sunday afternoon. Football had not yet appeared to occupy the time slot referred to as "the cultural ghetto." Later *Omnibus* would move to ABC, and then to NBC, where it remained until 1961—always noncommercial.

Shortly after the Ford Workshop was set up, the foundation turned its attention to educational television. Throughout the next decade the Ford Foundation was a major supporter of the infant medium. Ford established an independent program service, the Educational Television and Radio Center, which each week fed five hours of culture and public affairs and two and a half hours of children's programming—all Ford-funded—to ETV stations throughout the country. Unlike the commercial networks, none of the ETV stations were interconnected by telephone lines—long-lines charges would have wiped out the center's entire budget. Instead, kinescopes, and later tapes, were mailed from station to station in a process known as "bicycling." To save duplicating costs, one copy would go from station to station. Often months would pass before a given episode would reach all the stations wishing to run it.

In the first six years of its interest in educational stations, 1954–60, the Ford Foundation invested $14 million in the effort. Most of the money went into small grants for the "activation of noncommercial channels." The reasoning behind these grants was obvious: only 44 of the 242 channels the FCC had authorized in 1952 were functioning in 1959. In 1962 a Ford initiative brought about an instant change in the status of those channels. The Educational Television and Radio Center was moved from Ann Arbor, Michigan, where it had been totally occupied with the task of bicycling programs. Renamed National Educational Television (NET), the center was moved to New York, the undisputed heart of television activity at that time. The media industries began to take educational television seriously.

So did Washington—especially Senator Warren Magnuson, one of the most powerful chairmen ever to preside over the pivotal Commerce Committee. The Washington Democrat had been in Congress for thirty-six years and had a reputation as a canny politician who knew how to get things done. In *Politics of Broadcast Regulation*, Krasnow, Longley, and Terry quote "a highly placed FCC staff member" on the senator's effect on those around him: "[The FCC commissioners] bow and scrape. He doesn't have to ask for anything. The Commission does what it thinks he wants it to do."[8]

What Magnuson wanted—and got—was support for the 1962

Educational Television Facilities Act, which established the first federal funding for the medium, $32 million over five years. Tellingly, the act concentrated on two elements of the educational broadcasting function: hardware and the local stations. The act authorized a dollar-for-dollar matching fund. Educational stations were to be given an average of more than $6 million a year during a five-year period for updating their equipment and enlarging their capacities—but only if they succeeded in raising the same amount locally.

The second notable feature of the 1962 act, the mandate to use local funds, was to help shape public television to this day. Local funds required mobilizing local people around issues of fund-raising, stewardship, and operations. The $32 million provided a significant incentive for recruiting volunteers; it also preordained what would, of necessity, become an enormous ongoing local effort. That effort—again, of necessity—would spawn 354 local fund-raising entities.

Nevertheless, many of those who were active in educational television felt that this effort was far from adequate if the medium was ever to realize its potential. One of the most outspoken was Ralph Lowell of the Lowell Institute Cooperative Broadcasting Council, one of the fourteen institutions that established WGBH-TV in Boston. Lowell and his associates believed there should be a "a Commission to study the financial needs of educational television and the means by which they might be met."[9] They first broached the idea at a December 1964 conference convened by the National Association of Educational Broadcasters in cooperation with the U.S. Office of Education. Ralph Lowell and C. Scott Fletcher, who had moved to the NAEB, took the proposal to John S. Gardner, president of another highly regarded major foundation, the Carnegie Corporation.

Like the Ford Foundation, the Carnegie Corporation had been set up by a self-made industrialist. In 1848 Andrew Carnegie, at age thirteen, started his climb to fortune from bobbin boy in a textile plant. By the turn of the century, Carnegie produced 25 percent of all the steel manufactured in this country and owned iron mines, ore ships, and railroads. Also by 1900, he had endowed twenty-eight hundred libraries in the United States, as well as a number in his native Scotland. In 1901 he retired to concentrate on the Carnegie Corporation, to which he had given $350 million.

Andrew Carnegie was more far-sighted than most philanthropists of his or any generation. The deed to the corporation specifies: "Conditions upon the earth inevitably change [therefore] I give my trustees full authority to change policies or causes hitherto unaided when this, in their opinion, has become necessary or desirable."[10]

The Carnegie Corporation of New York, acting completely in accord with Andrew Carnegie's specified instructions, saw the state of educational television as a natural concern within the broad rubric of education and concern for underprivileged groups. It funded the commission proposed by Ralph Lowell and assigned Alan Pifer, then vice president, to oversee the effort. Gardner and Pifer—who would succeed Gardner as president before the report was issued—assembled a commission of outstanding citizens representative of the geographical, professional, and personal diversity the report would advocate.

The Transformation of Educational Television

The work of the Carnegie Commission on Educational Television took nearly three years, including one year of intensive study during which 225 interviews were conducted and the commission itself met en banc eight times for a total of twenty-eight days. The commission's final report took an astonishing tack: it spent little time on educational television—which it was careful to say it supported—and concentrated on a *third* form of television standing somewhere between educational (now called instructional) and commercial television. The title of the report gave the language a new term and foretold a new American institution: *Public Television: A Program of Action.*

Much of the impetus for the commission's statement that "we believe it to be urgently in the public interest that both categories [public and educational] be extended and strengthened"[11] may have come from the now-famous letter to the commission from the essayist E. B. White:

> Non-commercial television should address itself to the ideal of excellence, not the idea of acceptability—which is what keeps commercial television from climbing the staircase. I think television should be the visual counterpart of the literary essay, should arouse our dreams, satisfy our hunger for beauty, take us on journeys, enable us to participate in events, present great drama and music, explore the sea and the sky and the woods and the hills. It should be our Lyceum, our Chatauqua, our Minsky's, and our Camelot. It should restate and clarify the social dilemma and the political pickle. Once in a while it does, and you get a quick glimpse of its potential.

The report reprinted White's statement in a form and place that suggested the commission had adopted it as a mission statement. To accomplish such a mission, the commission set forth a dozen recommendations. They began with the need for adequate support to improve the facilities and increase the number of public stations. Providing such support, they contended, would require a concerted effort at the federal, state, and local levels.

To make that happen, their second recommendation called for "a federally chartered, nonprofit, nongovernmental corporation" to manage the funds, both governmental and private. To the commission, this recommendation was a deal breaker: if the Corporation for Public Television—as they called it—were not established, the commission would "be reluctant to recommend" other parts of the report. Although it is impossible to avoid comparison between "a federally chartered, nonprofit, nongovernmental corporation" and the BBC, the commission insisted that "this institution [public television] is different from any now in existence. It is not the educational television that we now know; it is not patterned after the commercial system or the British system or the Japanese system."[12]

The commission looked at those systems, as well as others in Canada, Italy, Germany, and the Soviet Union, and found that their success was rooted in their sensitivity to their own cultures. Therefore, "we propose an indigenous American system arising out of our own traditions and responsive to our own needs."[13]

The report's other recommendations included support for two national production centers, one of which would be NET; funding for research and development in programming; and a live interconnection of stations similar to those set up between commercial networks. AT&T, then the only telephone company in the country, would be required by law, however, to grant public television preferential rates, if not service at no cost at all.

Radical as that last proposal might have been, it was nothing compared to the commission's recommendation on funding. The report that would become known as *Carnegie One* called for funding the Corporation for Public Television and its activities through a trust fund derived from an excise tax on newly manufactured television sets. Such a trust fund, the commission believed, would provide more continuity than year-to-year congressional budgeting. And besides, there was a precedent in the dedicated tax that funded the federal highway system. The initial tax on television sets of 2 percent would grow to 5 percent—enough, the commission estimated, to fund public television at $100 million a year. One member of the commission, Joseph McConnell, the president of Reynolds Metal, filed a concurring opinion but objected to the excise tax on the grounds that it would tax the public "whose program preferences determine the television we have, to provide another service which we believe they should have as well." McConnell proposed that the burden of funding public television fall on the commercial broadcasters instead: "Those who are licensed to use the airwaves in the 'public interest'—the television stations—should . . . pay a franchise for that purpose."[14]

The commission and the Carnegie Corporation itself had done their homework. HEW Secretary John Gardner, the former president of the Carnegie Corporation, was on board at the very start of the process, as were key leaders in the House and Senate. The report came out in January 1967. In November, Lyndon Johnson signed into law the Public Broadcasting Act of 1967, which expanded the Carnegie Commission's vision to go beyond television and include public radio.

Unfortunately, Congress rejected both the commission's and McConnell's proposals for funding. The Treasury Department had historically objected to dedicated taxes, and the House Ways and Means Committee disliked any proposed taxes that did not come under conventional congressional control. As for the president, he was under considerable pressure to maintain his guns-and-butter policy for funding the Vietnam War and was loathe to push for a trust fund for public television, no matter how much he might have favored the concept.

The Corporation for Public Broadcasting (CPB) would, like federal agencies, be dependent on annual appropriations, a dependency that still endures, despite the Johnson White House's vow to seek a less volatile mechanism for funding. Even in that first year Congress authorized a paltry $9 million and then failed to follow through with any appropriation. Were it not for a $1 million grant from CBS to the proposed new broadcasting endowment, CPB would have been unable to open its doors.

The legislative process made other changes to the commission's recommendations. The CPB board membership was changed from six presidential appointees and six others chosen by them, to fifteen presidential appointees, confirmed by the Senate, with no more than eight to come from the party of the president. It is possible to imagine that the original commission design might have resulted in a nonpoliticized board; the act made politicization unavoidable.

Still other changes were made to definitions of what CPB would and would not control. The commission had envisioned an agency that would concentrate on programming and the interconnection of the stations. Instead, the act prohibited CPB from operating the interconnection on the grounds that doing so might result in centralized promotion and scheduling, which could, in turn, facilitate public television becoming a fourth network. The act also gave CPB the responsibility for dispensing the local station funds, thus attempting to insulate the stations from the kind of government intrusion that HEW oversight (as proposed) might entail.

Despite its shortcomings, the 1967 act made public broadcasting a national institution and largely determined what it has been ever since. Embodied in the legislation were numerous substantial legacies of *Carnegie One*. The report changed the name—and to a large degree, the perception—of noncommercial television. It established national production centers and interconnected the system. Arguably the most controversial—some might even say mischievous—recommendations, however, were those that enshrined localism.

The model came from the localized commercial radio (and later television) stations. At the time, and for those stations, localism had made good sense. The United States was a nation of localities as late as the 1920s. Most of the population was located on farms, in small towns, and in small cities. Moreover, the nation had moved across the continent, locality by locality, with the tradition of localism packed in the back of the wagon. Radio was quintessential, crackerbarrel local. Commercial television had established its own localities, the DMAs—dominant market (television market, that is) areas—which followed the signal across county lines, across state lines, and, on our northern and southern boundaries, across borders as well.

The logic of localism was less clear for the emerging public stations in 1967 and 1968. If anything, with the television markets already fixed, it would have been far more efficient to adopt that template. But once-compelling ideas die slowly, if at all. Independent local stations sprang up, sometimes in unlikely places, sometimes cheek by jowl with each other, yet always independent. As Richard

Somerset-Ward observes in *Quality Time?* "Local autonomy was, and remains, the birthright of every station."[15]

The 1967 Public Broadcasting Act clearly changed the course of public television. It also, as Somerset-Ward puts it, "legislated into existence most of the tensions that would give rise to conflict and argument within and about the system during the next twenty-five years."[16]

The most obvious example is the relationship between CPB and the other organizations in the field. Once the 1967 law was enacted, CPB realized that it had to find a way to operate the live interconnection. So an ad hoc committee made up principally of public television station managers devised the notion of a private not-for-profit organization, the Public Broadcasting Service, which came into being in 1969.

PBS is generally thought of by the public as a centralized network. In fact, it was created as—and remains to this day—a membership organization made up of nearly every public station. Initially the stations elected a board of station managers, together with representatives of CPB and NET and public members. (Today the thirty-five-member board consists of seventeen lay representatives from the stations' governing boards, thirteen professional representatives from station management, four general directors, and the PBS president.) PBS would serve as the distribution system for programs; CPB would hold and disburse the money. CPB had the authority to decide which programs would be funded by federal funds. Since PBS was the interface with the stations, however, it inevitably became involved in program planning and even funding. Over the years the relationship—and the power balance—between the two organizations and with America's Public Television Stations, an organization designed to lobby Congress on behalf of the stations' interests, would change many times. James Day (former NET and WNET president) notes in *The Vanishing Vision* that "strong national leadership might have articulated a mission for the medium when, in 1967, it was redefined as 'public television.' But Congress effectively neutered that prospect by placing 'leadership' in a hydra-headed structure of competing authorities."[17]

The problem of competing authority would surface within the act's first five years. That period, with station extension and upgrading so handsomely funded, was one of great growth in the number of stations. In 1967, 126 public stations had been on the air; by 1972 there were 233, an increase of more than 80 percent. The programming support was also showing results. *Civilization, The Forsyte Saga,* and *Masterpiece Theater* (all from the United Kingdom) had come on the air by 1972. So too had *Sesame Street.* Public television developed a higher profile as word of mouth brought more and more people to the quality programming Carnegie and the 1967 act promised and as hard-hitting documentaries and the patent success of *Sesame Street* stimulated intense press coverage. But publicity seldom comes without its costs. With the coverage, gratifying though it was, came what should not have been a completely unexpected problem.

The Public Broadcasting Act, in setting up the Corporation for Pubic Broadcasting, includes among its responsibilities: "full development of educational broadcasting in which programs of high quality obtained from diverse sources will be made available to . . . stations with strict adherence to objectivity and balance in all programs or series of programs of a controversial nature."[18] Interestingly enough, this section of the act makes it clear that public stations are to be held to a higher standard than are commercial stations. Commercial stations, even when the fairness doctrine was being enforced, could discuss one side of any controversial issue so long as they merely acknowledged other points of view, and not even on the same program but somewhere on their schedule.

Congress also realized another danger involving public funds. Section 396 of the act states that CPB must operate "in ways that will most effectively assure the maximum freedom . . . from interference with or control of program content or other activities." To bring the point home, section 398 specifically forbids any "direction, supervision, or control" of public television by officials of the U.S. government.[19]

In one of the most bizarre of those coincidences that seem to have marked so many significant developments in the history of public television, the success of two distinct program genres—public affairs and children's programs—brought about the apparent clash of those two sections of the law. In 1974 a genuine crisis came close to destroying public television. As Somerset-Ward sums it up, "The issue was bias. The 'cause' was localism. But the underlying problem lay in the structure and organization of public television."[20]

A peculiar scenario began to emerge in the early days of the first Nixon administration. Not only had the sociopolitical climate changed since the Kennedy-Johnson years, but public television had achieved far more prominence than before the 1967 act came into being. Its news and public affairs programs were gaining support in the press and among a growing audience. But not surprisingly, a White House that had assembled an "enemies list" was less than happy with strong documentaries and discussion programs that were often critical of the administration. Resentment over the perceived intrusion of politics into the deliberations of CPB—created to be an agency insulated from the government—caused several board members to resign. These resignations provided the White House with the opportunity to increase the proportion of like-minded members. CPB, with the power of the purse, took back the programming of public affairs programs from PBS. Most such programs disappeared, prompting the show business trade journal *Variety* to label public television's programming in 1972–73 the "Floppo Season." Supporters of public television and of open discourse mobilized friends in Congress to draft a generous appropriation bill.

The administration was careful not to use fairness or presumed bias as the reason for its next actions. Rather, they used localism in children's programming. The prominence of *Sesame Street* and the other CTW project, *The Electric Company,* was emblematic of the effect that CPB's money and PBS's programming had on local schedules. In 1964, 56 percent of all children's programs on public television had been local: by 1972 that figure was sliding toward 20 percent. Citing figures like those, in June 1972 President Nixon vetoed the two-year appropriation for CPB, $155 million, contending that these programs established that public television was forsaking localism.

Pat Buchanan, in an interview on *The Dick Cavett Show*, painted a very different picture of what was behind Nixon's action:

> I had a hand in drafting the veto message. And if you look at the public television, you'll find you've got Sander Vanocur and Robert MacNeil, the first of whom . . . is a notorious Kennedy sycophant, and Robert MacNeil who is anti-Administration. You have the Elizabeth Drew show on, which is, she personally, is definitely not pro-Administration. . . . *Washington Week in Review* is unbalanced against us . . . *Black Journal* . . . is unbalanced against us . . . you have Bill Moyers, which is unbalanced against the Administration. And then for a fig leaf they throw in William F. Buckley's program.[21]

The veto had an immediate impact within the public television community. Stations rallied behind the exceptionally skilled and diplomatic board chairman, Ralph Rogers of KERA–Dallas. Under his leadership, a volunteer and staff group drew up a plan. Rogers led the negotiations, which resulted in a newly defined partnership between CPB and PBS and a plan for CPB to devote half of its funds to local stations by 1977. Nixon announced the deal as a win for localism, and a reduced public television funding bill ($110 million over two years, a 30 percent reduction from the sum originally proposed) was signed into law.

The structure that emerged as a result of the crisis was far from perfect, but it did satisfy Congress and federal funding resumed. CPB had the statutory overall responsibility for the system, but with half of its funds going to the stations, it had less money to devote to programming. The new president of PBS, Hartford Gunn, devised a station program cooperative that enabled the stations to commission programs by pooling some of their CPB grant money. PBS ran the interconnection, while CPB paid for it.

By 1975 federal funding had taken an upward turn. There would be a five-year appropriation bill and a steep increase in federal funds in part owing to a program under which the federal government would give a station $1 for every $2.50 raised locally. In 1978 the Public Telecommunications Financing Act increased the matching-fund money by changing the formula to $1 federal to every $2 local. But at the same time the act decreased the authorization period from five to three years, and the actual funding period to two years.

In the late 1970s the Ford Foundation, after more than a quarter-century, wound down its efforts on the part of public television, hopeful of increasingly strong federal funding. Ford's last activity was the funding of the Station Independence Program (SIP). SIP creates a pool of funds dedicated, among other fund-raising techniques, to the production of special, highly promotable programming to be used during pledge drives. Some critics are uncomfortable with the concept because the programs have often featured performers—Peter, Paul, and Mary, for example, or "the Three Tenors"—who do not appear regularly throughout the year. Others see the programs as analogous to commercial television's sweep period specials.

This highly successful project is still in operation. In its first three years, 1974–77, Ford's matching grants helped the stations more than double viewer donations and bring the revenue stream up to 13.5 percent of total income. After fifteen years of SIP, $300 million a year (24 percent of total revenues) would come from viewers, a strong legacy of Ford's initiative.

The other major foundation supporter of public television, the Carnegie Corporation, convened a second commission in the late 1970s. In January 1979, it issued *A Public Trust: The Report of the*

The Underfunded Afterthought

Carnegie Commission on the Future of Public Television. The commission that drew up *Carnegie Two* was as distinguished as its predecessor, with even greater diversity, and its report went directly to the point.

> In less than a dozen years, among the most turbulent in our history, public broadcasting has managed to establish itself as a national treasure. . . . Millions now watch and hear, applaud, and criticize a unique public institution which daily enters their homes with programs that inform, engage, enlighten, and delight. In that sense the ideal has been realized: public broadcasting has made a difference.

Noting that "[t]here is a necessarily ambivalent relationship between public broadcasting—a highly visible creative and journalistic enterprise—and the government," the report goes on to discuss

> the fundamental dilemma that has revealed itself over and over again in public broadcasting's brief history . . . : how can public broadcasting be organized so that sensitive judgements can be freely made and creative activity freely carried out without destructive quarreling over whether the system is subservient to a variety of powerful forces including the government?[22]

The commission's second major concern was finding "public broadcasting's financial, organizational and creative structure fundamentally flawed." It described what we have been examining: the efforts to reconcile creative forces and funding sources with the public's needs. The commission concluded that those efforts had not been very successful: "Institutional pressures became unbalanced in a dramatically short time. They remain [in 1979]—despite the best efforts of the thousands within the industry and the millions who support it—out of kilter and badly in need of repair."[23]

Carnegie Two set out to make a midcourse correction to the direction charted for public television by the previous study. The most significant recommendations in *Carnegie Two* dealt directly with the structural problems the commission found during public television's first twelve years. "A properly constructed and effective public broadcasting system," the report promised, "can unleash the tremendous potential of America's creative artists so that the programming that comes into our homes can better educate and inform, entertain and delight."[24]

To achieve that end, the report recommended that the Corporation for Public Broadcasting and the Public Broadcasting System be renamed and refocused. CPB, which the commission felt was unable to fulfill a role of "national leadership," would be replaced by the Public Telecommunications Trust. The trust, a nongovernmental not-for-profit organization, would have a broad range of duties, including planning, disbursing federal funds, and evaluation. Its primary responsibility would be to insulate "the sensitive area of program making" from inappropriate interference, both from within and from "outside public broadcasting."[25] In addition to that awesome task, the trust would be responsible for a number of administrative functions, including, but certainly not limited to, facilities and signal coverage improvement, increasing involvement of women and minorities, and developing performance and accountability criteria for public funds.

As for PBS, it would be replaced by the Program Services Endowment. This entity, a "highly insulated, semi-autonomous, division" of the trust, would have "the sole responsibility of supporting creative excellence." The endowment would "underwrite a broad range of television and radio productions and program services." The fifteen-member endowment board would be appointed by the trust. The need to establish the endowment, the Carnegie Commission stated, sprang from the "desire to create a safe place for nurturing creative activity, which [would] otherwise become a casualty of the many other institutional priorities of this complex enterprise."[26]

Alas, this insight not only clearly described the experience of public broadcasting prior to 1979 but foretold its history for the next

The Underfunded Afterthought

twenty years. Lacking a Lyndon Johnson or a John Gardner, and with no Great Society galvanizing congressional activity and public support, *Carnegie Two* made little impact. Its recommendations were ignored, and public television continued on its twisted path—in James Day's words, "neutered by Congress," which had placed leadership in a "Hydra-headed structure of competing authorities."[27]

Ironically, *Carnegie Two* summed up the failure of the first twelve years and much of the disappointment of the next twenty with its description of what *Carnegie One* had envisioned:

> In retrospect, what public television tried to invent was a truly radical idea: an instrument of mass communication that simultaneously respects the artistry of the individuals who create programs, the needs of the public that form the audience, and the forces of political power that supply the resources.[28]

Sadly, we conclude that the invention did not work, or at least not very well.

If we were starting over in establishing public television, "would we do it the same way?" Somerset-Ward wondered in 1979. "Probably not. It would be more in tune with the times and the technology to create it centrally—as a superstation, like Turner Broadcasting System (TBS), or as a nationwide cable network."[29]

Whether or not Somerset-Ward's 1979 notion would be adopted today is highly questionable. It seems unlikely that we would accept one or two or three public superstations sending programs to slave transmitters, which would relay them, with no local input. Nor would the American people knowingly permit the 40 percent of its citizens who are least privileged to be disenfranchised, the inevitable result of replacing public television with cable. Somerset-Ward's proposal is provocative but moot. However much its critics might wish otherwise, public television is not simply going to disappear. But it is time to take a good hard look at what we now have and what we do not.

Public Television's Strengths

What are the strengths and weaknesses of the $1.5 billion public television industry in the United States as it approaches the millennium? As we see it, public television's strengths are many and considerable. Ten come readily to mind.

The Breadth of Public Television's Audience

In 1994, contrary to the widely held belief that public television audiences were in serious decline, 101 million persons tuned in to public television every week. This figure represents a 5 percent gain over the previous year, and the largest weekly audience in public television's history. During that same year commercial television audiences declined by the same percentage.

Yet another way to look at the audiences is the method advocated by *Carnegie Two*, the so-called cumulative or "cume" ratings. These numbers represent the number of different individuals in the total audience or in a particular demographic group who spend more than five minutes watching a given station during a specified time period. The cumulative ratings for public television show that 80 percent of all Americans watch public television every month.

These remarkably high figures point to two conclusions, each of which would represent a significant strength in any medium. First, most Americans see some benefit from the service, and second, to the extent that public television appeals to special audiences, a large number of those audiences are being reached.

But the demographic breadth of the public television audience is even more impressive. One of the persistent charges against public television is that it is irredeemably elitist, a view shared by many, including members of Congress, who are opposed to public funding for PBS. But the popular belief that public television appeals primarily to the rich and well-educated is seriously in error. For example, audience studies show that in 1995 three out of every four viewers of *The Metropolitan Opera Presents* had a household income below $40,000—hardly the upper crust.

In fact, the demographics of the public television audience may well be the second-best-kept secret in television. Nielsen's National Television Index (NTI) conducts continuous surveys of television audiences for the benefit of commercial stations and their advertisers; audiences are broken down by race, education, occupation, income, residence location (metropolitan, suburban, rural, etc.), whether or not the TV household has cable or pay cable, and by age and gender. Literally hundreds of groupings are available for comparison with the population of the United States as a whole.

Looking at full-day data (sign-on to sign-off) for the 1993–94 season, the public television audience was within 2 percent in twenty-three of the thirty-three principal population parameters. The largest single difference between the PBS audience and the population is less than 3.5 percent. (The percentage of PBS audience with family income under $20,000 is lower than the total population figures.) In prime time the same figures show a greater variance. The numbers for women over sixty-five and persons not in the labor force watching public television are each 6.4 percentage points higher than their representation in the total population. Even so, looking at each of the thirty-three audience groupings, there is remarkably little difference in composition between the public television audience and that of the country as a whole.

The Extensive Reach of Public Stations

Through its 354 stations, public television can reach 99 percent of the American public. Many of the shriller (and shallower) of public television's critics, those who bridle at the notion of public monies going to fund a medium that in other guises is enormously profitable, point to the fact that several of the program genres typically seen on public television are now appearing regularly on cable. Cable's subscriber level, however, is only 63 percent overall, and no single cable channel reaches anywhere near all of the cable subscribers. It is safe to say that public television's availability to 99 percent of *all* television households will never be matched by any cable channel or grouping of channels.

Public Television's Impressive Roster of Loyal Subscribers

Not only has public television become "firmly established in the experience and the culture of the American people," it has also enlisted a substantial number of active supporters.[30] In the spring of 1996, five million people were annual subscribers. The power of that number became unmistakable when the House of Representatives threatened, during the spring and summer of 1995, to put an end to federal funding for public television once and for all. Having been alerted, public station subscribers barraged their representatives with calls, faxes, and letters. The idea that federal funding would be cut off entirely was quickly dropped, although no one in the public broadcasting community believes that the issue is settled.

Congress underestimated the loyalty of the stations' subscribers in part because its members failed to appreciate two characteristics of the station-subscriber relationship. First, there is an obvious difference between public television subscribers and cable subscribers. The latter enter into a traditional *customer* relationship prompted by their inability to obtain the product otherwise. Public television subscribers, on the other hand, voluntarily become *members* of their local stations for unselfish reasons. They wish to show their support, they feel an obligation as responsible citizens, or they identify with the station's goals or some of its products.

The second point clearly establishes public television subscribers as a devoted group: they appear to tolerate, even if they do not forgive, their stations' seemingly endless pledge week sales pitches.

The Underfunded Afterthought

Finally, the viability of the subscriber system in public television is amply demonstrated by the growth in both the number of members and the total amount of their donations.

The Close Ties Between Public Stations and Their Communities

When it learned that the Newspaper Guild was about to strike San Francisco's two daily newspapers, KQED leapt into the breach. It was 1968, and although the station had been on the air for four-teen years, like virtually all public stations at that time KQED had no news department and, for that matter, no news broadcasts. As James Day, then the president of KQED, tells it, he made one phone call to Fred Friendly, at that time the television adviser at the Ford Founda-tion, requesting $50,000 to underwrite KQED's efforts to fill the news vacuum.

The ensuing broadcast, *Newspaper of the Air*, ran for the nine weeks of the strike. KQED hired reporters and a managing editor from one of the newspapers and, "in a radical departure" from the conventions of the day, sat them down at a long table to discuss, on camera, the stories they had covered that day. "It was news in the act of becoming a newscast—unedited, unformed, unfinished"— but it attracted an audience and met the community need.[31] It was also widely copied by commercial stations. For at least the next decade, the set for local news broadcasts would be a working news-room.

KQED's response to the newspaper strike may have been strik-ing, but it has been equaled or improved upon tens of dozens of times since. The public has always found public television stations to be responsive to community needs, and any station can cite a dozen examples. Moreover, the documentaries and special broadcasts that are the stations' stock in trade, as well as those made available by PBS, bring the stations into contact with community professionals and volunteers working in the areas covered by those programs.

Down the Tube

Doing so many broadcasts of that nature, no station, public or commercial, could avoid developing close community ties.

We should emphasize that we are talking here about perception as much as, and perhaps even more than, reality. Most commercial stations have community ties, and many commercial stations do exemplary work in this area, frequently doing even more than their public television counterparts could ever do on their limited budgets. Nonetheless, public stations are probably perceived to have stronger community ties, in large part because they produce programs that bring them into contact with many different components of the community, and also because many members take "ownership" of national programs and local outreach campaigns. In the final analysis, the identification of the station with its mission to serve as a major community resource may be the basis of the public's belief.

The Caliber of the Boards and Volunteers of Public Stations

The community leaders who serve on station boards and on the boards of CPB and PBS represent a major resource. In most communities the public television boards are considered prestigious and bring together civic, business, art, library, and educational leaders. Consider, for example, the traditional board of the PBS flagship station, WNET in New York. Among its fifty-four trustees, its thirty-three-member New York Community Advisory Board, the thirty members of its New Jersey Advisory Committee, and the twenty-seven members of the board of directors of the Friends of Thirteen, Inc., were household names and behind-the-scenes leaders in the arts, banking, communications, civic affairs, community action, construction, education, fashion, finance, foundations, government, labor, manufacturing, media, real estate, and retailing. Significant figures in every major commercial or noncommercial activity in the community are involved in the governance of the station. Like the members of any carefully selected board in a voluntary organization,

238

public television board members have access to leaders in every aspect of community life. Such links will undoubtedly remain critical to the effectiveness of many public stations.

Moreover, some board members are likely to be involved in the operation of the station. When Bill Baker first went to WNET as its president, he was taken on a tour of the station by George Miles, a former colleague who had left Westinghouse several years before and was then chief operating officer at the station. As they passed through studios and offices, storerooms and control rooms, Baker was struck by the physical similarity to other stations he had known. "George, he asked, "how does this place differ from commercial television?"

The answer surprised him. Miles opened a door to a room in which a number of people were busily at work and replied: "The biggest single factor is these people here. We couldn't keep the station running without our volunteers."

Over the next eight years Baker was to learn exactly how valuable—and dedicated—public television volunteers are. More than one hundred come in to WNET every week to do everything from licking envelopes to assisting on productions. The station maintains a video library for its members; it is operated and often staffed by a particularly generous volunteer. Several hundred volunteers show up to man the phones during pledge week.

The Quality of Public Television Programs

It is onerous—and maybe impossible—to quantify quality. Advertisers may count eyeballs and be satisfied that the most-watched program is the best venue for their wares. But surely none of us would ascribe excellence to the most-watched television spectacle of 1995, the O. J. Simpson trial. Numbers alone can hardly suffice to measure quality. As we have seen, the BBC has developed an index of viewer satisfaction. Absent any such measure in this country, we can defend our assertion of public television's quality only by pointing to the critical attention, the awards of peers, and the extent to which public television programs become the subject of discourse among those interested in ideas. *Nova, Great Performances, The National Geographic Specials, Sesame Street, The Civil War,* and *This Old House* serve as cases in point, as do other favorite public television series, mini-series, and one-off (specials and other nonseries) broadcasts. The record of programs public television has mounted—the very stuff of our medium—constitute, together with the artists public television has attracted, irreplaceable resources.

Public Television's Cadre of Artists

Over the past three decades, as public television has emerged as part of the fabric of contemporary life, the number of talented people who elect to do their work on public television, and virtually nowhere else, has grown exponentially. Some, like Bill Moyers, have moved to the commercial networks to gain a larger audience, only to return, by choice, to public television. Others, such as Jim Henson, Frank Oz, and their colleagues, developed into international stars through public television and went on to additional acclaim in other media while maintaining their public television ties. Still others—Ken Burns, for example—have worked exclusively in public television. The ability to draw upon such artists contributes to public television's image and enables programmers to envision and plan for long-term projects.

The Unique Credibility of Public Television's Programming for Children

Unlike all other television genres, children's programs represent a self-renewing resource. Commercial children's programmers estimate that their audiences turn over every five years; with its greater ability to do age-specific programming, public television's audiences turn over even faster. Unlike their commercial counterparts, however, public television stations do not have to maximize audiences every hour of the day to maintain and increase profitability. Instead, public stations can acknowledge the differences in children's understanding and interests as they develop from infancy through adolescence and provide programming to serve them at each stage of their growth. Commercial stations must aggregate several distinct age groups in order to attract advertisers, which need larger audiences. Public television puts the developmental needs of its several child audiences before any other considerations, although doing so may be more costly.

Thus, because they do what commercial children's programming cannot do, public television's children's programs are very rarely the subject of criticism, and they are virtually always considered beneficial, both in fulfilling traditional educational purposes and transmitting values.

Public Television's Strong Connections with the Educational Establishment

Public television's affiliation with education flows in part from its children's franchise. It also reflects the more than seventy years of determined efforts by a cadre of educators to see broadcasting used for more than entertainment and mere incidental learning. So intense was the educators' passion that in the pre-satellite 1950s they persuaded the Ford Foundation to underwrite a DC–6 equipped with two transmitters and the just-developed videotape machines. Circling at a height of several miles, the plane transmitted two channels of instructional television that were picked up by seventeen thousand classrooms in six midwestern states. The Midwest Program for Airborne Television Instruction was described at the time as the most expensive and bizarre experiment in educational television to date.

From their inception, the educational television stations in the United States carried instructional materials from kindergarten through college. Not surprisingly, the nexus between a public station and the educational institutions in its region is broad and deep. So too are the relationships between public stations and national education institutions.

Today most public stations continue this tradition. For example, WNET developed the National Teacher Training Institute (NTTI), which offers training in the integration of video and technology into science and math curricula from kindergarten throughout high school. Through teachers-teaching-teachers workshops, now held in twenty-six sites throughout the country, WNET has trained more than one hundred thousand teachers who, in turn, have influenced sixteen million students.

The station currently provides thirteen hundred hours a year of instructional programming for schools in its tristate coverage area. Monday through Saturday during the school year, from 2:00 to 5:30 A.M., teachers can tape a block of programs in math, science, language arts, social studies, health, art, history, and geography for classroom use the following school day. A special series is broadcast every morning at 6:30 and again during lunch hour for the benefit of adults who read at third-grade level or below. Also before the workday and during lunch, another series helps adults prepare for the high school equivalency examinations. Two days a week instruction is provided in Spanish and French.

Most important, numerous studies have shown that students comprehend and remember 80–90 percent more of the subject matter when the television materials are used than they do when the teacher covers the same subject matter without using the television component.

Public Television's Strong Brand Recognition

The strengths of public television, taken together, contribute to an asset that commercial marketers refer to, with great admiration, as *strong branding.*

Mothers remember their hours with Mr. Rogers and with Bert and Ernie. Children in the next generation remember their time with Barney. Grandmothers remember and identify their most cherished French dishes with Julia Child and her PBS series. A significant proportion of two generations of Americans remember setting their Sunday schedules so as not to miss *Masterpiece Theater.*

It would take hundreds of millions of dollars—if indeed it could be done at all—to build the identity and the trust that PBS enjoys and maintains. The high public regard for PBS has made it a surrogate for all public television. Like Coca-Cola and IBM, public television is clearly and strongly branded.

Public Television's Weaknesses

Having laid out what we believe to be public television's strengths, what do we see as its weaknesses? No organization is without some weaknesses, and from what we have already said, it should be clear that we believe several pressing matters must be addressed if public television is to flourish.

Public Television's Lack of a Clearly Articulated Mission

Everybody knows the mission of the fire department. Anyone can identify its priorities and articulate what society expects of it. Nearly everyone would describe the fire department's mission in essentially the same words: to get to the fire as quickly as possible and expeditiously and bravely save lives and property.

But what about a public television station? Or PBS? Surely average Americans know the mission of public television. Or do they? Despite its strong branding, neither PBS nor public television has managed to position itself clearly in the market.

Is public television's mission to educate? To inform? To entertain?

To do all three? And perhaps more? And in what proportion? What is public television's relationship to other institutions in our society? To commercial stations? To the public as a whole? To its audiences? The American public, we submit, is far less clear on public television's mission than it is on commercial television's.

Increasingly, businesses have found that they can no longer simply say to themselves, their employees, and their customers that they are in the widget business. They now find it helpful to think through their values, expectations, lines of business, priorities, and ways of reacting to change. One of the valuable tools, organizations have found, is a formal mission statement. These vary greatly in detail, style, and length, but all attempt to encapsulate, for all who need to know, what an organization is about.

The Boeing Company reviews its mission statement and elaborating material every six months. This "living document," as Boeing's vice president for continuing quality improvement put it, expresses the company's "long-range mission" of being "the number one aerospace company in the world and among the premier industrial concerns in terms of quality, profitability, and growth."[32] This statement leaves no doubt about Boeing's intentions. It wants to sell more airplanes than anyone else, and it wants to make money doing so. In its list of fundamental goals in pursuit of its mission, Boeing defines profitability as maintaining 20 percent average annual return on stockholders' equity, and the goal of growth as "greater than 5 percent annual real sales growth from 1988 base." Both goals support Boeing's mission, attest to the company's professionalism, and provide unambiguous direction to its employees.

It is difficult to imagine a single statement that would embrace the 349 stations PBS represents, PBS itself, the 5 stations who are not members of PBS, and all the other players.

Obviously, a mission statement alone cannot effect change. But as the Boeing example demonstrates, a well-conceived and well-crafted statement can go a long way toward making clear to all just what an organization stands for and what it seeks to do.

The Underfunded Afterthought

Public television's mission is hard to discern and nowhere clearly stated. PBS has expressed its mission as "serv[ing] its members with programming and services of the highest quality and the imaginative use of technology to advance education, culture, and citizenship."

This statement is not quite a call to storm the barricades. More like the interoffice memo that it in fact is, this mission statement talks of perceived organizational needs—of means, not of ends. Indeed, that is the problem we perceive: public television needs to sharpen its focus so that it can take the next step. It has become a national institution to which millions turn. It has even become an institution for which its members will fight. But unless most Americans can describe what it does as easily as they can talk about the fire department's mission, public television will never reach its potential.

The Duplication Issue

The May 22, 1995, issue of *Broadcasting & Cable* published the public television schedule for a typical weekday in Washington, D.C. It took six parallel columns to do so; Washington viewers, as the accompanying article pointedly emphasized, receive the signals of six public television stations. Two stations are licensed in the District of Columbia itself—WETA, a major community station, and WHMM, operated by Howard University. Stations operated by the Maryland Public Broadcasting Commission in Annapolis and Baltimore also come into the Washington market, as do two stations operated by the Central Virginia Educational Television Corporation, located in Fairfax and in Goldvein, suburbs of Washington.

One cannot help noticing in the side-by-side listing that *Sesame Street* is carried on three stations from 8:00 to 9:00 A.M., and on two stations from 10:00 to 11:00 A.M. *Sesame Street* is also carried on another station at 9:00 A.M. and on yet another at 5:00 P.M. *Barney* runs on two stations from 11:00 in the morning until noon. Another station carries it twice a day, at 9:00 in the morning and 5:00 in the afternoon.

At about the time Senator Larry Pressler was talking about privatizing public television, a Lehman Brothers document estimated that between $17 million and $34 million could be saved by public television between 1995 and 2000 if such duplications were eliminated by merger. A CPB report to the House Committee on Appropriations identified 53 markets in which the signals of a total of 135 public stations overlapped.

Signal overlap and the kind of duplication evident in the Washington, D.C., market have given the critics of public television in general, and of federal funding for public television in particular, a field day. They have called the duplications wasteful and used the studies to bolster their position against federal funding.

At first glance, criticism of duplication in public television's programming may seem warranted. Certainly, for most of the market, having the same program running on more than one channel represents an egregious waste of a limited resource. But the problem is more complex and less serious than it might appear to those living within the beltway. Issues of terrain, its effect on reception, and difference in mission—as well as programming—between instructional and public television are more important than mere duplication of schedule. Much of the problem can be traced to the initial allocation of channel space for educational stations and to the unforeseeable consequences of localism.

WETA in Washington came on the air thirty-five years ago, and the Baltimore station eight years later. Two other stations in the area have been broadcasting for more than twenty years, and the newest station for thirteen. When the allocations were made, no VHF frequency was reserved for education in either Washington or Baltimore. All of the public stations in the Washington area are on the UHF portion of the spectrum. With the possible exception of the Howard station—which came into being to serve the university and its students as well as the Washington area's large African American population—the stations did not overlap each other's coverage when they were founded, since ultra-high-frequency stations have far smaller coverage areas than do those in the very-high-frequency portion of the spectrum, channels 2–13.

Cable changed all that. Under the so-called must-carry rules, most cable systems are obligated to carry all broadcasting stations within fifty miles of their facilities. The result has been dramatic. As reported in *Current,* the public television trade journal, cable carriage enabled WPTD in Dayton, Ohio, to reach an audience six times larger than before. To a great extent, the development of cable has equalized the UHF and VHF stations. It has also highlighted the duplication problem.

Critics sometimes overlook, however, a critical fact: not everyone has access to cable. In the Washington area, four of every ten households do not subscribe to cable, most often because they cannot afford to buy access to all the programming listed in those newspaper columns.

During recent congressional discussions on the future of public television, the issue of duplication loomed large. PBS currently has 344 member stations in the fifty states and the District of Columbia, together with two in Puerto Rico and one each in American Samoa, Guam, and the Virgin Islands. No single commercial network has more than 208 stations covering the same territory.

Since reaching the entire country efficiently is of such critical importance to commercial networks and their stations, every county in the United States has been assigned to one and only one television market, based on which stations' signals are dominant. The commercial networks are able to reach every designated market area, and thus every county in the nation, with 136 fewer stations than public television covering the same area. Nineteen markets have more than one public station, and some of those markets, as in Washington, have six or more.

Admittedly, scheduling any program on two channels in the same market is not only impolitic in the present climate but, as PBS's opponents maintain, genuinely wasteful. However, while *Sesame Street* and *Barney* were running against themselves on some stations, another public station in the Washington market was running courses in foreign languages for an entirely different audience.

The problem, of course, is not necessarily that multiple PBS outlets air in one market. There is nothing intrinsically wrong in having two public stations serving the same area. Indeed, some public stations, most notably those in Pittsburgh, Dallas, and Boston, hold and operate two licensed broadcasting facilities. The problem lies in how stations in large metropolitan areas allocate their resources. Does it make sense for stations to have the same schedule? Or even the same mission?

Two public channels in most markets could be of enormous benefit to viewers. To begin with, most stations would make excellent use of having twice the airtime. Two different audiences, with distinct program needs, could be served at all times. For example, WNET's mission calls for the station to:

- Reflect and respect a diverse and complex world;

- Serve the underserved: new Americans, high school dropouts, illiterate populations, and urban youth;

- Foster lifelong learning opportunities;

- Offer cultural enrichment;

- Facilitate responsible citizenship;

- Create opportunities for experimentation.

A second channel in a market would provide a community with access to more items from a more varied menu, without doubling expenses. The private sector has known for a long time that, by pooling resources, two stations can operate more efficiently than one; commercial broadcasting is the very exemplar of the principle of economies of scale. Commercial station groups effect great savings by pooling accounting and payroll, purchasing, engineering, certain sales functions and program acquisition, and production—all critical functions for broadcasting organizations. In this age of computer networking, even nonprofit organizations have found that not every function needs to be performed within their own walls.

It is our belief that public stations could benefit greatly by pooling their resources to achieve vastly greater efficiencies while preserving station identity and nurturing volunteers and staff.

The Vagaries of Short-term Planning

The uncertainty of its financial future confines public television to short-term planning, which would limit any institution's vision and inhibit its long-term growth. Moreover, short-term planning fosters ad hoc solutions, which in the long run do not solve but merely postpone dealing with systemic problems. Planning is difficult and often wasteful when contending with short-term, inconsistent, and sometimes capricious funding sources.

WNET, for example, must start from scratch each year to raise more than $100 million. On more than one occasion when federal funds were cut back unexpectedly, the station had to shut down production to await the new funding cycle. It has seemed rather like firing a cohesive corps de ballet or a winning baseball team in midseason.

Public Television's Failure to Maximize All of Its Resources

Three of the ten strengths we identified in public television—the quality of its programs, its ability to attract and retain outstanding independent artists, and the credibility of its children's programming—are heavily dependent on an underused resource, the expertise of the major producing stations.

Seven stations have always been the originators of much of public television's prime-time and children's fare. Together they produce more than three hours a day of nationally distributed programming. *The Newshour with Jim Lehrer* and its predecessor, *The MacNeil/ Lehrer Newshour,* have been jointly originated by WNET in New York and WETA in Washington.

With its daily hour of news and such series as *Great Performances, Nature,* and *Charlie Rose*, WNET has been the most frequently watched source of programming, contributing more than five hundred hours a year. WGBH in Boston, with such titles as *Frontline, Nova,* and *Masterpiece Theater,* ranks second in number of hours produced. In third place is WETA, which originated *The Civil War* as well as regular series such as *Washington Week.*

Supplying more than thirty hours of prime-time programming a year are MPT (Maryland Public Television), the source of *Wall Street Week;* WTTW–Chicago, which originated *Lamb-Chop's Play-Along!* and *The New Explorers;* KCET–Los Angeles, from which *The Great War* emanates; and WQED–Pittsburgh, the longtime home of *Mr. Rogers' Neighborhood.*

Over the years the success of the major producing stations has secured PBS's reputation for high-quality programming. Their operations, though different, are sophisticated, creative, and highly professional. They have invested in the talent and business infrastructure necessary to support independently developed programming. Built on trust and mutual respect, their ongoing relationships with independent producers and other programming sources enable them to scout out promising programs in development and bring the very best to the system.

Clearly these stations' track records demonstrate their value as ongoing resources for PBS. One would expect the major producing stations—representing successful program developers whose aggregate local audiences constitute 25 percent of total PBS potential viewers—to be consulted regularly on national program planning. Yet they rarely are. Indeed, no mechanism is in place for drawing on their collective information and insights. There is, to be sure, an organization representing the top fifteen or so markets, the Community Station Resource Group (CSRG). That group, however, has never been formally authorized to advise PBS, help establish the national schedule, or even provide counsel to the PBS program chief.

We believe that CSRG's lack of involvement is emblematic of the weaknesses in the public television system. There is always hope, however, that PBS will recognize the value of the major producing stations.

Lack of Common Carriage

As we have seen, Congress and several administrations have taken steps, in the name of localism, to prevent public television from becoming or even looking like a conventional broadcasting network. In the process, public television programming has been severely hampered in achieving its potential. For fifteen years, from 1974 to 1989, national programming was controlled by the Station Program Cooperative (SPC), a cumbersome mechanism that made it very difficult to initiate or replace programs and was widely acknowledged as notably unresponsive to the marketplace.

The SPC was replaced by the chief program executive (CPE), but that change left unresolved the major problem with the previous system, the lack of common carriage—a substantial majority of stations carrying particular broadcasts at the same time. By the beginning of the 1990 season the CPE had raised participation of stations in the new system from less than 60 percent to more than 80 percent. Moreover, the chief program executive herself, Jennifer Lawson, and her troops pulled off a major coup. Through their prodding, most public television stations carried a nine-episode series on the same days and at the same times. Duplicating stations in some markets adjusted their schedules to provide a planned alternative scheduling.

The results were every bit as satisfying as anyone could have hoped. *The Civil War* became the most watched limited series in PBS history. The series began on Sunday night against the commercial networks' highly publicized season premieres and attracted more viewers than a heavily touted new series on CBS, a premiere on NBC, and all but one of the series on Fox that week. An average of fourteen million Americans watched each night. *The Civil War* proved that well-scheduled, high-quality programming that provides a significant shared experience brings viewers to television. CBS's head of audience research estimated that the total over-the-air audience increased on the first night by 3–4 percent as a direct result of the PBS series.

Many public stations, concerned that they might lose their autonomy, have resisted common carriage, perhaps believing that scheduling will lead inevitably to their having no voice in programming. But the impact of localism goes beyond who is calling the shots on program production. Corporations are understandably reluctant to commit dollars for production up front and then find out that a number of local stations have decided not to carry the program. On the other hand, *The Civil War* established that in this age of highly mobile populations, of cellular telephones, fax machines and E-mail, it is still possible to share a cultural experience. It also reminded us that we can still benefit from one of earlier television's much lamented characteristics: its ability to serve as the national hearth. All it takes is a superior program that all can share at the same time, and plenty of advance notice.

Insufficient Audience Leveraging

It is somewhat problematic, in many people's minds, to speak of generating public television audiences. Should public stations be looking at rating books? Aren't they supposed to be above all that? The answer lies in reframing the question. Isn't it in the public interest to inform people about forthcoming programs?

The list of the twenty-five most-watched programs distributed by

The Underfunded Afterthought

PBS as of September 1990 is heavily laden with titles in two series. The earliest broadcast on the list occurred on October 28, 1975, and the lesson it conveys remains relevant. The broadcast captured its time period on Channel 13, WNET in New York, with a phenomenal 36 share—nine to twelve times the share the station normally showed in the 9:00–10:00 P.M. Tuesday time slot. Similarly, it drew 36 percent of the total viewing audience in Pittsburgh, 30 percent in Boston, 28 percent in Washington, and 20 percent in Houston. Nineteen million persons saw the broadcast on the 250 PBS stations that carried it, the largest audience in the history of public television to that date.

What accounted for the broadcast's success? It wasn't lack of competition: the three commercial networks had each scheduled first-run episodes of strong shows, and it was early in the new season. Admittedly, the public television offering was an episode in a well-known series, *National Geographic*, which had been on network television for nine previous years. Furthermore, "National Geographic" had been a household term for decades, thanks to the society's magazine. Yet such recognition might even have negative associations. Some viewers might think the series or its usual subject matter, wildlife, old hat. The series had never, in all its nine years, garnered anything like the audience attracted to "The Incredible Machine," the series' public television debut.

The subject matter, the inside of the human body captured on film, was fascinating. Health and biology teachers assigned the broadcast as required viewing. But schoolchildren doing their homework, even with their parents looking on, could not add up to a 36 percent share of audience. What did account for that share was the most massive promotion campaign ever mounted for a public television broadcast.

In PBS's largest single corporate grant to that time, Gulf Oil Corporation underwrote twelve *National Geographic* specials broadcast over a three-year period. Gulf's first entry into public television was a grant of $3.7 million. In addition to the program grant, Gulf also pledged at least $1 million a year to promote the programs. Although "The Incredible Machine" cost only $250,000 to produce, a spokesman for Gulf reportedly said that "around $900,000" was spent to promote the first broadcast in the series.

WNET sources outlined the campaign's seven parts: thirty-second spots on CBS and NBC; newspaper ads in every PBS market; a saturation radio campaign in twenty-five markets; a broad magazine campaign in both mass and selected publications; bill stuffers sent to three and a half million Gulf credit card holders; posters sent to nineteen thousand gas stations; and internal promotion to Gulf employees.

"The Incredible Machine" proved twenty-one years ago that when PBS is able to mount a complete advertising and promotion campaign for a program of quality, public television can be competitive with commercial networks. Anything less than coordinated national scheduling and adequately funded advertising and promotion fails to serve the potential audience—and thus the public whose interest public television was created to serve.

Organization and Governance

Localism reaps some great benefits. We would agree with the argument that public television has been accepted as a significant and valued American institution in large part because of the role the local station plays in its community.

But there is a dark side to localism. Welcomed by public television's detractors in the Nixon administration, the autonomy of local stations has hampered public television ever since. PBS's member stations each have equal voice on every issue that comes before the body. Thus, one vote apiece goes to WNPE in Watertown, New York, with eighty-two thousand households; KEET in Eureka, California, a market with fifty-two thousand; and Bowling Green, Kentucky, with forty-four. At the same time, the three votes of the stations in the three largest markets in the country—WTTW–Chicago, KCET–Los Angeles, and WNET–New York—represent more than fifteen million households.

Unattractive though it may be to consider the size of public television audiences in many contexts, PBS is a representative body by law and by custom, as well as by nature. Shouldn't the principle of one vote per transmitter be modified in order to come closer to representing the public that supports public television and is served by it?

There are a number of models that have sought to address this issue. The bicameral Congress of the United States seeks to represent states in the Senate and individuals in the House. The United Nations gives one vote in the General Assembly to nations not much more populous than Rapid City, while reserving some issues for the Security Council, where membership bespeaks the extent of resources that can be brought to bear on the UN's chief mission, maintaining and fostering world peace.

PBS's major concern is the development of programs that can be made available to a national audience. The specter of a few markets depriving most of the nation of the programming it should be seeing—or conversely, insisting that programming of narrow regional interest supersede all others—is too real to ignore. A mechanism that balances the legitimate interests of the stations with the primary responsibility to the audience could surely be found.

The Politicization of the Industry

The calculus of power in the public television apparat is byzantine. The public television model foreordained by the insistence on "the bedrock of autonomy" may well represent the worst of all worlds. Stations must be responsive to underwriters, to philanthropists, and to governments. In the process of serving all those masters, the system has devolved a structure that makes internal conflicts inevitable. The Corporation for Public Broadcasting is the agency that allocates federal funds; PBS is the station-run programming agency. The Association for Public Broadcasting (APB)—formerly the National Association of Public Television Stations (NAPTS), more recently calling itself America's Public Television Stations (APTS)—is involved in "representing the stations on legislative and regulatory issues, research and planning, and communications." Then there are the regional networks, such as the Central Educational Network (CEN) and the Eastern Educational Network (EEN); state networks; and a host of other agencies whose mandates range from funding to technology to children's programs to Latino issues.

Merely reciting that abbreviated list may make one breathless; thinking about the political implications of such an array of power centers may make one ill. Little wonder that lengthy, costly, and wasteful bottlenecks are routinely encountered in the world of public television.

Lack of Independence

Stations are beholden to a broad array of funding sources: the federal government, state and local governments, foundations, members, and sponsors. In some ways public stations are more beholden to sponsors than are commercial broadcasters. The commercial broadcast sponsorship contract is based on a clear-cut economic exchange with measurable outcomes, both of which elements are missing with public television. Public stations are also beholden to subscribers and to audience members who are or might become contributors.

Diverse support does offer some benefits. Having a number of discrete funding sources is as sound a practice as diversifying investments: should any single source withdraw support, the entire enterprise is not necessarily in jeopardy. The downside is that a tremendous amount of time and effort is required to maintain a steady flow of income. One source or another always seems to be at risk. Bill Baker estimates that he must devote 50 percent of his time to out-and-out fund-raising and about 20 percent to his board. Only 30 percent can be devoted to such matters as planning and programming.

Because public television, like all not-for-profit organizations, must spend considerable time and money on fund-raising, federal and state dollars are particularly welcome. Government funds are the most efficient sources of money because they take comparatively little time and money to raise.

Options for the Twenty-first Century

Having looked at public television's strengths and weaknesses, the obvious question is, where do we go from here? What follows is our agenda for public television.

The problems have been addressed by others, including the reports of the Carnegie Commissions and the Twentieth Century Fund Task Force on Public Television. Ours is a short list in both senses of the word. We have only six recommendations to make, but we believe that each one is essential to the survival of the medium.

1: Rationalize the system to make it modern and more efficient and to increase viewer choice. Reduce the cost and improve the quality of station operations. Stations in larger markets should, at the very least, agree to differentiate their missions and coordinate scheduling to avoid duplication. Other options worth considering include comanagement, outsourcing, or reconfiguring administrative tasks. Marketwide cooperation should result in increased operating efficiency and greater program variety, thus serving many more constituencies. Smaller stations, with the cooperation of the larger, should seek out and serve niche audiences. Above all, stations and their boards should take immediate action to eliminate the wide-spread and counterproductive cannibalism of resources, both monetary and otherwise. Stations in smaller markets should set up regional or statewide mechanisms to share services and should seek out innovative collaborations with natural allies such as cable access facilities.

Change of this nature is never easy, but the need is easy enough to demonstrate. The literature of the not-for-profit sector is rich with examples of both the urgency of the need and the probability of success. When volunteers become convinced of the need for change and exercise their stewardship, the task becomes far less daunting and the indisputable benefits are seen to be within grasp. We believe that with leadership the system will thrive as it has never been able to do before.

2: Establish coordinated national common carriage and promotion.

3: Develop new revenue streams.

4: Strengthen ties with other institutions such as libraries and museums to broaden and solidify a natural political base.

5: Strengthen the educational role to assist schools and colleges as their societal roles change. Sesame Street can be viewed as a deliberate societal/educational intervention to ameliorate a significant problem. A revitalized public broadcasting system could imaginatively meet such needs as worker retraining, distance learning, volunteer development and training, and parenting.

6: Work to ensure long-term funding. There are four options, the first of which would be for public television to remain a combined *government-private system.* The only possible change would be to modify the relative percentages of funding received from the various sources in order to respond to changes in the economy and minimize dependence on any one source.

A second option would be for public television to become a *commercialized system*. This could actually work, but the cost would be unacceptable: the medium would be irreversibly changed. Commercial values such as those described in chapters 3 and 4 would prevail. Some would counter that public television could model itself after the BBC and the Japanese NHK, providing a much more varied menu by producing and programming sports, game shows, and comedy. We believe it is far too late to consider this option, for two reasons. For one thing, the BBC and NHK began and gained audiences for this kind of service before commercial television arrived on the scene. For another, the costs of such a schedule are far greater now than then, and the number of competitors in the United States—four commercial networks, two netlets—WB and UPN—and two others in the process of becoming—would make start-up very difficult at best. Inevitably, commercials would be shown as frequently as they now are on the commercial networks.

A third option is a variation of the second: out-and-out *privatization*. Under this option, the stations would be sold to shareholders and the resulting capitalization would pay for start-up. Under such an arrangement, a station could turn a modest profit with only a minimum number of commercials every hour. What makes this option impossible, however, is the cost of money.

Let's look at how that might work. In 1995, New York City sold its city-owned UHF station, WNYC-TV, for $200 million. What if a group of investors could have been found who were willing to invest $200 million in that station with the understanding that it would continue as a public station but would sell enough commercials to pay the expenses and a modest level of interest on their loan? It is reasonable that if they had not put their money into the public station, these investors could have put it into the market and earned more than 10 percent given today's market conditions. Let's assume that they are willing to accept only 5 percent. At that rate, the interest on $200 million amounts to $10 million a year, or $40,000 a day.

It is easy to see what might have happened, even if the investors were all deeply committed to the mission of the station. Inevitably, through death or financial vicissitude, first one and then another would find it necessary to sell his or her shares on the open market. If the station could not find enough backers to put up the money with the expectation that the profit would be virtually nil, it would have to sell the shares on the basis of their ultimate profitability.

The so-called opportunity cost of that much money would require the station to take in $27,500 a day before paying the electricity bill to light the studios and fire up the transmitter and before paying a penny for salaries or royalties. Even more important, advertisers would demand a total of impressions (the sum total of the audiences for each of the day's commercials).

The fourth, and by far the most appealing, option would be the creation of a *federal trust fund*, not unlike the Federal Highway Trust or the various state highway, bridge, and tunnel trusts, such as the Port Authority of New York and New Jersey, which owns the World Trade Center, a rapid transit system operating between New Jersey and Manhattan, the George Washington Bridge, and the Holland and Lincoln Tunnels. Tolls, train fares, and rents from the Trade Center and other real estate have built up the trust to the point where it can finance other projects.

A public broadcasting trust fund could be financed by dedicated radio and television receiver excise taxes, by the auction or sale of portions of the electromagnetic spectrum, or by licenses to use spectrum. It would almost certainly have to be started with a massive federal grant or loan in order to generate the $4 billion that is the minimum estimated to produce enought interest to make a real difference. But it holds out the best hope for public broadcasting to become independent and to reach the level of performance the American people have every right to expect.

* * *

The Underfunded Afterthought

As we write these words, the fate of public television remains an open question. To be sure, canceling all public funds, a very real possibility during the first session of the 104th Congress, was taken off the table. For now. But the funding of public broadcasting, like the funding of the arts, can never be taken as a given in this country, in part because of persistent misunderstandings about both institutions: the myth that they are exclusively elitist; the failure to recognize their place in the nation's overall economy; and the misapprehension that they are nowhere nearly as popular as sports events.

The similarity between the demographics of *Live from the Met* and the general population should dispel the myth of elitism. Those who hold that the arts and entertainment are merely a luxury ignore the fact that American television and film production constitute one-sixth of the national economy, according to Jack Fields, former chairman of the House Telecommunications subcommittee. And despite the eagerness of city administrations throughout much of the country to pony up hundreds of millions of dollars to construct new stadia at the barest hint that a sports team might be thinking about relocating, the fact is that museum admissions exceed the paid admissions totals for all sports. And public television's audiences exceed sports attendance by many millions.

Newt Gingrich may have stopped openly referring to public television as a "sandbox for the rich," and federal funding may not have been completely abandoned, but it did fall from 86 percent of public television's total revenue in 1980 to 16 percent in 1995. Corporate funding, on the other hand, has increased in the same period by more than 50 percent. As of 1995 it had reached 17 percent of all public broadcasting funds. William F. Fore of the Yale Divinity School, writing in *Christian Century*, described public television's dilemma:

> Pressures to commercialize public broadcasting continue and have created a classic Catch-22. If PBS and NPR were to depend entirely on congressional support they would be out of business. But if they

accept commercial sponsors and grovel through "pledge weeks," then they are accused of selling out. They are damned if they do, defunct if they don't.[33]

The pressures will continue. The reduced federal funding, still as much as 14 percent of many stations' budgets, is in place only through 2000 and must be renewed every year thereafter. In making the case for recent cuts, many commentators have suggested that public television competes with cable or can be replaced by cable. Our experience in the commercial television industry tells us that nothing could be further from the truth, no matter how many cable channels are available.

Public television, in our view, is irreplaceable. To be sure, several cable networks rerun and even produce programs in subject areas or genres that have been hallmarks of public television: nature, documentaries, opera, ballet, and theater. Those networks provide a genuine service to those American households that can afford cable. But paradoxically, the for-profit cable networks simply cannot produce new programs that match the quality that public television provides. Networks such as Arts and Entertainment do documentaries in six weeks; PBS often takes six months or a year. The difference is in the research and in the validation of the content. Public television programs are given the same degree of peer review that scientific journals provide. PBS nonfiction programs are typically vetted by panels of experts. Similarly, only public television can spend $1 million to produce an opera: a cable network's shareholders would simply not permit it to do so. Public television considers the money an investment in the preservation of our cultural heritage.

The one inescapable difference between the two systems is that commercial television must always make a profit; indeed, it must almost always maximize its profits. As one public television manager put it, the task of the commercial station manager is to make a dollar; the task of the public television manager is to make a difference.

Americans benefit from a strong commercial television industry.

It is a significant part of our economy, and its ratings-driven creativity brings us many hours of pleasure. But it doesn't bring our children much of value, and it doesn't bring the arts to millions. Its news programming often focuses on the sensational and neglects more serious matters.

We deserve both strong commercial television and strong public television. National parks, public libraries, and public schools are not profitable ventures, so the marketplace takes little interest in them. Because these public resources add to the quality of our lives and the well-being of our nation, we provide for them ourselves, as a society. The same is true for public television.

If we always aim for the bottom line, we aim too low. During the congressional debates on public television, polls showed that 80–90 percent of Americans "want public television to survive and to grow."[34] It will do so only if it remembers E. B. White's adjuration to "address itself to the ideal of excellence, not the idea of acceptability."

(9)

The Road Ahead

W HAT WILL THE ROAD ahead be like? Will it be the promised superhighway, bulldozing its way across the continents, wide and swift and relentless, interested only in its destination? Will it be a meandering secondary road, respecting the mountains, coming into the lives of the county seats, the crossroad towns, the suburbs, and the endless grids of modest housing that encompass and nourish the central business districts of our cities?

Will it be democratic, accessible to all, bringing delight and enrichment? Or will it be simply another impersonal source of noise, pollution, and stress? What vehicles will travel this road? For whose sake? Under whose direction? What will they carry? Will we like it? Will it help? And will we have any say in the matter? Will it reflect our choices? Is it too late to shape our information future? What does that future portend for programming, for children, for broadcast journalism, and for public television? What will be the fate of the viewer? Will we be even further commodified?

Do we stand at a crossroad, or have we traveled too far?

When the Clinton administration set out to develop the necessary broad support for the bill that ultimately became the Telecommunications Act of 1996, the term "information superhighway" entered the vocabulary. Vice President Al Gore was dispatched to sing its praises. And praiseworthy it certainly seemed. If you were lost in the woods, at sea, or in an unfamiliar city, your location would be instantly pinpointed and whatever help was needed would soon be at hand. If you were injured on the highway, your medical records would be summoned up and the nation's foremost surgeons would be in video contact with the paramedics, who would have been en route to the scene from the very instant the accident occurred. Every school in the country could, at any time, summon up the leading authorities in every field.

The technology for most of this had been developed; only two elements still needed to be put in place: infrastructures to establish and maintain linkages among the various institutions, and a vastly improved broad-band network to distribute the signals. Indeed, the administration's dog-and-pony show was addressing the latter concern. The United States could not maintain its preeminence in international finance without a complete overhaul of the data networks involved. Since the 1980s, the amount of money that passed through New York City in any three-day period was at least equal to the gross domestic product (GDP)—the country's entire output of goods and services in a year. Every ten days the amount flowing through New York was equal to the world's GDP. With electronic financial transactions increasing exponentially, the United States had no choice but to upgrade its capacity. Hyping the emergency and education capabilities seemed a lot safer politically than asking members of Congress to underwrite a system that would help Wall Street when they were busy explaining to their constituents why the local military base had to be closed.

Television would play into the information superhighway through convergence. Computers, telecommunications, and mass media would soon interchange signals as their technologies began to look and function alike. Then, the argument ran, we could have five, hundred channels. To make all this happen, we would need to reform the communications laws.

We were at a crossroads indeed. A new, comprehensive telecommunications act, long anticipated but not possible until the mid-1990s, appeared to be imminent. Not only that, but many of the promises of the information superhighway were already coming to pass as the Internet seemed to be exploding from a university-based research tool into a popular electronic communications system. Most important, a new era in television technology was coming to fruition after a frustrating twenty years of development.

A new regulatory framework could provide hope that a reactivated public interest standard would answer the perennial questions about television fare: Why is so much television so unfulfilling? Why must it be so formulaic? Why must it be so offensive that many people would welcome the government setting the criteria for acceptability?

Any regulatory framework attempting to address these issues is constrained by three resources: money, time, and content. For at least the last twenty years, media scholars have been watching the principle of relative constancy at work. As mentioned in chapter 4, the principle holds that as the population grows, the total amount of money spent on information and entertainment will grow, but the proportion of the GDP representing communications expenditures remains relatively fixed from year to year, despite the appearance of new technologies, new media, or new content.

For example, in 1996, $113.7 billion was spent on advertising in the United States. That amount, which had risen over the previous five years, paid for a high proportion of radio, television, cable, newspapers, and magazines. The amount that consumers spent directly on cable, motion pictures, home video, recorded music, newspapers, books, magazines, business information services, and interactive digital media of all kinds—$103 billion—had also risen. Pay-per-view movies on cable grew by 44 percent. The sum of all expenditures for communications, $290.7 billion, represented 3.8 percent of the GDP. Despite the fluctuations in individual components, despite the appearance and growth of VCRs, home video, personal computers, and the Internet, that percentage had varied only by two-tenths of a percent for more than twenty years. It is estimated that it will rise to 3.8 percent by the end of the century.

Another way to describe the principle of relative constancy is to say that the public's expenditures on media in the United States represent a zero-sum game. For every dollar spent on a new medium, a dollar is taken from older media. Every additional dollar put into television production must be met with a dollar coming out of advertising at the expense of radio or print or outdoor advertising or a dollar coming out of profits. Americans will not tap into the rent or food money to pay for media.

Closely related to the money issue is the management of that other scarce resource, time. Analyses by Veronis Suhler & Associates show that the average person, twelve years and older, spent nine hours and eighteen minutes a day on all communications in 1996. The yearly total has not varied by more than two hours since 1989, nor is it estimated to do so for the rest of this decade. This is not surprising in light of the increasing number of two-income families, the greater time demands placed on job holders, and the decrease in leisure time. It is also not surprising that 46 percent of the average person's communications time was spent with television, and 32 percent with radio. What may be surprising is that while reading accounted for about one hour a day, less than 6 minutes a day was spent on computer on-line services and the Internet. Despite all the hype about the information superhighway and its components, the amount of time the average person spends on these pathways is not expected to reach much more than an hour a month. The average American will spend only thirty hours on-line during the entire last year of the century.

What of television—will we like it?

In that same year, 1999, each American will spend an average of 1,645 hours with television. A little more than two-thirds of that time will be spent with broadcast television. Less than 5 percent of the time will be spent watching movies and special events on premium cable channels and pay-per-view. Ironically in this age when the prospect of five hundred channels is casually spoken of, there is a growing scarcity of prime-time programming.

Network prime time has been the staple of American program supply, both broadcasting and cable. It has also historically supplied an average of 21 percent of European programming. The decline in broadcast network shares has inevitably diminished the amount of money available to develop and produce prime-time entertainment. Even more important, the short-term, bottom-line obsession of management for most of the last ten years has decreased the supply by 20 percent, and the magazine shows have proliferated. These series were scheduled primarily because they are relatively inexpensive to produce. Admittedly, cable has been producing more and more original programming. But the money cable provides to make programs amounts to 5–12.5 percent of what the networks pay. Network shares have stabilized and are expected to remain where they are for the balance of the century. But if network shares once again begin to drop, can sufficient audiences be aggregated to ensure advertiser support for twenty-two hundred hours of new prime-time programming a year?

Programming genres are cyclical. We seem to be in a particularly formulaic period. But relief may be on the way—the baby boomers are reaching their fifties. People in their fifties watch more television than ever before. The first generation raised with television—and the largest generation before or since—will bring more people to the set every year for at least the next decade. Will the networks seek their patronage? For that matter, will advertisers recognize that baby boomers have more disposable income than younger groups? Or will the advertisers, in their desire to capture the much smaller next generation, drive the boomers to cable reruns?

The Europeans have contended for the last ten years that there is a worldwide dearth of programming. The number of channels in Europe has grown by 50 percent since 1987, when nearly fifty thousand hours of American programming were showing up each year on European television sets. Even though the European Community has placed a 25 percent quota on programming from non-European sources, there will still be a demand for seventy-five thousand hours of imported programs. Because our population base is so big and our popular culture so widely accepted, it is unlikely that any nation will supersede the United States as the primary source of exported programming. Admittedly, the seventy-five-thousand-hour figure is an artifact: any episode of *Baywatch,* a popular export, will appear on television in several countries and each appearance counts as one hour. But if new programming does not increase in the United States, will we be able to meet the demands of Europe, or will we see more TeveGlobos emerging to fill the gap?

The European problem is small compared with the domestic shortfall. As we pointed out in chapter 4, cable networks now number more than 150, and for the past five years or more at least 150 new networks have been scrambling for shelf space at the annual cable markets. Many will not succeed, but they all put together pilot programs or, in some cases, a pilot day of programming. More than one broadcast entertainment executive has privately complained that these projects, as well as the increased demand from established cable networks for original programming, have made it difficult to put together production teams for their projects.

Is the road ahead the fabled information superhighway?

Probably not. At least, not as it was envisioned. NBC is coming closest with its joint venture with Microsoft, MSNBC. Both that channel and CNBC are now seen internationally. Also, in June 1997, MSNBC mounted a substantial promotion campaign to announce that its 10:00–11:00 P.M. news broadcast was the only "network-produced," hourlong nightly news program.

Many broadcasters throughout the country have experimented with web pages that permit viewers to summon up ancillary data. Public broadcasters have been heavily engaged in such experiments. But so far none feature interconnectedness to the extent possible with MSNBC. And even that channel comes nowhere near providing the level of interactivity that the envisioners of a video Internet promised. Their vision of a robust democratization of television will remain only that, a vision, for the next decade at least. Nor, for that matter, will we see five hundred channels. Given the low level of pay-per-view activity seen now and projected for the rest of the century, we will not see video-on-demand (VOD) either. VOD is the setting aside of, say, nine channels to accommodate a single pay-per-view movie with start times every ten minutes, thus making it possible to sit down with popcorn at 8:00 and watch your choice on channel 401, or at 8:10 on channel 402, or at 8:15 . . .

The future of television will be driven by two factors: the fate of regulation and our national preoccupation with technology. Never mind what kind of programs we present, or what kind of programs the audience deserves. If we build it—whatever it may be—they will buy.

For whose sake, and under whose direction?

For several years we knew that 1996 could mark a significant turning point. In that year Congress would address telecommunications—not only television and radio but telephone and computerized communications, direct satellite delivery services, cable, and all the ways these separate technologies can converge with, interact, replace, augment, and enhance each other. The trade press had been speculating on communications reform for more than two years, reflecting the industries' mood swings from critical concern to eager anticipation.

From a business perspective, the mood was optimistic. In a September 1995 interview in *Broadcasting & Cable*, the managing director of the major investment firm Lazard Freres and head of its communications group, Steve Rattner, foresaw an increasing bullishness for media stocks. Mergers and acquisitions throughout the American economy were about to reach an all-time high. The proportion of mergers in the media industries was running 50 percent higher than in other sectors of the economy. The investment community ascribed this activity to a number of factors, including technological change, the economy itself, and, especially, regulation. The financial interest and syndication rules (see chapter 4) had already been lifted, and the telecommunications bill seemed to be on track. Rattner was particularly impressed by the impact of the three new networks, Fox, WB, and UPI, which were scurrying to line up affiliates: "It's created a game of musical chairs. . . . Indeed, there may not be one chair too few, there may be two or three chairs too few in a given market."[1]

Will television be accessible to all, bringing delight and enrichment?

In February 1996, President Clinton signed the Telecommunications Act of 1996. The new law did nothing to address the concerns we've expressed in this book, but very few people were surprised. The 104th Congress had come into power a year earlier, championing smaller government, less regulation, and the unbridled primacy of the marketplace model.

Broadcasting & Cable, with its usual restraint, ran a banner on its cover: "The Future Begins Now."[2] The chairman of the House Commerce Committee, Thomas Bliley of Virginia, somewhat anachronistically announced: "This is the first major overhaul of telecommunications law since Marconi was alive and the crystal set was state of the art."[3] At least a dozen visionaries, Edward R. Murrow among them, turned over in their graves.

There have been three regulatory (generally Democratic) periods and three deregulatory periods in American history. Each began with a "watershed election in which . . . a new alignment of party presidential voting—resting on a new coalition—was established, which kept its essential shape for at least twenty years." Kevin Phillips, who served as Richard Nixon's chief political analyst, enumerates the characteristics that our deregulatory period shares with the two previous eras, the 1890s and the Roaring Twenties:

Conservative politics; Reduced role for government; Difficulties for labor; Large-scale economic and corporate restructuring; Tax reduction; Disinflation or deflation; Two-tier economy (Difficult times in agricultural, energy and mining areas; good times in emerging industry, service and financial centers); Concentration of wealth; Increased debt and speculation; Speculative implosion.

He adds: "It is no fluke that the Republican supremacies coincided with and helped generate the three major capitalistic heydays in which wealth became more concentrated—the post–Civil War Gilded Age, the Roaring Twenties and the Reagan years."[4]

A "capitalist heyday" is precisely what Wall Street, and many in the television industry, saw coming with the passage of the 1996 Telecommunications Act. The act addresses eighty issues ranging from cable rates to how businesses might benefit from combining their particular competencies with those of companies in other areas of the field. The promise, as with mergers and acquisitions, is that the result will be greater than the sum of the parts.

The act specifically removes all regulatory barriers to long-distance telephone companies providing local service, and vice versa. It permits cable systems to enter the telephone business, and vice versa. It permits broadcasters to enter the cable system business, except in markets where they have stations.

Moreover—and this item has attracted more attention than any other—the act permits the single ownership of an unlimited number of television stations, provided only that the total audience thus reached is less than 35 percent of all American television households.

Within the next ninety days, David Smith, CEO of the Sinclair Broadcast Group in Baltimore, had acquired River City Broadcasting LP. The resulting Sinclair Communications, with twenty-nine television stations, became the largest television station group in the country and, with thirty-four radio stations, the seventh-largest radio group. The combined operating income of Sinclair and River City made it the fifth-largest broadcast group in cash flow. With that cash flow, Smith's "very practical objective" of owning one hundred television stations "in the next few years" does not seem like an idle boast, considering that Sinclair's twenty-nine stations, mainly in medium markets in the Midwest, reach only 14.3 percent of the nation's television households.[5] And although less than 15 percent of the nation's audience may not seem significant, some monopoly watchers might be concerned by the observation of the media broker Steve Pruett: Sinclair, with stations from Raleigh-Durham to San Antonio, now owns "the whole middle of the United States almost in contiguous markets."[6]

Proponents of the Telecommunications Act contended that competition would be fostered by unleashing media-owning companies from restrictions on how much they could own. Many others, however, remember what happened when the airlines were deregulated. The handful of airlines that had controlled 80 percent of the market increased their share to 95 percent. Similarly, the consent decree (see chapter 3) ended network production, resulting in a greatly increased share of market for the eight production companies. The most watchful of the media analysts looking at the question of oligopoly formation and control has been the former assistant managing editor of the *Washington Post*, Ben Bagdikian, who first published his warnings of the increased control of a few media owners in the early 1980s. In 1993, in his preface to the third edition of *The Media Monopoly*, he wrote:

> Seven years ago, I suggested that sooner or later a handful of corporations would control most of what the average American reads, sees and hears. Today the leaders of the media industry are themselves predicting this development and are moving rapidly and eagerly to bring it about. They believe that the same few corporations will control all the important mass media not just in the United States but globally. Nevertheless, there is a close to total silence in the mainstream news on the social consequences of this concentration. . . . Now that the media owners are so large that they are part of the highest levels of the world economy, the news and other public information become heavily weighted in favor of all corporate values.[7]

After the giant mergers in the last quarter of 1995 and throughout 1996, twelve companies stand out as the major forces in U.S. media industries. Ranked by their 1996 revenue, the Mega-Media Twelve are:

1. Time Warner Inc. Revenue: $20.9 billion. Operating income: $2.1 billion. WB Television network; Warner Bros. Television; international Warner Bros. CNN 5 networks; HBO 3 networks; TBT: TBS Superstation; Cartoon Network. Cable systems serving 12.3 million subscribers. Warner Bros. Studios; Warner Home Video; Warner Bros. International Theaters. Time Inc: *People, Sports Illustrated, Time, Entertainment Weekly, Fortune.* Time Warner Trade Publishing; Warner Books; Little, Brown; Warner Music Group: Atlantic, Elektra, Warner Bros. Music International,

Warner/Chappel Publishing Co.; 50 percent of Columbia House. Warner Bros. Consumer Products; Warner Bros. Studio Stores worldwide; Book-of-the-Month Club; Warner Bros. theme parks; CNN Interactive.

2. The Walt Disney Co. Revenue: $18.7 billion. Operating income: $3 billion. Walt Disney Television (International); Touchstone Television; Walt Disney Television Animation; Buena Vista Television; ABC Inc.: ABC Television Network (ABC News and ABC Sports), 10 television stations; Disney/ABC International Television. ESPN; The Disney Channel; A&E; The History Channel; Lifetime Television. ABC Radio Network; 26 ABC radio stations, 11 AMs, 15 FMs. Walt Disney Pictures; Touchstone Pictures; Hollywood Pictures; Caravan Pictures; Buena Vista International; Buena Vista Home Video; Buena Vista Home Entertainment; daily newspapers; 50 trade publications; *W, Discovery*, and family magazines; books, comics. Walt Disney Records, Hollywood Records; 101 Disney stores worldwide; clothing, toys licensing ventures; Disney theme parks; Walt Disney Theatrical Productions; Disney Online, Disney Interactive; Disney Cruise line; interests in international broadcasting companies and partnership with Ameritech to develop new cable TV networks.

3. News Corp. Ltd. Revenue: $14.3 billion. Operating income: $1.4 billion. Fox Broadcasting Co.; 23 U.S. TV stations; 20th Century Fox Television; 20th Century; Twentieth Century/Astral Television Distribution Ltd.; Evergreen Television Productions, Inc.; Fox Children's Network, Inc. Fox Pay-Per-View services; Fox networks; Fox Motion Pictures; 20th Century Fox Film; Columbia TriStar Films; 21st Century Film; Cinemascope Products; Fox Animations Studios; Mirror Pictures; Van Ness Films; Fieldmouse

Production; Fox West Pictures; San Antonio Film Features; Fox Home Entertainment; HarperCollins US Inc.; Murdoch Publications; News T Magazines; News America Publications; *New York Post, TV Guide*; Fox Music Inc.; Fox Records; Fox Film Music; Fox On Air Music; Fox Broadcast Music; Fox Movietone News; Fox Net; Fox Sports Productions. News Corp. owns and operates STAR TV in Hong Kong and has extensive interests in the UK: BSkyB; *The London Times* and other newspapers; and in Australia: *The Australian* and other newspapers.

4. Viacom. Revenue: $12.1 billion. Operating income: $2.2 billion. Television Signal Corp.; Riverside Broadcasting Co.; 13 TV stations; Paramount Communications Inc.; 75 percent of Spelling Entertainment Group, Inc.; MTV; Showtime; Nickelodeon/Nick at Night; VH1; USA Networks; Comedy Central; All News Channel; 12 radio stations; Paramount Pictures; Viacom Productions; Simon & Schuster; Macmillan Publishing USA; Prentice-Hall Co.; technical and professional books; Music by Video Inc.; Blockbuster Entertainment Corp.; Discovery Zone; 5 theme parks; Games Productions Inc.

5. Tele-Communications Inc. Revenue $8 billion. Operating income: $2.3 billion. Cable systems serving 14.4 million subscribers; Liberty Media; Bravo Classic Movies Ltd.; Cable Accounting Inc.; Cable Television Advertising Group; Discovery Communciations Inc.; Home Sports Network; local cable networks; Direct Broadcasting Satellite Service Inc.; Netlink USA; United Paging Corp.; UCT Aircraft Inc.; United Corporate Communications; United Hockey Inc.; Intelligent Electronics.

6. Sony Corp. Revenue $7.9 billion. Operating income: $517.7 million. Sony Pictures Entertainment (television programming and syndication); Columbia TriStar Television; Sony Pictures Entertainment Inc.; Columbia Pictures; TriStar Pictures; Sony Pictures Classics; Triumph Films; Columbia Records; Epic Records Group; Sony Classical.

7. General Electric. Revenue: $5.2 billion (from media alone). Operating income: $953 million (from media alone). NBC Network, 11 TV stations; 7 cable/satellite networks, including CNBC and Court TV; MSNBC—joint venture with Microsoft.

8. Westinghouse Electric Corp. Revenue: $4.4 billion (from media alone). Operating income: $1.4 billion (from media alone). CBS TV Network; CBS Entertainment; 14 TV stations; CBS News/Sports; 175 radio stations. (On December 1, 1997, Westinghouse's assets, together with Infinity Broadcasting and CBS, became CBS Corporation.)

9. Gannett Co. Revenue: $4.4 billion. Operating income: $1.4 billion. 18 TV stations; USA Radio Partners; *USA Today*; 95 Gannett newspapers; *USA Weekend*; Cape Publications Inc.; billboards; Advanced Media Solutions.

10. General Motors. Revenue: $4.1 billion (from media alone). Operating income: $259.8 million (from media alone). Hughes Electronics Corp.; DirecTV; Hughes Galaxy; Hughes Network Systems; VSAT; PanAmSat.

11. Comcast Corp. Revenue: $4 billion. Operating income: $1.2 billion. Cable systems serving 4.3 million subscribers; cable systems in the UK; QVC electronic retailing; wireless telephone service; satellite television. Joint ventures in Primstar, DBS service, and Spring Spectrum.

12. Seagram Co. Ltd. Revenue: $3.7 billion. Operating income: $379 million. Universal television productions; 10 percent of Time Warner; 50 percent of USA Networks; Universal Pictures; 49 percent of United Cinemas International Multiplex; 49 percent of Cinema International Corp.; 49 percent of Cineplex Odeon Corp.

These numbers tell only a small part of the story. More important is information on what portion of the nation's and the world's audiences these companies control. In addition to owning all of the commercial broadcasting networks in the United States, together with the new hopefuls WB and UPN, the Mega-Media Twelve own no fewer than 89 television stations. The overwhelming majority of stations in the nation's top ten markets are owned by the Twelve. Since they also own more than 600 radio stations, one of the three major news magazines, virtually all 24-hour news channels, and more than 92 daily newspapers, including *USA Today* and the *New York Post*, the Twelve have enormous influence over the nature and amount of news disseminated to the American people.

In entertainment their holdings are even more significant. The Twelve own all of the major motion picture studios and virtually all of the producers of network entertainment broadcasting. Every cable channel that manages to attract more than one million viewers per week is controlled by the Mega-Media Twelve. Thirty-one million cable households—more than half of all cable subscribers in the United States—are customers, and therefore dependent on the channel choices of the Twelve. Moreover, the other cable systems in the country are dependent solely on the Twelve for nearly half of the basic and pay channels they carry.

Among them, the Twelve control, in addition to their television and radio interests, more than twelve major trade book publishing companies, more than sixty magazines, and most of the recorded music in the United States.

The Mega-Media Twelve are arguably both the largest oligopoly and the largest oligopsony in the United States. Since there are only twelve major *sellers* of programming—as we have shown in chapter 4, the studios and the networks control the development process—the price set by any one of them may well affect the entire market. Similarly, since the Twelve include the major *purchasers* of programming—the networks, cable networks, and major station groups—the market leverage of any one of the Twelve can affect the price any distribution system is willing to pay.

Internationally, the Twelve have significant interests in the Scandinavian Broadcasting System; cable channels in Germany; children's programming in China; Nickelodeon UK; HBO Olé and El Canal in South America; NBC Super Channel in Europe; satellite channels in Europe, Asia, and South America; and numerous other interests in many other countries. Disney, Time Warner, and Seagram dominate the world's theme-park industry. Murdoch's empire includes 123 daily newspapers around the world as well as BSkyB, the direct broadcast satellite system in Northern Europe. He also controls the largest potential television audience, the 1.6 billion persons in the footprint of STAR TV (see chapter 7).

Since 1988 there have been at least fifteen hundred significant mergers and acquisitions in the United States. How did this merger mania come about? The frequently heard and often accepted explanation is that mergers are driven by three phenomena: the maturity of traditional forms, the appearance of new technologies, and the prospect of convergence.

Maturity in this context is analogous to the transition from adolescence into adulthood: many businesses, like young adults, reach their maximum growth. Television stations are not mature businesses, however, and broadcast networks even less so. Even though their share of audience had declined, the average network prime-time ratings reached an all-time high in 1994, owing to the increase in television households—up nearly 20 percent from the more than eighty million in 1983. The number of television households will inevitably continue to increase as long as the population continues to rise. The networks lost share relative to cable largely because of their preoccupation with short-term profits during the early 1990s. During that period the more cheaply produced magazine programs came to occupy one out of five hours of prime time on the networks. In turn, magazine programming drove viewers to the independents, which were able to offer more and more first-run syndicated entertainment programming. From a revenue standpoint, network television will continue to thrive because it remains the most efficient means for advertisers to reach a mass audience.

Cable, on the other hand, is becoming a mature business. The nation is almost completely wired. More than 98 percent of all television households have been passed by feeder cables and could have cable tomorrow if they subscribed. However, as we pointed out earlier, nearly 40 percent of the households passed by cable will probably never become subscribers.

We discussed in chapter 4 that cable was deregulated in 1984 and subsequently reregulated in 1992 as a result of intense customer dissatisfaction with rate hikes and poor service. Certain cable rates have been deregulated again in the 1996 Telecommunications Act. But the cable operators seem not to have learned their lesson. Even before the act took effect, several major MSOs were raising the rates yet again by changing the number of channels in premium packages offered to their customers.

The marvels to come—what do they portend?

The much-heralded new technologies are DTH (direct to home) and HDTV (high definition television). DTH uses broadcast satellites that relay signals directly to eighteen-inch reception dishes that deliver a clearer picture than cable ever could. Until recently, dishes cost more than $500. Investment companies have maintained that DTH—even with the current promotional campaigns and the expanded number of channels it offers, owing to digitalization—will not reach 5 percent penetration of the market until the dishes become less expensive. They predict that prices will not drop until sometime in the next century.

As we write, however, discount retailers have brought the price point down to less than $150. Five operators are already engaged in or prepared to enter DTH: Hubbard, Echostar, Primestar, the consortium of Hughes and AT&T, and Murdoch's News Corp. A *Broadcasting & Cable* editorial, while suggesting that DTH boded real competition to cable, aptly commented, "That leaves terrestrial TV holding at least two aces: remaining the only free TV medium and the only local one. In mass media audience terms, that's still the hand to beat."[8]

The editorial might also have spoken of AT&T's hedging its bets. In a clear example of convergence—the third phenomenon said to be driving the merger movement—the long-distance company is getting involved in a state-of-the-art medium that may be able to deliver telephone services as well as programming without expensive house-to-house optical fiber wiring. Convergence describes the coming together of previously discrete technologies and the businesses that have provided their services. One of the barriers to convergence disappeared with the passage of the 1996 Telecommunications Act. Cable systems may now use their fiber optic cables to deliver telephone services; "telcos" may enter the video delivery business; and broadcast networks may once again own cable systems.

In all mergers, the ideal is synergy: A telco brings its switching capability and a cable company supplies its knowledge of programming. Then the whole is indeed greater than the sum of the parts.

Much to the surprise of many media watchers, high definition television is presenting the most synergistic possibilities of all. In fact, HDTV may provide us with the very opportunity for change we have advocated throughout this book.

The concept of high definition television has been around for decades. The phrase has been used several times simply to distinguish a new piece of equipment as state-of-the-art. Since the 1960s the term has been attached to a particular technology that increases resolution, that is, improves picture quality. Television sets in this country have conformed to a standard set in the 1940s by an industry committee that fixed the resolution at 525 lines per screen, the so-called NTSC (National Television Standards Committee) standard. Every television station, every television camera, and every television set sold for use in this country adhered to this standard, thus permitting everyone in the country to have access to every broadcasting channel located within range, no matter where they might be. The NTSC standard was a compromise: some picture quality was sacrificed in the interest of accommodating as many stations as possible. Most developed countries have a standard that provides a much sharper picture.

For at least the last twenty years American engineers have sought a way to provide a better service without increasing the bandwidth of the signal and thus using more of the limited electromagnetic spectrum. The chief figure in this effort has been Joseph Flaherty, CBS's senior vice president for technology, who persuaded the NHK Laboratory, the television research facility serving the Japanese industry, to try solving the problem. By the summer of 1981 NHK's engineers had developed a prototype camera. When a group of American television executives visited the laboratory on the outskirts of Tokyo that summer, the camera, set up to shoot out of a second-story window, was focused on a street corner two blocks away. Wires snaked across the floor and down from the ceiling. The engineers apologized for the "breadboarding" of the guts of the camera: transistors attached to pieces of plywood hung out both sides of the camera. But the picture seen on the camera's viewfinder was unlike anything they had ever seen. It was clearer than any television anywhere in the world and every bit as good as 35mm film, the standard for theatrical motion pictures.

In 1982 CBS arranged demonstrations in Washington, Los Angeles, and New York. We attended these demonstrations, which included at least two cameras, their components all neatly out of sight. The reaction of the audience was the same: Hollywood producers, FCC commissioners, and industry executives gasped in amazement and delight. There appeared to be no doubt that HDTV was the wave of the future. But although the Japanese, in partnership with CBS, had been working on HDTV since the 1960s, at least five barriers, some of them enormous, had to be overcome before that future would arrive.

The most obvious was that the bandwidth question had not been resolved. Each station broadcasting HDTV would require six times the bandwidth of NTSC channels. Since the spectrum was already crowded to capacity, either as many as five out of every six stations would have to be shut down or some other portion of the spectrum would have to be used. Clearly the first alternative was politically and practically unacceptable. The United States solved the problem by appealing to the International Telecommunications Union to use spectrum space set aside for the Japanese system, by then known as MUSE.

Meanwhile, European countries became concerned that MUSE would allow the Japanese electronics companies to overwhelm their industries, as had already happened in the United States. Thomson and Philips combined forces to introduce their own HDTV system.

By 1988 several American production companies had begun to shoot television series in MUSE instead of on 35mm motion picture film, the industry standard it closely resembled. MUSE was a much less expensive process, and it also would save them a step in entering the inevitable HDTV syndication market. Meanwhile, just as with 35mm film, the masters could easily be transferred to NTSC or other video formats. At the same time the Japanese had managed to reduce the spectrum needs for MUSE. By 1991 they were broadcasting eight hours of programming in HDTV every day. The audience was greatly limited: MUSE television sets cost $18,000 and were only partially compatible with other broadcasts.

Compatibility was an issue every bit as thorny as spectrum space.

Down the Tube

The FCC, as it had done when color television was introduced, long held out for a system that would permit television sets to receive both NTSC and HDTV.

In 1988, in part to resolve that issue, the FCC established the Advisory Committee on Advanced Television Service (ACATS) under the chairmanship of Richard Wiley, an energetic and effective former FCC chairman. Joe Flaherty, who, like a new-tech Ancient Mariner, had continued to champion CBS and NHK's MUSE, was a dominant member of the committee. ACATS proved to be catalytic: no fewer than twenty different systems were proposed for adoption by the FCC. Some, like MUSE, were analog systems; others were digital and thus at least potentially compatible with computer technology.

Operating without government funds but with donations of $8,000 from each of the nineteen committee members, ACATS set up a laboratory in Alexandria, Virginia, to provide a peer-reviewed process for testing prototypes. During this period one and then another manufacturer saw opportunities to combine forces. Finally, four systems emerged successfully from the test process. Wiley announced that another round of "very expensive" tests would be necessary to make the desired improvements by a certain date. When the manufacturers objected, Wiley offered an alternative: "Form a single, Grand Alliance system."[9]

It took another year to complete the design of the equipment. But the result, Wiley contends, is "the greatest advance ever in television technology. . . . It's what I characterize as the theater in the home. Larger, wider screens. Almost photographic images."[10]

Wiley has every right to be proud of having put the system together. Getting Zenith, General Instrument, AT&T, the Massachusetts Institute of Technology, and a consortium led by Philips Electronics, NBC, and the David Sarnoff Research Center to combine their strengths and produce a system both compatible with the international standard and acceptable to all the networks, commercial and public, is a prodigious accomplishment.

But the public has a $75 billion stake in its television sets, to say nothing of its VCRs and NTSC home video equipment. Whether they will be willing to buy ten million big-screen (thirty-five-inch) sets at one or two thousand dollars more than the most expensive sets on the market today is a significant question. Jerry Pearlman, chairman of Zenith during the Grand Alliance process, thinks Americans will buy the new sets, and Richard Wiley agrees: "I've heard the arguments that there is no public demand for it. My answer is that the public hasn't seen it yet. When we build it, they will come."[11]

Pearlman compares the situation to color sets and VCRs, both of which began to sell when the $500 price point was reached. He is confident that thirty-five-inch sets, the minimum recommended for HDTV, will quickly go down to less than $500 more than today's price for NTSC sets.

As we pointed out in chapter 3, consumer sets represent the largest investment in television equipment. Replacing one receiver in each of the nation's television homes with a $2,500 HDTV set would cost nearly $250 billion.

The broadcasting industry also faces large expenditures. It is estimated that conversion to HDTV will cost each of the nation's sixteen hundred television stations between $10 million and $35 million. The industry as a whole will spend an estimated $12–42 billion.

Those costs, however, do not include the cost of the transitional broadcasting. Stations may have to maintain duplicate studios and duplicate transmitters for the period of nine years permitted by the Telecommunications Act before turning in their NTSC frequencies.

The last question may be the most interesting one of all. Who will broadcast in high definition? And under what circumstances? This question may seem meaningless on its face: the 1996 Telecommunications Act clearly states that, at least initially, the only entities eligible to obtain advanced television (ATV) licenses are broadcasting stations now on the air and others already approved to construct stations. The term advanced television embraces all digital television, both the system the Grand Alliance has settled on, HDTV, and SDTV (standard digital television), which is an improved type of

NTSC. Some stations are contemplating going to digital—converting the television pictures into the on–off signals computers use—but not adopting HDTV. Instead, they will use the new wider bandwidths to broadcast several simultaneous commercial services by "multiplexing" their signals. *Multiplexing* is a term for ways of reducing the amount of spectrum needed to send a signal. A simple example is the practice of using the pauses between words in a conversation to insert words from a second conversation. They are later separated into their correct sequences at the receiving end. No licenses will be granted, however, until Congress settles one contentious issue.

In the early 1990s Congress approved the auctioning of portions of the spectrum to prospective cellular phone users. The sum thus raised greatly exceeded expectations and attracted considerable attention at a time when Congress and the Clinton administration were both expressing concern over the national debt. The National Association of Broadcasters immediately began to lobby against any such auction for high definition spectrum, citing the enormous costs that stations would incur in developing the new technology. Nonetheless, to the surprise of many of his pro-business colleagues in the 104th Congress, Majority Leader Robert Dole described the idea of turning over spectrum to the broadcasters as a "giveaway" and threatened to hold up passage of the Telecommunications Act in the Senate. He later withdrew his opposition in exchange for a commitment from the FCC to issue no licenses for ATV until Congress resolved the issue.

Not just the camel's nose but the camel himself was already in the tent. The idea of auctioning or leasing spectrum is clearly on the table. Moreover, Congress instructed the commission to permit ATV licensees to offer "'ancillary or supplementary services' consistent with the public interest." If a subscription fee is charged for any such services, the station must pay a fee to the commission. Fees are to be designed, in part, "to recover for the public a portion of the value of the public spectrum resource made available for such commercial use."

The act adds that licensees will pay an amount equivalent to what would have been obtained had there been competitive bidding. Congress thus adopted, it seems to us, the concept of an assigned value to the electromagnetic spectrum.

What does the Telecommunications Act portend for public television?

Under the new law, every public licensee should be eligible for an ATV spectrum license. The critical question is how public stations—all of which are not-for-profit, educational, or local government entities—will pay for the construction of digital facilities. The most recent studies show that it will take $1.7 billion to convert all public broadcasters (including radio) to the new technology. It will take great creativity to fund that transition and simultaneously devise a long-term permanent funding mechanism to sustain public broadcasting. During the last two years, a variety of funding proposals have been considered and rejected.

One potential source of future funding is the analog spectrum. Once the transition from analog to digital broadcasting is complete (when at least 85 percent of consumers in each market have access to digital signals), broadcasters will be required to return their portion of the analog spectrum. Those frequencies will then be auctioned by the FCC for other telecommunications purposes. Even a small percentage of the proceeds of such an auction would allow for the creation of a trust fund that could sustain public broadcasting far into the future.

Although the public television stations are seeking matching grants from the federal government, from their local communities, and from state governments, it is questionable at this point whether public television will be able to raise enough money for the transition solely from these traditional methods. What is clear, however, is that additional channels for public television would be of enormous benefit to audiences throughout the country. Such an expansion, sufficiently funded, would enable public television to fulfill its promise of cultural, educational, and intellectual diversity while also serving, in fresh, enriching, and effective ways, the socioeconomically underserved. It is possible that the new technologies will, after all, result in beneficial new regulations.

Where are we in the regulatory cycle?

What is also clear is that, at the very least, the current regulatory cycle may soon be moving us toward a closer look at the role of regulation in American society. We have seen several harbingers of change. Polls show that public sentiment strongly supports the Food and Drug Administration in its efforts to halt the exploitation of children by the tobacco industry; airline safety and reinstatement of an effective and modernized Federal Aviation Administration are being called for after the ValueJet and other airline disasters. Concern over health care costs and dismay over the role of almost completely unregulated insurers are mounting rapidly.

In this climate, the Telecommunications Act of 1996, surely an opportunity for regulatory reform, seems to us disappointing. Its stated purpose is "to promote competition and reduce regulation in order to secure lower prices and higher quality services for American telecommunications consumers and encourage the rapid deployment of new telecommunications technologies." One wonders how increasing the number of stations an oligopoly can own or manage serves the interests of competition.

There is one ray of hope. Section 201, "Broadcast Spectrum Flexibility," which covers the allocation of spectrum for ATV, does not preclude the FCC from setting up an auction or setting a fee for spectrum use. The mention of the "public interest, convenience, and necessity" standard no fewer than four times in less than fifty lines suggests a genuine concern on the part of Congress that the new frequencies be put to other than trivial or completely commercial, non-program, use. And then, of course, there is the fee question, which establishes, as the 1934 act never did, that spectrum is a scarce resource that belongs to the public.

The 1996 act begins its consideration of ATV with: "If the Commission determines to issue additional licenses for advanced television services, the Commission should . . ." The FCC is not directed to issue ATV licenses at all, nor is the possibility of an auction ruled out. Congress neatly sidestepped the issue and left open the possibility of negotiation. We believe that if ways are found for the public to benefit from the issuance of ATV licenses, the 1996 act may stand out as the first legislation to consider the public interest rather than what interests the public.

It has been our argument that misregulation and its unintended effects are a bane not only to broadcasters and others in the industry but also to the public. It has kept us from the realization of E. B. White's vision; we have neither Chautauqua nor Minsky's, neither Lyceum nor Camelot. Our civilization has been judged and found wanting.

When the 1996 Telecommunications Act came to a vote, it was during a period of deregulation, of unrestrained mergers and acquisitions. The act's major achievement was to make them even easier across the traditional barriers between the various communications industries. But the Telecommunications Act was not the only regulation emerging at that time. Concerns about program content were beginning to be expressed in several quarters. By May 12, 1997, *Broadcasting & Cable* was sufficiently alarmed to editorialize on the issue. Pointing out that one hundred members of Congress, led by Newt Gingrich, had signed a letter to the heads of the television networks requesting that they once again program 8:00–9:00 P.M. as the family hour, the editorial raised the specter of "programming to the tastes of a national nanny with a political agenda."

Let's recap. At least one governmental entity wants to dictate the type of children's programs broadcasters have to air, the kinds of programs they put on at 8–9 P.M., the content ratings system they employ (V-chip, age-based ratings, etc.), how many and what kinds of public service announcements they carry, the times they may program adult-oriented material—i.e., content that registers on some bureaucrat's sex or violence meter—how much broadcasters can or cannot charge for their own advertising time if the client is a well-heeled political machine and whether they may carry truthful advertising about a legal product.

At this rate, the government is going to price speech right out of the market.[12]

We don't think so. We have shown that the profit margins and cash flows of broadcasting and cable are very sound compared with most other American industries and are likely to remain so. But we differ with *Broadcasting & Cable* in an even more important way. The real impetus behind this list, we would contend, was not the agenda of a national nanny, but the failure of the industry to address public needs as well as the desires and preferences of audiences.

There are several reasons for this failure. Public apathy about the deinstitutionalization of America has led to lowered expectations, thus facilitating the reshaping of broadcasting institutions as mere profit centers. The relentless drive to maximize profits at any cost by maximizing audiences has fostered pandering to the lowest common denominator of public taste at the expense of expanding public sensibilities. Any doubt on this point can be instantaneously dispelled by viewing a single episode of the Entertainment Channel's *Talk Soup*, a review of the most egregious segments of the current week. Similarly, the commodification of local news programs and their audiences has diminished public discourse.

Also contributing to the industry's failure are three other factors: the entry of a generation of managers with little or no commitment to the product and absolute devotion to the ever-increasing profitability of their television properties; the trend to globalization and the rush toward mergers and acquisitions; and finally, the popularity of broadcasting stocks in the investment community, fueled by deregulation.

Ultimately, however, most problems in our medium, public as well as commercial, come back to issues of deregulation, misregulation, and reregulation. Our position is clear. We subscribe to the trusteeship model. Broadcast licenses should carry a commitment to the public interest, articulated in policy, embedded in well-conceived legislation, and monitored consistently and helpfully. We believe that neither excessive regulation nor unbridled laissez-faire market forces serve the American public, especially with respect to news, public affairs, and children's programming. Television is far too influential to leave to chance, and far too fragile to be hobbled with misconceived and unexamined restrictions.

We are not alarmed by the six proposals emanating from the 104th Congress. What does disturb us are the conditions that prompted them. Broadcasters trying to palm off *Gilligan's Island* as educational programming, airing fewer and fewer public service announcements, and ignoring parental concern about making commonplace the tasteless exploitation of scatological, sexual, and violent material—these are trends that should raise alarms.

We have a unique opportunity before us, if we but seize it. Technology is about to drive us into a new era. The digital revolution will, at the very least, require a complete replacement of the equipment that makes television possible. But this technological advance is different from previous ones. We know the calendar: the system will not be fully operational for eight to ten years. Those years are a gift that must be used carefully and purposefully. We propose nothing less than using the period to draw up a national television policy. The discourse should take place on at least five levels: the government (both the FCC and Congress), the industry, the professional societies, the academic community, and the public.

Agenda items come to mind immediately: ensuring the future of public broadcasting; spectrum assignment issues; the role of television in the political process; television and the education of our children; a definition of the public interest for the twenty-first century.

We have been given a chance to right the wrongs of the past. The alternative—failure to confront the issues—is unacceptable. We are in peril of discovering the prescience of Edward R. Murrow's comment that without human determination to use television, our marvelous medium, for higher purposes, it is "merely wires and lights in a box."

Notes

Chapter I
What Hath Mammon Wrought?

1. Erik Barnouw, *A Tower in Babel: A History of Broadcasting in the United States*, vol. 1: *to 1933* (New York: Oxford University Press, 1966), 247–48.
2. Adam Smith (1737), *An inquiry into the nature and causes of the wealth of nations*, ed. Edwin Cannan (New York: The Modern Library, 1937), 128.
3. Philip K. Howard, *The Death of Common Sense: How Law Is Suffocating America* (New York: Random House, 1994), 45.
4. Susan J. Douglas, *Inventing American Broadcasting: 1899–1922* (Baltimore, Md.: Johns Hopkins University Press, 1987), xxi.
5. Ibid., 23.
6. Ibid., xxii.
7. James Truslow Adams "Our Dissolving Ethics" (1926), in Louise Desaulniers, ed., *Highlights from 125 Years of* The Atlantic (New York: The Atlantic Monthly, 1977), 314 (emphasis added).
8. Kevin Phillips, *The Politics of Rich and Poor: Wealth and the American Electorate in the Reagan Aftermath* (New York: Random House, 1990), 61.

Notes

9. Owen D. Young and James G. Harbord (1926), "Announcing the National Broadcasting Company, Inc.," Radio Corporation of America advertisment reproduced in Barnouw, *Tower in Babel*, 187.

10. Harry P. Davis, "The History of Broadcasting in the United States," delivered before the Graduate School of Business, Harvard University, April 21, 1928, 10.

11. Ibid.

12. Barnouw, *Tower in Babel*, 96.

13. Joy Elmer Morgan, *Harper's* (November 1931), quoted in ibid., 282.

14. Barnouw, *Tower in Babel*, 283.

15. Paul Johnson, *Modern Times: The World from the Twenties to the Eighties* (New York: Harper & Row Perennial Library, 1983), 241.

16. David Savilla Muzzey and Edgar Eugene Robinson, "United States of America, History, the Stock Market Crash," *Encyclopaedia Britannica* (Chicago: Encyclopaedia Britannica, 1958), 848–48A, s.v.

17. Barnouw, *Tower in Babel*, 219.

18. Erik Barnouw, *The Golden Web: A History of Broadcasting in the United States*, vol. 2: *1933 to 1953* (New York: Oxford University Press, 1968), 169.

19. Ibid.

20. Ibid., 173.

21. Ibid., 176.

22. Ibid., 189.

23. Sally Bedell Smith, *In All His Glory: William S. Paley the Legendary Tycoon and His Brilliant Circle* (New York: Simon and Schuster, 1990), 293.

24. Davis, "History of Broadcasting."

25. Douglas H. Ginsburg, Michael H. Botein, and Mark D. Director, *Regulation of the Electronic Mass Media: Law and Policy for Radio, Television, Cable and the New Technologies*, 2nd ed, American Casebook Series (St. Paul, Minn.: West, 1991), 443–47.

26. "Justice Department Asking FCC to Postpone ITT Merger," *New York Times*, January 2, 1967, A7.

27. Les Brown, *The Bu$iness Behind the Box* (New York: Harcourt Brace Jovanovich, 1971), 359.

28. Newton H. Minnow and Craig LeMay, *Abandoned in the Wasteland: Children, Television, and the First Amendment* (New York: Hill and Wang, 1995), 26.

29. John Gregory Dunne, Review of *Your Time Is My Time—To the End of Time: The Seduction and Conquest of a Media Empire,* by Richard M. Clurman, *New York Review of Books* 39, no. 8 (April 23, 1992): 4.

30. Charles H. King, in John E. Coon, ed., *Freedom and Responsibility in Broadcasting*, proceedings from the Conference on Freedom and Broadcasting, Northwestern University School of Law, 3 and 4 August 1961 (Evanston, Ill.: Northwestern University Press, 1961), 46.

31. James M. Poterba and Lawrence H. Summers, "A CEO Survey of U.S. Companies' Time Horizons and Hurdle Rates," *Sloan Management Review* (Fall 1995): 45–53.

Notes

32. *The Veronis Suhler & Associates Communications Industry Forecast: Historical and Projected Expenditures for 10 Industry Segments*, 9th annual ed. (New York: Veronis Suhler, 1995), 224.

33. Todd Gitlin, *Inside Prime Time* (New York: Pantheon Books, 1985), 334.

Chapter 2
The Road Not Taken

1. Quoted in Walter B. Emery, *National and International Systems of Broadcasting: Their History, Operations and Control* (East Lansing: Michigan State University Press, 1969), 82.

2. John Scupham, *Broadcasting and the Community* (London: C.A. Watts, 1967), 22–23.

3. Emery, *National and International Systems of Broadcasting*, 83.

4. Ibid.

5. Leonard Maill, "BBC Television: The End of the Beginning," in *BBC Television: Fifty Years* (New York: The Museum of Broadcasting, 1986), 9.

6. John Reith, quoted in Asa Briggs, *The Birth of Broadcasting: United Kingdom*, vol. 2 (Oxford: Oxford University Press, 1985), 55.

7. Alasdair Milne, "A Word from the Director General," in *BBC Television*, 37.

8. Maill, *BBC Television*, 15.

9. John Reith (1949), quoted in Sydney W. Head, *World Broadcasting Systems: A Comparative Analysis* (Belmont, Calif.: Wadsworth, 1985), 298.

10. Peter Black, in "The BBC: A Critic's View," in *BBC Television*, 28.

11. Reith in *Report of the Broadcasting Committee 1949*, Cmnd 8117, Appendix H, 363, HHMS, 1951, quoted in Scupham, *Broadcasting and the Community*, 14.

12. Lord John Reith, "The future of British Broadcasting," *Manchester Guardian*, 29 December 1960, quoted in Scupham, *Broadcasting and the Community*, 15.

13. *Report of the Broadcasting Committee 1960*, quoted in Emery, *National and International Systems of Broadcasting*, 92.

14. Ien Ang, *Desperately Seeking the Audience* (London: Routledge, 1991), 108.

15. Sir Frederick Ogilvy (1946), letter to the *London Times*, quoted in Head, *World Broadcasting Systems*, 91.

16. Anthony Smith, *British Broadcasting* (1974), quoted in Head, *World Broadcasting Systems*, 91.

17. Ang, *Desperately Seeking the Audience*, 115.

18. Briggs, *The Birth of Broadcasting*, 324.

19. T. Burns, *The BBC: Public Institution and Private World* (London: Macmillan, 1977), 25.

20. Black, in "The BBC: A Critic's View," 31.

21. *Report of the Committee on Broadcasting 1960* (June 1962), quoted in Emery, *National and International Systems of Broadcasting*, 91.

Notes

22. Ibid.
23. Eileen Opatut, quoted in George Dessart, "Of Tastes and Times: Some Challenging Reflections on Television's Elastic Standards and Astounding Practices," *Television Quarterly* 26, no. 2 (November 1992).
24. *Report of the Committee on Broadcasting 1960* (June 1962), 34–35.
25. Ibid.
26. Emery, *National and International Systems of Broadcasting*, 89ff.
27. Ibid.
28. Independent Broadcasting Authority (1992), quoted in Head, *World Broadcasting Systems*, 201.
29. Martin Jackson, "Entertaining Auntie," in *BBC Television*, 18.
30. *BBC Annual Report and Accounts 1991–92 and Guide to the BBC* (London: British Broadcasting Corporation, 1992).
31. Black, "The BBC: A Critic's View," 32.
32. Alasdair Milne, in *BBC Television*, 37.
33. Great Britain (1977): 235, quoted in Head, *World Broadcasting Systems*, 82.
34. Milne, in *BBC Television*, 37.
35. *BBC Annual Report and Accounts 1991–92 and Guide to the BBC*, 57.
36. Scupham, *Broadcasting and the Community*.
37. *BBC Annual Report and Accounts 1994–95 and Guide to the BBC* (London: British Broadcasting Corporation, 1995).
38. Ibid.

Chapter 3
Eyeballs for Sale

1. Sydney W. Head, *Broadcasting in America: A Survey of Television and Radio* (Boston: Houghton Mifflin, 1956), 362.
2. Ibid., 116.
3. Erik Barnouw, *A Tower in Babel: A History of Broadcasting in the United States*, vol. 1: *to 1933* (New York: Oxford University Press, 1966), 111.
4. Ibid., 94.
5. *Radio Broadcast* (May 1922), quoted in Barnouw, *Tower in Babel*, 95.
6. Thomas A. DeLong, *The Mighty Music Box: The Golden Age of Musical Radio* (Los Angeles: Amber Crest, 1980), 41; Barnouw, *Tower in Babel*, 214.
7. Sidney W. Head, Christopher H. Sterling, and Lemuel B. Schofield, *Broadcasting in America: A Survey of Electronic Media*, 7th ed. (Boston: Houghton Mifflin, 1994), 41.
8. Ronald Coase, "The Federal Communications Commission," *Journal of Law and Economics* 2, no. 1 (1959), in Douglas H. Ginsberg, Michael H. Botein, and Mark D. Director, *Regulation of the Electronic Mass Media: Law and Policy for Radio, Television, Cable and the New New Technologies*, 2nd ed., American Casebook Series (St. Paul, Minn.: West, 1991), 31.

9. Ibid., 25.
10. *Federal Reporter* (1946): 628, in Head, Sterling, and Schofield, *Broadcasting in America*, 463.
11. *Federal Reporter* (1975): 536, in ibid., 462.
12. Erik Barnouw, *The Sponsor: Notes on a Modern Potentate* (New York: Oxford University Press, 1978), 23.
13. Barnouw, *Tower in Babel*, 242.
14. Ibid., 158–59.
15. Barnouw, *The Sponsor*, 24.
16. Ibid., 25.
17. Eulogy for the late Betty Furness, NBC Memorial, 1997.
18. Archibald Crossley, quoted in Ien Ang, *Desperately Seeking the Audience* (London: Routledge, 1991), 55.
19. John A. Schneider, then President, CBS Broadcast Group, personal communication, February 1977.
20. Quoted in *Broadcasting & Cable*, 20 February 1995, 18.

Chapter 4
The Scarcity of Abundance

1. Rich Brown, "Original Cable Programming '95," *Broadcasting & Cable,* 20 February 1995, 22.
2. Ibid., 40.
3. Raymond Timothy, personal communication, May 1987, September 1997.
4. Don Hewitt, remarks to the CBS Affiliates Meeting, Century Plaza Hotel, Los Angeles, May 1987; Ken Auletta, *Three Blind Mice: How the TV Networks Lost Their Way* (New York: Random House, 1991), 244.
5. Howard Stringer, remarks to the CBS Affiliates Meeting, May 1988.
6. Ibid.

Chapter 5
Where the Action Is

1. Martin Mayer, *Making News* (Garden City, N.Y.: Doubleday, 1987), 15.
2. Julius K. Hunter and Lynne S. Gross, *Broadcast News: The Inside Out* (St. Louis, Mo.: C. V. Mosby, 1980), 125.
3. Mayer, *Making News*, 19.
4. Philip McHugh, "The Role of the Consultant," address to the International Radio and Television Society Fifth Annual Faculty-Industry Seminar, Tarrytown Conference Center, Tarrytown, New York, 12 November 1975, in George Dessart, ed., *Television in the Real World: A Case Study in Broadcast Management* (New York: Hastings House, 1978).

5. Ibid., 104*n*6.

6. Federal Communications Commission Statement of Program Service, Form FCC 303-C (p. 2), in National Association of Broadcasters, *NAB Legal Guide to FCC Broadcast Regulations* (Washington, D.C.: National Association of Broadcasters, 1984), App. 1B, 1.

7. Mitchell Stephens, *A History of News: From the Drum to the Satellite* (New York: Penguin, 1988), 9.

8. William Peter Hamilton, Letter to the Editor, *Wall Street Journal,* 31 January 1994, A3.

9. Herb Altman, quoted in Edwin Diamond, *Good News, Bad News* (Cambridge, Mass.: MIT Press, 1980), 125.

10. Dan Rather, "Courage, Fear and the Television Newsroom," *Television Quarterly* 27, no. 1 (1994): 91.

11. Personal communication, June 1997.

12. Arthur Unger, "'Uncle Walter' and 'The Information Crisis'," *Television Quarterly* 25, no. 1 (1990): 32.

13. "There's a Heap of Persuasion Between Networks and Longer News: If It Weren't for the Honor, the Affiliates Would Rather Walk," *Broadcasting,* 3 May 1976, 28; Pierce, quoted in Maureen Christopher, "Walters' Plea for Expanded Net News Gets Icy Greeting from ABC Affiliates," *Ad Age,* 31 May 1976, 2A.

Chapter 6
Kinderfeindlichkeit

1. Richard K. Doan (1970), "Kindergarten May Never Be the Same Again," reprinted in *TV Guide: The First 25 Years,* comp. and ed. Jay S. Harris, in association with the eds. of *TV Guide* (New York: Simon and Schuster, 1978), 172–73.

2. Ibid.

3. Martin Mayer, *About Television* (New York: Harper & Row, 1972), 133.

4. Thomas S. Rogers, "How Can Television Serve the Public Interest?" in Stuart Oskamp, ed., *Television as a Social Issue: The Eighth Applied Social Psychology Annual,* sponsored by the Society for Psychological Study of Social Issues (SPSSI) (Newbury Park, Calif.: Sage, 1988), 80.

5. Ellen Wartella, "The Public Context of Debates About Television and Children," in Oskamp, ed., *Television as a Social Issue,* 62.

6. George Dessart, "Of Tastes and Times: Some Challenging Reflections on Television's Elastic Standards and Astounding Practices," *Television Quarterly* 26, no. 2 (November 1992).

7. Ibid.

8. Ellen Wartella and B. Reeves, "Historical Trends in Research on Children and the Media: 1900–1960," *Journal of Communication* 35 (1985): 118–33.

Notes

9. Harry Castleman and Walter J. Podrzik, *Watching Television: Four Decades of American Television* (New York: McGraw-Hill, 1982), 44.

10. Peggy Charen, interview with George Dessart, Boston, June 1995.

11. Joan Ganz Cooney, interview with George Dessart, June 1995.

12. Cy Schneider, *Children's Television* (Lincolnwood, Ill.: NTC Business Books, 1989), 22.

13. Ibid., 26.

14. Ibid., 28.

15. Peggy Charren, interview with George Dessart, Boston, June 1995.

16. Ibid.

17. Evelyn Kaye, *The Family Guide to Children's Television: What to Watch, What to Miss, What to Change and How to Do It,* under the guidance of Action for Children's Television with the cooperation of the American Academy of Pediatrics (New York: Pantheon, 1974), 122.

18. National Association of Broadcasters Code Authority, *Broadcast Self-Regulation: Working Manual of the National Association of Broadcasters Code Authority*, 2nd ed. (Washington: National Association of Broadcasters, 1977), Television Code, Standard X–4, Presentation of Advertising.

19. Ibid., Standards for Non-Program Material.

20. Peggy Charren, interview with George Dessart, Boston, June 1995.

21. Ibid.

22. William Strauss and Neil Howe, *Generations: The History of America's Future, 1584 to 2069* (New York: William Morrow, 1991), 98.

23. Ibid., 97.

24. Ibid.

25. Dean Burch, address to the International Radio and Television Society, Waldorf Astoria Hotel, New York, 16 September 1970.

26. National Association of Broadcasters Code Authority, *Broadcast Self-Regulation* (1984), II–29.

27. Kaye, *The Family Guide to Children's Television*, 73–74.

28. Schneider, *Children's Television*, 5.

29. Jerome S. Bruner, *Toward a Theory of Instruction* (New York: W. W. Norton, 1966), 113.

30. John Holt, *How Children Learn* (New York: Pitman, 1967), 8.

31. Kaye, *The Family Guide to Children's Television*, 15.

32. Peggy Charren, interview with George Dessart, Boston, June 1995.

33. Richard M. Polsky, *Getting to Sesame Street: Origins of the Children's Television Workshop* (New York: Praeger, 1974), 95.

34. Ibid., 93.

35. Ibid., 95.

36. Ibid., 31.

37. Ibid., 3.

38. Joan Ganz Cooney, interview with George Dessart, June 1995.

39. Dessart, "Of Tastes and Times."

Notes

40. George Heinemann, Vice President for Children's Programs, NBC, personal communication.

41. Peggy Charren, interview with George Dessart, Boston, June 1995.

Chapter 7
World Television

1. International Council Executive Committee meeting held on the 52nd floor of the GE Building, March 1994.

2. Richard Parker, *Mixed Signals: The Prospects for Global Television News.* A Twentieth Century Fund Report (New York: The Twentieth Century Fund Press, 1995), 38.

3. R. I. Davis, "Rupert the First," *World Business* (January 1995): 22–27.

4. *Clyne Committee Report of 1979,* quoted in John M. Eger, "Information: Predicates for International Regulation," in George Gerbner and Marsha Siefert, eds., *World Communications: A Handbook* (New York: Longman, 1984), 11.

5. Sydney W. Head, *World Broadcasting Systems: A Comparative Analysis* (Belmont, Calif.: Wadsworth, 1985), 117.

6. Davis, "Rupert the First," 23; William Shawcross, *Murdoch* (New York: Simon & Schuster, 1992), 349.

7. Parker, *Mixed Signals,* 38.

8. Julian Mounter, Presentation to the International Council of the National Academy of Television Arts and Sciences, Hong Kong, 1992.

9. Laurence Zuckerman, "Satellite TV Makes Broadcasting Waves," *International Herald Tribune,* 10 December 1992, unpaginated reprint.

10. Jonathan Karp, "Marketing: Medium and Message," *Far Eastern Economic Review,* 25 February 1993, unpaginated reprint.

11. Ibid.

12. Zuckerman, "Satellite TV Makes Broadcasting Waves."

13. Charles P. Wallace, "Frontier India: 'Dish Wallas' Plug India into the World," *Los Angeles Times,* 20 October 1992, H–2.

14. Pratap Anita/New Delhi, "Challenge or Threat?" *Time,* 21 October 1991, 51.

15. Zuckerman, "Satellite TV Makes Broadcasting Waves."

16. Karp, "Marketing," p. 2 of reprint.

17. Zuckerman, "Satellite TV Makes Broadcasting Waves."

18. Simon Twiston Davies, "Wishing on a STAR," *Asia Inc.,* November 1996, 40.

19. Ibid.

20. Geraldine Fabrikant, "Murdoch Bets Heavily on Global Vision: Despite the Risks, News Corp. Pursues an Aggressive Expansion," *New York Times,* 29 July 1996, D1, D8.

21. Jesse Wong, "Murdoch's Sudden Zeal for China May Not Be Requited in Beijing," *Asian Wall Street Journal,* 13 September 1993, 1.

22. Janine Stein, "Twelve to Watch in 1996: STAR TV's Gary Davey," *Electronic Media,* 22 January 1996, 150.

23. Felipe Rodriguez, "TeveGlobo at 30: 'Just the First Step'," *ALMANAC: The Annual of the International Council of NATAS for 1995/1996* (New York: International Council, 1995), 45.

24. Zuckerman, "Satellite TV Makes Broadcasting Waves."

25. Sandra Burton, "A STAR Is Born Over Asia," *Time,* 21 October 1991, 50.

26. Mitsuko Shimomura, "The 25-Year-Old from Hong Kong Who Is Making the Asian Village a Reality: From the News Lounge Column," *Asahi Shimbun,* 24 October 1992, unpaginated special media report to STAR TV.

Chapter 8
The Underfunded Afterthought

1. Erik Barnouw, *A Tower in Babel: A History of Broadcasting in the United States,* vol. 1: *to 1933* (New York: Oxford University Press, 1966), 281.

2. Ibid., 96.

3. Erik Barnouw, *The Golden Web: A History of Broadcasting in the United States,* vol. 2: *1933 to 1953* (New York: Oxford University Press, 1968), 24.

4. Ibid., 25.

5. Ibid., 294.

6. Erik Barnouw, *The Image Empire: A History of Broadcasting in the United States,* vol. 3: *from 1953* (New York: Oxford University Press, 1970), 72.

7. Ibid., 73.

8. Erwin G. Krasnow, Lawrence D. Longley, and Herbert A. Terry, *The Politics of Regulation,* 3rd ed. (New York: St. Martin's Press, 1982), 88.

9. *Public Television: A Program for Action,* The Report and Recommendations of the Carnegie Commission on Educational Television (New York: Harper & Row, 1967), viii.

10. "Carnegie Trusts: Carnegie Corporation of New York," *Encyclopaedia Britannica* (1958 ed.), s.v.

11. *Public Television,* 3.

12. Ibid., 4.

13. Ibid.

14. Ibid., 72.

15. Richard Somerset-Ward, "Public Television: The Ballpark's Changing," background paper in *Quality Time?* The Report of the Twentieth Century Fund Task Force on Public Television (New York: The Twentieth Century Fund Press, 1993), 77.

16. Ibid., 84.

17. James Day, *The Vanishing Dream: The Inside Story of Public Television* (Berkeley: University of California Press, 1995), 5.

18. Sidney W. Head, Christopher H. Sterling, and Lemuel B. Schofield, *Broadcasting in America: A Survey of Electronic Media,* 7th ed. (Boston: Houghton Mifflin, 1994), 268.

Notes

19. Ibid.

20. Ibid., 269.

21. Somerset-Ward, "Public Television," 86.

22. *A Public Trust: The Report of the Carnegie Commission on the Future of Public Broadcasting*, published by arrangement with the Carnegie Corporation of New York (New York: Bantam Books, 1979), 9–10.

23. Ibid., 11.

24. Ibid., 12.

25. Ibid., 13.

26. Ibid., 14–15.

27. Day, *The Vanishing Dream*, 5.

28. *A Public Trust*, 11.

29. Somerset-Ward, "Public Television," 77.

30. Ibid., 76.

31. Day, *The Vanishing Dream*, 54.

32. Patricia Jone and Larry Kahaner, *Say It and Live It: The 50 Corporate Mission Statements That Hit the Mark* (New York: Doubleday, 1995), 36, 33.

33. William F. Fore, "Public Media, Public Discussion: In Defense of PBS," *Christian Century*, 5–12 July 1995, 669.

34. Ibid.

Chapter 9
The Road Ahead

1. "What's Going On?" *Broadcasting & Cable*, 18 September 1995.

2. *Broadcasting & Cable*, 13 January 1997.

3. Ibid., 4.

4. Kevin Phillips, *The Politics of Rich and Poor: Wealth and the American Electorate in the Reagan Aftermath* (New York: Random House, 1990), 34.

5. Steve McClenna, "Sinclair's $2.3B Powerhouse," *Broadcasting & Cable*, 15 April 1996, 8.

6. Ibid.

7. Ben Bagdikian, *The Media Monopoly*, 3d ed. (Boston: Beacon Press, 1993), x.

8. "Getting Crowded Up There," editorial, *Broadcasting & Cable*, 29 January 1996.

9. "Dick Wiley: Delivering on Digital," interview in *Broadcasting & Cable*, 4 December 1995, 32.

10. Ibid., 40.

11. Ibid., 32.

12. Editorial, *Broadcasting & Cable*, 12 May 1997.

Bibliography

Adib, Jorge. "TeveGlobo Goes Global." *ALMANAC: The Annual of the International Council of the National Academy of Television Arts and Sciences, 1993/1994.* New York: International Council, 1993.

Adler, Richard P., Gerald S. Lesser, Laurene Krasny Meringoff, Thomas S. Robertson, John R. Rossiter, and Scott Ward, with Bernard Z. Friedlander, Leslie Isler, Ronald J. Faber, and David B. Pillemer. *The Effects of Television Advertising on Children: Review and Recommendations.* Lexington, Mass.: Lexington Books, 1980.

Ang, Ien. *Desperately Seeking the Audience.* London: Routledge, 1991.

Auleta, Ken. *Three Blind Mice: How the TV Networks Lost Their Way.* New York: Random House, 1991.

Baker, William F. "Public TV Irreplaceable: Cable Can't Fill Void; I Know—I Worked in Cable." *USA Today,* November 21, 1995.

Balanoff, Neal. "New Dimensions in Instructional Media." In *The New Media and Education,* edited by Peter H. Rossi and Bruce J. Biddle. Garden City, N.Y.: Anchor Books, 1967.

Balfour, Frederik. "Rock Around the Clock: MTV's 24-Hour Programming Targets the Young." *Far Eastern Economic Review,* February 25, 1993. Unpaginated reprint.

Bibliography

Barnouw, Erik. *A Tower in Babel: A History of Broadcasting in the United States.* Vol. 1. *–to 1933.* New York: Oxford University Press, 1966.

———. *The Golden Web: A History of Broadcasting in the United States.* Vol. 2. *1933–1953.* New York: Oxford University Press, 1968.

———. *The Image Empire: A History of Broadcasting in the United States.* Vol. 3. *–from 1953.* New York: Oxford University Press, 1970.

———. *The Sponsor: Notes on a Modern Potentate.* New York: Oxford University Press, 1978.

Barone, Michaela, and Grant Ujifusa. *The Almanac of American Politics 1986.* Washington, D.C.: National Journal, 1985.

Barwise, Patrick, and Andrew Ehrenberg. *Television and Its Audience.* Sage Communications in Society series. London: Sage, 1988.

BBC Annual Report and Accounts 1991–92 and Guide to the BBC. London: British Broadcasting Corporation, 1992.

BBC Handbook 1977. London: British Broadcasting Corporation, 1976.

BBC Television: Fifty Years. New York: The Museum of Broadcasting, 1987.

Berry, Gordon L., and Joy Keiko Asamen. *Children & Television: Images in a Changing Sociocultural World.* Newbury Park, Calif.: Sage, 1993.

Besen, Stanley M., Thomas G. Krattenmaker, A. Richard Metzger, Jr., and John W. Woodbury. *Misregulating Television: Network Domination and the FCC.* Chicago: University of Chicago Press, 1984.

Blessington, John P. *Let My Children Work!* Garden City, N.Y.: Anchor Press/Doubleday, 1974.

Bluestone, Charles. "Life, Death and 'Nature' in Childrens' TV." In *TV as Art: Some Essays in Criticism.* Papers originally commissioned by the Television Information Office for the National Council of Teachers of English Television Festival, edited by Patrick D. Hazard. Champaign, Ill.: National Council of Teachers of English, 1966.

Boyer, Peter J. *Who Killed CBS?: The Undoing of America's Number One News Network.* New York: Random House, 1988.

Broadcasting, 1989–March 1, 1993.

Broadcasting. "Fifty Years of *Broadcasting.*" October 12, 1981.

Broadcasting & Cable: The Newsweekly of Television and Radio. "Broadcasting & Cable Top 25 Media Groups." July 7, 1997.

Broadcasting & Cable: The Newsweekly of Television and Radio, March 1, 1993–.

Broadcasting/Cable Yearbook. Washington, D.C.: Broadcasting Publications, 1989.

Brooks, Tim, and Earle Marsh. *The Complete Directory to Prime Time Network TV Shows 1946–Present.* 5th ed. New York: Ballantine Books, 1992.

Brown, Les. *Television: The Bu$iness Behind the Box.* New York: Harcourt Brace Jovanovich, 1971.

Brown, Rich. "Original Cable Programming: From Series to Movies, Cable Programming Comes of Age." *Broadcasting & Cable,* February 20, 1995, 22–50.

Bruner, Jerome S. *Toward a Theory of Instruction.* New York: W. W. Norton, 1966.

Bibliography

Burton, Sandra. "A STAR Is Born Over Asia." *Time,* October 21, 1991, 50.

Carnegie Commission on Educational Television. *Public Television: A Program for Action.* New York: Harper & Row, 1967.

Carnegie Commission on the Future of Public Television. *A Public Trust: The Report of the Carnegie Commission on the Future of Public Broadcasting.* Published by arrangement with the Carnegie Corporation of New York. New York: Bantam, 1979.

Castleman, Harry, and Walter J. Podrazik. *Watching: Four Decades of American Television.* New York: McGraw-Hill, 1982.

Chester, Giraud, Garnet R. Garrison, and Edgar E. Willis. *Television and Radio.* 4th ed. Englewood Cliffs, NJ: Prentice-Hall, 1971.

Coase, Ronald H. "The Federal Communications Commission." *Journal of Law & Economics* 1 (1959).

Coles, Robert. *The Moral Life of Children.* Boston: Houghton Mifflin, 1986.

Davis, Harry P. "The History of Broadcasting in the United States." Delivered before the Graduate School of Business, Harvard University, April 21, 1928.

Davis, R. I. "Rupert the First." *World Business,* January 1995, 22–27.

Day, James. *The Vanishing Vision: The Inside Story of Public Television.* Berkeley: University of California Press, 1995.

DeLong, Thomas A. *The Mighty Music Box: The Golden Age of Musical Radio.* Los Angeles: Amber Crest, 1980.

Dessart, George. "Of Tastes and Times: Some Challenging Reflections on Television's Elastic Standards and Astounding Practices." *Television Quarterly* 26, no. 2 (November 1992).

———. *Television in the Real World: A Case Study Course in Broadcast Management.* New York: Hastings House, 1978.

———. "A Twenty-one Inch Medium for Thirty-six Inch Receivers." In *TV as Art: Some Essays in Criticism.* Papers Originally Commissioned by the Television Information Office for the National Council of Teachers of English Television Festival, edited by Patrick D. Hazard. Champaign, Ill.: National Council of Teachers of English, 1966.

Dikkenberg, John. "A Star Is Born." *Asia Magazine,* September 6–8, 1991.

Doan, Richard K. "Kindergarten May Never Be the Same Again." (1970.) Reprinted in *TV Guide: The First 25 Years,* compiled and edited by Jay S. Harris, in association with the editors of TV Guide. New York: Simon and Schuster, 1978.

Doubleday, Catherine N., and Kristin L. Droege. "Cognitive Developmental Influences on Childrens' Understanding of Television." In *Children & Television: Images in a Changing Sociocultural World,* edited by Gordon L. Berry and Joy Keiko Asamen. Newbury Park, Calif.: Sage, 1993.

Douglas, Susan J. *Inventing American Broadcasting: 1899–1922.* Baltimore: Johns Hopkins University Press, 1987.

Emery, Walter B. *Broadcasting and Government: Responsibilities and Regulations.* East Lansing: Michigan State University Press, 1971.

Bibliography

————. *National and International Systems of Broadcasting: Their History, Operations and Control.* East Lansing: Michigan State University Press, 1969.

Fabrikant, Geraldine. "Murdoch Bets Heavily on Global Vision: Despite the Risks, News Corp. Pursues an Aggressive Expansion." *New York Times*, July 29, 1996, D1, D8.

Fortner, Robert S. *International Communication:History, Conflict and Control of the Global Metropolis.* Belmont, Calif.: Wadsworth, 1993.

Friendly, Fred W. *The Good Guys, the Bad Guys, and the First Amendment: Free Speech vs. Fairness in Broadcasting.* New York: Vintage Books, 1977.

————. *Due to Circumstances Beyond Our Control.* New York: Random House, 1967.

Garry, Ralph, F. B. Rainsberry, and Charles Winick. (Eds.). *For the Young Viewer: Television for Children . . . at the Local Level.* New York: McGraw-Hill, 1962.

Gates, Gary Paul. *Air Time: The Inside Story of CBS News.* New York: Harper & Row, 1978.

Ginsburg, Douglas H., Michael H. Botein, and Mark D. Director. *Regulation of the Electronic Mass Media: Law and Policy for Radio, Television, Cable and the New Technologies.* 2d ed. American Casebook Series. St. Paul, Minn.: West, 1991.

Goldenson, Leonard, with Marvin J. Wolf. *Beating the Odds: The Untold Story Behind the Rise of ABC: the Stars, Struggling, and Egos that Transformed Network Television.* New York: Scribners, 1991.

Green, Maury. *Television News: Anatomy and Process.* Belmont, Calif.: Wadsworth, 1969.

Greene, Sir Hugh. *The Future of Broadcasting in Britain.* The Granada Guildhall Lecture 1972. London: Hart-Davis, MacGibbon, 1972.

Gunter, Barrie. "The U.K.: Measured Expansion on a Variety of Fronts." In *Audience Responses to Media Diversity: Coping with Plenty*, edited by Lee B. Becker and Klaus Schoenbach. Hillsdale, N.J.: Lawrence Erlbaum Associates, 1989.

Halberstam, David. *The Powers That Be.* New York: Alfred A. Knopf, 1979.

Hamilton, William Peter. Letter to the Editor. *Wall Street Journal*, January 31, 1994.

Harris, Jay A. (Ed.). *TV Guide: The First 25 Years.* New York: Simon and Schuster, 1978.

Hazard, Patrick D. (Ed.). *TV as Art: Some Essays in Criticism.* Papers originally commissioned by the Television Information Office for the National Council of Teachers of English Television Festival. Champaign, Ill.: National Council of Teachers of English, 1966.

Hazell, Ann. "European Television: The Next Decade." *ALMANAC: The Annual of the International Council of the National Academy of Television Arts and Sciences.* New York: International Council, 1989.

Head, Sydney W., Christopher H. Sterling, and Lemuel B. Schofield. *Broadcasting in America: A Survey of Electronic Media.* 7th ed. Boston: Houghton Mifflin, 1994.

Bibliography

Head, Sydney W. *World Broadcasting Systems: A Comparative Analysis.* Belmont, Calif.: Wadsworth, 1985.

———. *Broadcasting in America: A Survey of Electronic Media.* Boston: Houghton Mifflin, 1956.

Himmelstein, Hal. *Television Myth and the American Mind.* 2d ed. Westport, Conn.: Praeger, 1994.

Holt, John. *How Children Learn.* New York: Pitman, 1967.

Howard, Philip K. *The Death of Common Sense: How Law Is Suffocating America.* New York: Random House, 1994.

Hoynes, William. *Public Television for Sale: Media, the Market, and the Public Sphere.* Boulder, Colo.: Westview, 1994.

Jankowski, Gene F., and David C. Fuchs. *Television Today and Tomorrow: It Won't Be What You Think.* New York: Oxford University Press, 1995.

Johnson, Paul. *Modern Times: The World from the Twenties to the Eighties.* New York: Harper & Row/Perennial Library, 1983.

Joyce, Ed. *Prime Times, Bad Times.* New York: Doubleday, 1988.

Karp, Jonathon. "Medium and Message." *Far Eastern Economic Review*, February 25, 1993. Unpaginated reprint of cover story.

Kaye, Evelyn. *The Family Guide to Children's Television: What to Watch, What to Miss, What to Change, and How to Do It.* Under the guidance of Action for Children's Television with the cooperation of the American Academy of Pediatrics. New York: Pantheon Books, 1974.

Kraar, Louis. "A Billionaire's Global Strategy." *Fortune*, June 29, 1992. Unpaginated reprint of cover story.

Krasnow, Erwin G., Lawrence D. Logley, and Herbert A. Terry. *The Politics of Broadcast Regulation.* New York: St. Martin's Press, 1982.

Lesser, Gerald S. *Children and Television: Lessons from Sesame Street.* New York: Vintage Books, 1974.

MacNeil, Robert. *The People Machine: The Influence of Television on American Politics.* New York: Harper & Row, 1968.

Markel, Lester. *What You Don't Know Can Hurt You: A Study of Public Opinion and Public Emotion.* 2d ed. New York: Quadrangle/New York Times Book Co., 1973.

Mattelart, Armand. *Advertising International: The Privatisation of Public Space.* Translated by Michael Chanan. New York: Routledge, 1992.

Mayer, Martin. *Making News.* Garden City, N.Y.: Doubleday, 1987.

———. *About Television.* New York: Harper & Row, 1972.

Mercado, Edward. "SABADO GIGANTE: Pan-American Solidarity Every (Giant) Saturday Night." *ALMANAC: The Annual of the International Council of the National Academy of Television Arts and Sciences, 1993/1994.* New York: International Council, 1993.

Minow, Newton N., and Craig L. LeMay. *Abandoned in the Wasteland: Children, Television, and the First Amendment.* New York: Hill and Wang, 1995.

Bibliography

Moss, Nicholas. *This Is BBC Television.* London: BBC Network Television, 1994.

————. *BBC TV Presents: A Fiftieth Anniversary Celebration.* London: BBC Data Publications, 1986.

National Association of Broadcasters. *Legal Guide to FCC Broadcast Regulations.* 2d ed. Washington, D.C.: National Association of Broadcasters, 1984.

————. *Legal Guide to FCC Rules, Regulations, and Policies.* Washington, D.C.: National Association of Broadcasters, 1977.

National Association of Broadcasters Code Authority. *Broadcast Self-Regulation: Working Manual of the National Association of Broadcasters.* 2d ed. Washington, D.C.: NAB Code Authority, 1977.

————. *The Television Code.* 22d ed. Washington, D.C.: NAB Code Authority, July 1981.

Noll, Roger G., Merton J. Peck, and John J. McGowan. *Economics of Television Regulation.* Studies in the Regulation of Economic Activity. Washington, D.C.: The Brookings Institution, 1973.

Over 40,000 Hours of Programming a Year. Hong Kong: STAR TV, 1992.

Owen, Bruce M., and Steven S. Wildman. *Video Economics.* Cambridge, Mass.: Harvard University Press, 1992.

Paley, William S. *As It Happened: A Memoir.* Garden City, N.Y.: Doubleday, 1979.

Paper, Lewis J. *Empire: William S. Paley and the Making of CBS.* New York: St. Martin's Press, 1987.

Parker, Richard. *Mixed Signals: The Prospects for Global Television News.* A Twentieth Century Fund Report. New York: Twentieth Century Fund Press, 1995.

Pember, Don R. *Mass Media Law.* 6th ed. Dubuque: Wm. C. Brown, 1993.

Personal, Parental and Peer-Group Value Conflicts as Catalysts of Complex Educational and Psychological Issues Confronting Children in a Contemporary Society or . . . : Fat Albert and the Cosby Kids. New York: CBS, 1972.

Phillips, Kevin. *The Politics of Rich and Poor: Wealth and the American Electorate in the Reagan Aftermath.* New York: Random House, 1990.

Polsky, Richard M. *Getting to Sesame Street: Origins of the Children's Television Workshop.* New York: Praeger, 1974.

Postman, Neil. *The Disappearance of Childhood.* New York: Vintage Books, 1982.

Postman, Neil, and the Committee on the Study of Television of the National Council of Teachers of English. *Television and the Teaching of English.* New York: Appleton-Century-Crofts, 1961.

Pratap, Anita. "Challenge or Threat?" *Time,* October 21, 1991, 51.

Public Broadcasting System. *Setting the Record Straight: The Facts About Public Television.* Alexandria, Va.: Public Broadcasting System, 1995.

Public Service Broadcasters Around the World: British Broadcasting Corporation. A McKinsey Report for the BBC, April 1993. London: McKinsey, 1993.

Rembar, Charles. *The End of Obscenity: The Trials of Lady Chatterley, Tropic of Cancer, & Fanny Hill.* New York: Random House, 1968.

Bibliography

Rodriguez, Felipe. "TeveGlobo at 30: 'Just the First Step.'" *ALMANAC: The Annual of the International Council of the National Academy of Television Arts and Sciences, 1995/1996.* New York: International Council, 1995.

Rogers, Thomas S. "How Can Television Serve the Public Interest?" in *Television as a Social Issue: The Eighth Applied Social Psychology Annual,* edited by Stuart Oskamp. Sponsored by the Society for Psychological Study of Social Issues (SPSSI). Newbury Park, Calif.: Sage, 1988.

Rohrer, Larry. "Miami: The Hollywood of Latin America." *New York Times,* August 18, 1996, sec. 2, 1–3.

Routt, Edd, James B. McGrath, and Frederic A. Weiss. *The Radio Format Conundrum.* New York: Hastings House, 1978.

Schneider, Cy. *Children's Television.* Lincolnwood, Ill.: NTC Business Books, 1989.

Schneider, Cynthia, and Brian Wallis. (Eds.). *Global Television. wedge,* no. 9/10. Special issue of *wedge* made possible in part by a grant from the New York State Council on the Arts. New York: wedge Press and Cambridge, Mass.: MIT Press, 1988.

Schumach, Murray. *The Face on the Cutting Room Floor: The Story of Movie and Television Censorship.* New York: Da Capo Press, 1975.

Schwartz, Deanna, and Pearl Smith. *National Audience Handbook: 1993–1994.* Alexandria, Va.: PBS Research, 1995.

Scupham, John. *Broadcasting and the Community.* London: C. A. Watts, 1967.

Sennett, Ted. *The Old-Time Radio Book.* New York: Pyramid Books, 1976.

Shanks, Bob. *The Cool Fire.* New York: W. W. Norton, 1976.

Shawcross, William. *Murdoch.* A Touchstone Book. New York: Simon and Schuster, 1992.

Sherman, Barry L. *Telecommunications Management: The Broadcast and Cable Industries.* New York: McGraw-Hill, 1987.

Singer, Dorothy G., and Tracey A. Revenson. *A Piaget Primer: How a Child Thinks.* New York: Plume, 1978.

Smith, Adam. (1737.) *An inquiry into the nature and causes of the wealth of nations,* edited by Edwin Cannan. New York: Modern Library, 1937.

Smith, Sally Bedell. *In All His Glory: The Life of William S. Paley: The Legendary Tycoon and His Brilliant Circle.* New York: Simon and Schuster, 1990.

Somerset-Ward, Richard. "Public Television: The Ballpark's Changing." A Background Paper in *Quality Time?: The Report of the Twentieth Century Fund Task Force on Public Television.* New York: Twentieth Century Fund Press, 1993.

Stanley, Robert H. (Ed.). *The Broadcast Industry: An Examination of Major Issues.* New York: Hastings House, 1975.

"STAR TV Reports Reaching 11 Million Households." News release, February 8, 1993. Hong Kong: STAR TV.

Stein, Janine. "Twelve to Watch in 1996: STAR TV's Gary Davey." *Electronic Media,* January 22, 1996, 50.

Bibliography

Steinberg, Cobbett. *TV Facts*. New York: Facts on File, 1980.

Stephens, Mitchell. *A History of News: From the Drum to the Satellite*. New York: Penguin, 1988.

Strauss, William, and Neil Howe. *Generations: The History of America's Future, 1584 to 2069*. New York: William Morrow, 1991.

The Power to Choose. Hong Kong: STAR TV, n.d.

"The Twentieth Annual International Emmy Awards Gala: The 1992 Directorate Award for Personal Executive Achievement." *ALMANAC: The Annual of the International Council of the National Academy of Television Arts and Sciences, 1992–1993*. New York: International Council, 1992.

The Veronis Suhler & Associates Communications Industry Forecast: Historical and Projected Forecasts for 9 Industry Segments. 9th annual ed. New York: Veronis Suhler, 1995.

The Veronis Suhler & Associates Communications Report: Five-Year Historical Report of 349 Public Companies. 11th annual ed. New York: Veronis Suhler, 1993.

The Veronis Suhler & Associates Communications Report: Five-Year Historical Report of 349 Public Companies. 13th annual ed. New York: Veronis Suhler, 1995.

Turner Broadcasting System, Inc. *History of Turner Broadcasting System, Inc.* Atlanta, Ga.: Turner Broadcasting System, 1994.

Twentieth Century Fund Task Force on Public Television. *Quality Time?: The Report of the Twentieth Century Fund Task Force on Public Television*. New York: Twentieth Century Fund Press, 1993.

Udell, Jon G. (and contributing authors). *The Economics of the American Newspaper*. Publication sponsored by the American Newspaper Publishers Association Foundation, Communications Arts Books. New York: Hastings House, 1978.

Unger, Arthur. "'Uncle Walter' and 'The Information Crisis'." *Television Quarterly* 25, no. 1 (1990): 32.

Vogel, Harold L. *Entertainment Industry Economics: A Guide for Financial Analysis*. Cambridge: Cambridge University Press, 1994.

Wallace, Charles P. "'Dish Wallahs' Plug India into the World." *Los Angeles Times*, October 25, 1992, H8.

Wartella, Ellen. "The Public Context of Debates About Television." In *Television as a Social Issue: The Eighth Applied Social Psychology Annual*, edited by Stuart Oskamp. Sponsored by the Society for the Psychological Study of Social Issues (SPSSI). Newbury Park, Calif.: Sage, 1988.

Williams, Huntington. *Beyond Control: ABC and the Fate of the Networks*. New York: Atheneum, 1989.

Willis, Edgar E., and Henry B. Aldridge. *Television, Cable and Radio: A Communications Approach*. Englewood Cliffs, N.J.: Prentice Hall, 1992.

Winick, Charles, Lorne G. Williamson, Stuart F. Chuzmir, and Mariann Pezzella Winick. *Children's Television Commercials: A Content Analysis*. Praeger Special Studies in U.S. Economic, Social and Political Issues. New York: Praeger, 1973.

Bibliography

Winick, Charles, and Mariann Pezzella Winick, "Television and the Culture of the Child: *Exploring* on the Renaissance." In *TV as Art: Some Essays in Criticism,* edited by Patrick D. Hazard. Papers originally commissioned by the Television Information Office for the National Council of Teachers of English Television Festival. Champaign, Ill.: National Council of Teachers of English, 1966.

Wolber, Joseph Mallory. "The U.K.: Constancy of Audience Behavior." In *Audience Responses to Media Diversity: Coping with Plenty,* edited by Lee B. Becker and Klaus Schoenbach. Hillsdale, N.J.: Lawrence Erlbaum, 1989.

Wong, Jesse. "Murdoch's Sudden Zeal for China May Not Be Requited in Beijing." *Asian Wall Street Journal,* September 13, 1993, 1.

You're Invited to Participate in the Future of Television. Hong Kong: STAR TV, n.d.

Zuckerman, Leonard. "Satellite TV Makes Broadcasting Waves." *International Herald Tribune,* n.d. [after July 1992].

Zuckman, Harvey L., and Martin J. Gaynes. *Mass Communications Law in a Nutshell.* St. Paul, Minn.: West, 1977.

Index

Index

Index

Index

Index

Index

Ford Foundation Television Workshop, 218

Ford Motor Co., 86

Fore, William F., 261

Forsyte Saga, The, 227

Fowler, Mark S., 27, 28, 29, 31, 170, 177

Fox, 97, 118, 124, 195, 200, 271; news and, 147; programming and, 112

Fox O, 158

France, television in, 196

Frankfurter, Felix, 61

FRC. *See* Federal Radio Commission

Freedman, Lewis, 180, 181

"Freedom and Responsibility in Broadcasting" (Northwestern University School of Law), 29

Friendly, Fred W., 146, 237

Friends of Thirteen, Inc., 238

Frontline, 250

Furness, Betty, 86–87

FX, 147

Gannett Co., 277

Garden, Mary, 79

Gardner, John S., 220, 221, 224

Garfunkel, Frank, 153

General Electric, 11, 67, 71, 277

General Instrument, 284

General Motors, 14, 277

General Motors Family Party, 81

Georgetown University Law Center, 177

Gerald McBoing Boing, 163

Germany, television in, 196, 223, 279

Getting to Sesame Street: Origins of the Children's Television Workshop (Polsky), 179

Ghostwriter, 182, 183

Gigantic Saturday (Sábado Gigante), 209, 210, 211

Gillette Cavalcade of Sports, The, 86

Gimbel's, ix

Gingrich, Newt, 261, 289

Gitlin, Todd, 31

Global television, 188. *See also* World television

Globo, 208. *See also* TeveGlobo

Globo Radio, 208

Go, 169

Gold Dust Twins, The, 76

Goldenson, Leonard, 139

Goldman Sachs, 204

Goldwyn, Samuel, 64

Goodson, Mark, 181

Goodson-Todman, 181

Gorbachev, Mikhail, 59

Gore, Al, 265

Government, television and, 39, 40, 189–92. *See also* British Broadcasting Corporation; Congress; Deregulation; Federal Communications Commission; Federal Radio Commission; Misregulation; Regulation

Granada, 44, 57

Granath, Herb, 187

Grange, Red, 14

Granger, Richard, 176

Great Atlantic and Pacific Tea Company, 76

Great Depression, 14–15

Great Performances, 240, 250

Great Train Robbery, The, 155

Great War, The, 250

Greene, Hugh, 49

Group W stations, xii, 23, 131

Guide to the BBC 1992, The, 53

Gulf Oil Corporation, 253–54

Gunn, Hartford, 230

Haley's M-O, 81

Hamilton, William Peter, 134

Handler, Elliot and Ruth, 165, 166

Hanna-Barbera, 143

Happiness Boys, The, 76

Happy Days, 104, 193

Hard Copy, 178

Hargis, Billy James, 20

Hatfield, Henry, 215

Hausman, Louis, 180–81

Index

Index

Index

Multi-system operators. *See* MSOs

Muppet Show, The, 25, 183

Murder, She Wrote, 113

Murdoch, Rupert, 144, 145, 188, 195–96, 204–6, 212, 279, 281

Murphy, Thomas S., 134

Murrow, Edward R., 19, 272, 292

MUSE, 283

Must-carry rule, 104, 247

My Beautiful Launderette, 56

NAB. *See* National Association of Broadcasters

NAPTS. *See* National Association of Public Television Stations

Nardino, Gary, 117

NASA, WESTAR and, 198

Nashville Network, xii

National Academy of Television Arts and Sciences, International Council of, xiii, 187

National Advisory Council on Radio in Education, 14

National Association of Broadcasters (NAB), 15, 17, 21–22, 82, 168, 286

National Association of Educational Broadcasters (NAEB), 151–52, 220

National Association of Public Television Stations (NAPTS), 256

National Broadcasting Corporation, 12. *See also* NBC

National Cable Television Association, 113

National Carbide Company, 76–77

National Committee on Education by Radio, 14

National Educational Association, 13

National Educational Television (NET), 219, 223, 226

National Geographic Specials, The, 240, 253

National PTA, 169

National Teacher Training Institute (NTTI), 242

National television, policy for, 291–92

National Television Standards Committee. *See* NTSC

Nature, 250

NBC (National Broadcasting Company, Inc.), ix, 86, 87, 88, 93, 112, 114–16; ABC and, 16; advertising and, 80, 81, 82; audience ratings and, 93; Aylesworth and, 79; cable news and, 147; Chicago School, 158–59, 169; children's television and, 158–59, 162, 163, 169, 180; CNBC and, 270; commercials and, 86, 87, 88; deregulation and, 27; development process and, 114–16; formation of, 77–79; HDTV and, 284; MSNBC and, 269–70; news and, 127–38, 141–42, 146; prime-time access rule and, 24; prime-time television audience of, 97; programming and, 112; public affairs programming and, 19; quiz show scandals and, 18–19; radio and, 16, 79, 80, 85; STAR TV and, 205, 212; sustaining programs and, 85; television demonstrated by, 17–18; Tinker and, 114–15; Weaver and, 88–89, 90; WJZ and, 79; WLBT-TV and, 20; world television and, 187, 188

NBC Children's Theater, 169

NBC Nightly News, The, 141, 142

NBC Super Channel, 279

NBC Symphony Orchestra, 16, 85

NET. *See* National Educational Television

Networks: advertising and, 121, 123; cable television and, 122–23, 124, 280; domestic economy and, 123; Fox as competition of, 124; independent stations and, 104–5, 124, 280; magazine programs and, 280; news and, 130–31, 139, 147; Paley and, 80–81; prime-time ratings and, 279–80; programming and, 98, 99, 112, 113, 118, 119–21; radio and, 77

325

Index

Index

Perth, Rod, 113

Philco, 86

Philips Electronics, 283, 284

Phillips, Kevin, 192, 272

Pierce, Frederick, 148–49

Pifer, Alan, 221

Pilkington Committee, 44, 50–53

Piracy, cable systems and, 103

Piston, Walter, 183

Pitroda, S. G., 202

PM Magazine, xii, 25

Politics of Broadcast Regulation (Krasnow, Longley, and Terry), 219

Polsky, Richard, 179

Popeye, 162

Poterba, James, 30

Povey, Terry, 205–6

Pressler, Larry, 246

Primestar, 281

Prime time: magazine programs and, 280; programming and, 117, 118, 268–69

Prime-time access rule (PTAR), 24–25, 124, 148–50, 183–84

Primo, Al, 129–30

Program-length commercials, 173

Programming: cable television and, 97, 99–100, 110–13, 121–23, 124–25, 268, 269; current criticisms of, 289; development process, 113–25; economics of, 99; Europe and, 269; future and, 268–69; independent stations and, 280; limited choices of, 96–125; magazine, 280; media companies controlling, 279; networks and, 98, 99, 112, 113, 118, 119–21; prime-time, 268–69; public television and, 240, 250, 251–52; scarcity of, 268–69; studios and, 99

Program Services Endowment, 232

Prohibition, liquor advertising and, 15

PROJAC. *See* Centro de Producas de Jacarepagua

Pruett, Steve, 273

PSAs. *See* Public-service announcements

PTAR. *See* Prime-time access rule

Public affairs programs, definition of, 132–33

Public Broadcasting Act of 1967, 224–25, 226–28

Public Broadcasting Service (PBS), xii; audience leveraging and, 253–54; audience of, 234, 235; board of, 238; brand recognition of, 243; British Broadcasting Corporation and, 197; children's programs and, 159; common carriage and, 251–52; community of, 237; Corporation for Public Broadcasting and, 226, 229, 230; creation of, 226; development process and, 121; duplication and, 247–48; issues covered by, 126; mission needed by, 244, 245; news and, 149, 150; news for hearing-impaired and, 139; organization and governance of, 255, 256; Program Services Endowment and, 232; resources, 250–51; value of, 262

Public Broadcasting System, 232. *See also* Public Broadcasting Service

Public interest standard, 73, 74–75, 85, 138, 173

Public-service announcements (PSAs), 23

Public Service Responsibility of Broadcast Licensees, 17

Public Telecommunications Financing Act, 230

Public Telecommunications Trust, 232

Public television, xii, 214–63; artists working on, 240; audience of, 234–35, 261; boards and volunteers of, 238–39; brand recognition and, 242–43; cable television versus, 262; children's television and, 177, 179–83, 228–29, 240–41; commercialization of, 259, 261–62; commercial television versus, 262–63; common carriage lack and, 251–52, 258; Congress and, 215, 216,

327

Index

Public television (*cont.*)
224–25, 226–29, 230, 234, 236, 246, 247, 251, 261–62; dependence on funding sources of, 256–57; development of, 221–33; duplication and, 245–49; educational television and, 151–52, 172, 177, 215–21, 241–42, 258, *see also* Children's Television Workshop; failure to maximize all resources of, 249–51; federal trust fund for, 260; in government-controlled systems, 212; as government-private system, 258–59; increasing efficiency of, 257–58; localism and, 225–26, 228–29, 251, 254; long-term funding of, 258–60; loyal subscribers of, 236–37; mission needed by, 243–45; modernization of, 257; options for twenty-first century for, 257–60; organization and governance of, 254–55; politicization of, 255–56; privatization of, 259–60; program quality of, 239–40, 250, 251–52; promotion of, 252–54, 258; reach of stations of, 235–36; short-term planning by, 249; sponsorship of, 75; strengths of, 234–43; Telecommunications Act of 1996 and, 287–88; ties between stations and their communities and, 237–38; weaknesses of, 243–57; web pages and, 270

Public Television: A Program of Action (Carnegie One), 221–23, 225, 233

Public Trust: The Report of the Carnegie Commission on the Future of Public Television, A (Carnegie Two), 230–33, 234

Pulitzer, Joseph, 127

Q score, 135, 136–37

Quality and Value Cable (QVC), 66, 100

Queensborough Corporation, 70, 75, 76

Quiz show scandals, 18–19, 98

QVC. *See* Quality and Value Cable

Radio: advertising on, 81–84; AM and FM, 28; America's Cup race (1899) covered by, 9–10, 34; audience measurement for, 91; cable television similar to, 100; CBS/BBC project and, 3–4; commercialization of, 66–71, 73; concerns over children listening to, 156; educational, 215; establishment of, 8, 10, 34; KDKA and, 12, 68, 70, 71, 75, 131; misregulation of, 7, 8–17, 21, 32, 66–67, 71–75; news and, 145; offshore pirate radio stations and, 193–94; Paley and, 80–81, 82; public, 224; sense of delicacy in early days of, ix–x; sponsorship of, 75–79; sustaining programs and, 85; in United Kingdom, 34–38, 41, 43, 46, 47, 49, 58

Radio Act of 1912, 10, 72

Radio and Television News Directors Association, 137

Radio Association of Great Britain, 36

Radio Corporation of America. *See* RCA

Radio Luxembourg, 47

Radio stations: department stores establishing, ix; media companies owning, 278

Radiotelevisione Italiana (RAI), 194, 195

Radiovision, 17

RAI. *See* Radiotelevisione Italiana

Raposo, Joe, 183

Rather, Dan, 137

Ratings: audience, 91–93; television news and, 135–36

Rattner, Steve, 271

RCA (Radio Corporation of America), 11, 12, 71; NBC formation and, 77–79; WEAF and, 70

Reader's Digest, 144–45

Index

Index

Index

Index